CHURCHES *on* MISSION

OTHER BOOKS IN THE EMS SERIES

ABOUT EMS
www.emsweb.org

The Evangelical Missiological Society is a professional organization with more than 400 members comprised of missiologists, mission administrators, reflective mission practitioners, teachers, pastors with strategic missiological interests, and students of missiology. EMS exists to advance the cause of world evangelization. We do this through study and evaluation of mission concepts and strategies from a biblical perspective with a view to commending sound mission theory and practice to churches, mission agencies, and schools of missionary training around the world. We hold an annual national conference and eight regional meetings in the United States and Canada.

Evangelical
Missiological
Society
Series

no. **25**

CHURCHES*on*
MISSION

GOD'S GRACE ABOUNDING TO THE NATIONS

GEOFFREY HARTT, CHRISTOPHER R. LITTLE, JOHN WANG | EDITORS

WILLIAM CAREY
LIBRARY

Churches on Mission: God's Grace Abounding to the Nations

Published by William Carey Library
1605 E. Elizabeth St.
Pasadena, CA 91104

Melissa Hughes, editor
Joelle Bridges, copyeditor
Pear Creative, cover design
Joanne Liang, interior design

William Carey Library is a ministry of
Frontier Ventures
www.frontierventures.org

Printed in the United States of America
21 20 19 18 17   5 4 3 2 1   BP600

Library of Congress Cataloging-in-Publication Data
Names: Hart, Geoffrey, editor.
Title: Churches on mission : God's grace abounding to the nations. / Geoffrey Hart, Christopher R. Little, John Wang, editors.
Description: Pasadena, CA : William Carey Library, 2017. | Series: Evangelical Missiological Society series ; no. 25 | Includes bibliographical references. |
Identifiers: LCCN 2017019357 (print) | LCCN 2017021348 (ebook) | ISBN 9780878086696 (eBook) | ISBN 9780878085293 (pbk.) | ISBN 0878085297 (pbk.)
Subjects: LCSH: Missions. | Church. | Mission of the church.
Classification: LCC BV2063 (ebook) | LCC BV2063 .C525 2017 (print) | DDC 207/.2--dc23
LC record available at https://lccn.loc.gov/2017019357

CONTENTS

Part Three

CHURCH ON MISSION IN NORTH AMERICAN PERSPECTIVE

Part Four

CHURCH ON MISSION IN PRACTICAL PERSPECTIVE

CONTRIBUTORS

K. ROBERT BESHEARS (ThM) is an ordained teaching pastor at Mars Hill Church in Mobile, AL and serves as an adjunct instructor in the School of Christian Studies at the University of Mobile. He holds a BS from Moody Bible Institute and a ThM from Southern Baptist Theological Seminary where he is also a PhD student. He is a member of the American Academy of Religion, Evangelical Theological Society, and Evangelical Missiological Society.

DAVID R. DUNAETZ (PhD) is assistant professor of leadership and organizational psychology at Azusa Pacific University. His research program focuses on conflict processes in Christian organizations. He was a church planter in France for seventeen years with WorldVenture.

NATHAN GARTH (MA) is the pastor of international missions at Sojourn Community Church in Louisville, KY. Before becoming a pastor, Nathan served as a missionary in Kathmandu, Nepal. He is also a consultant for the Upstream Collective helping local churches grow as sending churches. Nathan is finishing his DMiss at the Southern Baptist Theological Seminary.

GEOFFREY HARTT (DIS), serves as the executive director of Hispanics for Christ. He is ordained by the North American Baptist Conference and teaches at North Portland Bible College. He is currently the Regional VP for the Northwest Region of the Evangelical Missiological Society.

J. Scott Horrell (ThD) is professor of theological studies at Dallas Theological Seminary and teaches widely in non-Western seminaries and conferences. In Brazil he taught at several schools, while serving as coordinator of graduate studies at the Baptist Theological Seminary of São Paulo. He has authored multiple books and articles in Portuguese and English including *From the Ground Up: Biblical Foundations for the 21st Century Church* (Kregel 2004), *Jesus in Trinitarian Perspective*, eds. F. Sanders and K. Issler (B & H 2007) and *Exploring Christian Theology*, Vol. 1, eds. N. Holsteen and M. Svigel (Bethany 2014).

Jerry M. Ireland (PhD) serves as a missionary with the Assemblies of God, and lives with his wife and daughter in Lomé, Togo. He holds a PhD in theology and apologetics (Liberty Univ.), and also serves as vice provost of Pan Africa Theological Seminary (PAThS). He is the editor of PneumAfrica Journal and his publications include *Evangelism and Social Concern in the Theology of Carl F. H. Henry* (Pickwick 2015) and *For the Love of God: Principles and Practice of Compassion in Missions* (Wipf and Stock 2017), for which he served as editor.

Mehari Korcho (MA) served in student ministry in Ethiopia with EvaSUE–IFES as a Southwestern regional coordinator. He holds a BS in sociology from Lund University, Sweden, and a MA in global studies from Columbia International University. He currently serves in the USA with One Challenge International as a mobilizer for diaspora churches.

Christopher R. Little (PhD) has advanced the glory of God among the nations through mission in Europe, Africa, and the Middle East and in higher education for over three decades. He is the author of *The Revelation of God Among the Unevangelized* (WCL 2000), *Mission in the Way of Paul* (Peter Lang 2005), and *Polemic Missiology for the 21st Century* (Amazon Kindle 2013), as well as numerous articles in various journals. He presently serves as a consulting missiologist-at-large to the church.

GUILLERMO MAC KENZIE (DMin) was born and raised in Buenos Aires, Argentina. He studied there for his first theological degrees, was ordained at the age of twenty-four, and served as pastor for six years. In 2008, he moved to the States to complete a Master of Theology and a Doctor of Ministry at Covenant Theological Seminary. Having returned to Argentina, Guillermo is currently serving as pastor in a multicultural church, stated clerk of his presbytery, translator for the Nehemiah Project, and invited professor at different seminaries.

MURILO MELO (MD, PhD) is currently in the last semester of the ThM at Dallas Theological Seminary and about to start his doctoral education in theological studies in the same institution. He is a board member of CDL (Leadership Development Center), an evangelical seminary in Maputo, Mozambique. He was a professor of molecular medicine for ten years at Santa Casa Medical School in his native São Paulo, Brazil. He published over sixty papers in scientific journals and was director of several medical societies and clinical laboratories.

J. D. PAYNE (PhD) serves as the pastor of church multiplication for The Church at Brook Hills in Birmingham, Alabama. He is also a missiologist, seminary professor, podcast host (Strike the Match), and blogger at jdpayne.org. He is the author and editor of thirteen books including *Strangers Next Door* (IVP 2012), *Developing a Strategy for Missions* (Baker 2013), and *Apostolic Church Planting* (IVP 2015). He formerly served as a regional vice-president and executive vice-president of administration for the Evangelical Missiological Society.

MICHELLE RAVEN (PhD) is passionate about African Americans participating in global missions, capacity building, and reaching the least reached. A retired Air Force Lt Colonel, attorney, and ministry leader, she served as director of personnel for Christar and founded Capacity Builders International, a nonprofit committed to increasing participation in global missions through up-reach, in-reach, and outreach initiatives. She holds an MA in global studies from Liberty University and is in a PhD intercultural studies program at CIU.

DANIEL A. RODRIGUEZ (PhD), a native of California, has served the Churches of Christ as minister in Central and Southern California, and as a missionary in Puebla, Mexico (1985–1994). He is currently professor of religion and Hispanic studies at Pepperdine University, where he teaches missiology including multiethnic ministry and cross-cultural mission. He has published numerous scholarly articles as well as chapters in edited volumes. His book *A Future for the Latino Church: Models for Multilingual and Multigenerational Hispanic Congregations* challenges the assumption that Hispanic ministry in the United States is synonymous with ministry conducted almost exclusively in Spanish.

BORIS J. SARLABOUS DÍAZ is a professor of Hebrew, exegesis, and theology at the Los Cedros del Libano Theological Seminary in Cuba. He earned graduate degrees at the Southern Baptist School for Biblical Studies, Los Cedros del Libano Theological Seminary, and has studied at Tyndale House in Cambridge, UK. He is ordained by the Free Baptist of Cuba.

LINDA P. SAUNDERS (MAGS) is co-founder of Ambassadors for Christ Ministries and has served as a career missionary in Venezuela since 2003. Her passion is equipping and involving African American young adults in missions. Her desire to educate and train the African American church for missions prompted her to develop a cross-cultural training program. Currently Linda is in the developmental phase of creating a missions training center. This center would offer missions education and training to equip young adults, specifically African American young adults, for global missions. This center was born out of Linda's thesis research.

EDWARD L. SMITHER (PhD) is professor and dean of intercultural studies at Columbia International University. He served for fourteen years in intercultural ministry in North Africa, Europe, and the USA, and his books include *Mission in the Early Church* and *Missionary Monks*.

JOHN WANG (PhD) serves as the pastor of Chinese and Spanish ministry of First Baptist Church of Flushing, a multiethnic, multilingual, and multi-congregational church in New York City. He is currently the regional VP for the Northeast Region of the Evangelical Missiological Society. Prior to his ministry career, he was a professional engineer for fourteen years.

ZHIQIU XU (PhD) grew up in mainland China, studied in Renmin University (BA 1993) and Beijing University (Juris Master 1996) prior to arriving in the States. He continued his education in Westminster Theological Seminary (MDiv 2001) and Boston University (PhD 2014). He had served as pastor in two local churches for fifteen years. His first book *Natural Theology Reconfigured* was published in 2016. He has been teaching theology at Columbia International University since 2014.

ACKNOWLEDGMENTS

The editors of this year's annual EMS volume would like to acknowledge that the completion of this strategic project would not have been possible without the assistance, contribution, and support of many, many others. To begin with, we would like to express our gratitude to the EMS President Robert Priest for his valuable guidance and feedback in producing this volume. The regional vice presidents of EMS deserve mention as well, as their dedication to organizing their respective regional conferences, and the papers which are produced as a result, surpasses the call of duty and has contributed to the quality of materials readers will find herein. In addition, we would like to sincerely thank the numerous peer reviewers who labored alongside us to select, improve, and bring to print each of the chapters in this book. We would also like to convey our heartfelt appreciation to each of the authors who demonstrated patience and perseverance in striving with us to produce their best possible work. Moreover, the commitment of William Carey Library to publish EMS's annual volumes is without parallel in the publishing world, and as a consequence, the entire evangelical missiological community is indebted to it. Our last and most important acknowledgment is reserved for our Lord Jesus Christ without whose sustaining grace would not have made this endeavor possible. It is to him we dedicate this volume with the prayer that he would be pleased to use it to empower his church in mission "so that the grace which is spreading to more and more people may cause the giving of thanks to abound to the glory of God" (2 Cor 4:15).

INTRODUCTION

Geoffrey Hartt, Christopher R. Little, and John Wang

What are the global giants in the world? What are the problems that affect billions of people, not millions? Spiritual emptiness, self-centered leadership, poverty, disease, illiteracy. There aren't enough doctors to solve all the issues in the world. There aren't enough teachers to solve all the issues in the world, and there aren't enough missionaries to solve all the issues in the world. But there is an army of believers sitting in churches waiting to be mobilized. (Saddleback Church)

These are the opening words of the introductory video for the missions initiative PEACE Plan of the Saddleback Church in Southern California. It not only shows the enormous magnitude of the global missionary task in front of us, but also points to the great potential of believers and their local churches in our world-wide missionary pursuit.

Claude Hickman, Steve C. Hawthorne, and Todd Ahrend wrote about four major practices of a World Christian lifestyle: going, welcoming, sending, and mobilizing (2013, 725–30). All World Christians in some way will be engaged in these four practices, although to different extents. If they imply different roles Christians play, then collectively the local church will also be engaged in all these responsibilities. The church is a place where missionaries, or goers, are produced. However, short-term missions, business as mission, tentmaking, and other innovative means of missionary work also allow many members of local churches to go. Today, the massive global migration movement encourages the church and its members to be engaged in the practice of welcoming. When domestic migrants or foreign immigrants come to our cities, it is not enough to receive them with domestic missionaries as our representatives. Many of these newcomers live side-by-side with other Christians. They are our neighbors, coworkers, classmates, service providers, or clients. It is the members of local churches who need to show hospitality.

But the church does not only welcome foreigners. The practice of welcoming should also extend to creating a friendly environment for the unreached, unevangelized, and unengaged population of our societies. Local churches have traditionally served well as senders. We provide financial resources, relational support, prayer, and care to loved ones who have gone to the mission field. Often, local churches not only support missionaries when they go, but also provide a safe and warm environment when they come home for furlough or retirement. The missionaries are part of us! Mobilization for world mission happens when the local church has a clear vision of its role and potential in contributing to the kingdom of God. The local church is responsible to mobilize all its members and should function as a discerning body to confirm missionary calls.

This volume is an attempt to bring missiology into closer connection with congregations. Authors represented herein have gone through an extensive peer review process to be included in this volume. In addition, some of the authors are not native English speakers, yet the editors worked hard to include their writings in order to give a voice to what God is doing in their particular ethnic communities. The authors come from diverse backgrounds and offer biblical and historical reflections, expand our understanding of mission through local churches in North American and global contexts, and provide practical strategies to empower God's people as they engage in missionary work.

In Part One, the authors present their viewpoints on biblical and historical subjects. In contrast to the image of a centralized kingdom of God in the Old Testament, Scott Horrell argues for a decentralized form of the kingdom for the church in the New Testament. He suggests that Scripture allows for significant diversity among the transcultural and transgenerational manifestation of Christ's followers. He also recognizes New Testament flexibility regarding forms and the primacy of New Testament functions in church planting efforts. Missionaries and indigenous leaders are free to adapt forms and organize in such a way that encourages the full expression of these activities. Edward Smither reviews five missionary-monk-bishops who served between the fourth and eighth centuries, prior to the rise of monastic missionary orders. He challenges Ralph Winter's proposal of the two structures of redemptive mission—modalities and sodalities. Instead he argues for the church as the sole means of missionary sending during that early stage of the history of Christianity. Jerry Ireland argues from the book of Acts on the concept of solidarity as a vital ingredient in the emergence of indigenous mission movements. He believes missionaries should avoid taking a primary role in compassionate ministries and instead allow national leaders the opportunity of leading, engaging, and demonstrating solidarity in local compassionate needs.

In Part Two, attention is given to a series of case studies in the Majority World regarding how local churches and church movements engage in missionary work. Boris Sarlabous offers a Cuban perspective of how local churches survived under the communist regime, and the development and projection of the evangelical movement in that country. Murilo Melo describes the fast growing Neocharismatic movement in Brazil and analyzes its strength and weaknesses. He also informs readers about the state of its rapid global expansion. Zhiqiu Xu helps us understand the history, evangelistic strategies, and missionary potential of the Chinese church through the study of three specific urban churches. Lastly, Guillermo Mac Kenzie, by comparing two immigrant Presbyterian churches in Argentina, highlights the difficult path of immigrant churches in shifting their focus from the first-generation immigrant community to outreach of people beyond their own ethnic group.

In Part Three, the focus shifts to the North American context. Two chapters deal with the important topic of mission emerging from the African American context. Michelle Raven's paper provides a historical analysis of the ups and downs within this community regarding mission. She also presents as an example a local church's experience in missionary engagement. Linda Saunders writes about the importance of education and training among African American churches. She very helpfully offers a concrete proposal to mobilize and develop the potential of African American churches for world mission. Daniel Rodriguez describes the evangelistic opportunities and theological challenges presented by the Hispanic evangelical church in America. Considerations are given to issues of outreach to US-born Latinos, the transnational potential of the Latino community, its cultural preservation, and theological resistance among the Latin American diaspora. Mehari Korcho introduces the Ethiopian immigrant churches in America, explaining how mission is defined and practiced among them. He addresses such topics as mobilization, recruitment, intergenerational responsibilities, and transnationalism within this community.

The focus of Part Four is on the practical aspects of mission in the context of the local church. Kyle Beshears covers the challenge of contemporary apatheism in the West with its characteristics of lacking reason, motivation, and will to believe. He offers a well-reasoned strategy for churches to embrace in order to confront this growing adversary to the gospel. Nathan Garth discusses the responsibility and the advantage of local churches doing missionary assessment. He describes the experience of a local church in creating a formal procedure for such assessment.

David Dunaetz uses mathematical models to analyze the relationship between missionaries and their supporting churches. He offers useful advice to maintain productive and healthy relationships between these two entities for mutual benefit. Reflecting his personal experience as a missions pastor and missions professor, J. D. Payne believes that in order to mobilize and lead congregations to a stronger engagement in mission, the role of the pastor is of fundamental importance. He provides six guidelines for educating pastors on the topic of mission today.

With the advancement of technologies for communication and transportation, the rapid transformation of Western society as a mission field, the decline of mission agencies, and the cultural shift toward grassroots participation, local church involvement in mission has become increasingly possible and necessary. Facing the new challenges of this era, it is important for local churches to engage the practices of going, welcoming, sending, and mobilizing in a creative way. As editors for this publication, it is our prayer that the papers included in this volume will offer some practical advice to leaders in local churches, inspiration to practitioners and missions agencies, and new challenges to the academic community of missiologists.

REFERENCES CITED

Saddleback Church. "Missions: Global PEACE." http://saddleback.com/connect/ministry/the-peace-plan (accessed March 25, 2017).

Claude Hickman, Steve C. Hawthorne, and Todd Ahrend. 2013. "Life on Purpose." In Perspectives on the World Christian Movement: A Reader, edited by Ralph Winter and Steven Hawthorne, 725–30. Pasadena, CA: William Carey Library.

Part One
CHURCH ON MISSION
IN BIBLICAL AND
HISTORICAL PERSPECTIVES

BASIC CHURCH

FREEING CROSS-CULTURAL CHURCH PLANTING WITH NEW TESTAMENT ESSENTIALS*

J. Scott Horrell

Missionaries today are aware that much of what has been exported or repeated in missional church planting remains freighted with North Atlantic and traditional institutionalism that is often peripheral to New Testament (NT) church essentials. These same ecclesial structures and ways of doing church have been and sometimes are perpetuated by well-intentioned second- and third-generation leaders who replicate these forms— forms through which they themselves responded to the gospel in years past. For all of us, loyalties to particular ecclesiologies (if not denominations) lie embedded in our experience with the God we love. Yet what worked well in one generation and culture does not necessarily transfer to another. In church planting, a living ecclesiology is as vital to missions as vigorous missions is to ecclesiology.

One group of pastors in São Paulo, Brazil lamented that the concept of *church* in their own congregations—said to be typical of tens of thousands of congregations around the world—centers in four images: a church building (or "temple"); Sunday as the "Christian Sabbath"; the worship service (the more powerful the better); and the full-time pastor ("the man of God" and mediator) (Kivitz 1995, 37–56). In the mind of most believers, if one of these four standards is lacking then one does not truly have a church.

Many in evangelical missions agree that these kinds of preconceived ecclesiologies undermine effective cross-cultural

---

*A version of this chapter original appeared under the title, "Freeing Cross-Cultural Church Planting with New Testament Essentials," *Bibliotheca Sacra* 174 (April–June 2017): 210–25.

church planting as well as the growth of existing churches. Yet a glance around the world suggests that most church planters, whether indigenous or cross-cultural, repeat traditional or preconceived concepts of what the church is. By so doing, some church planters assume that they protect "sound doctrine," others that they continue a denominational heritage, still others seek to clone the megachurch or nouvelle structure through which they have been commissioned. I suggest, however, that the need is to return to the primal experiential dimensions of NT Christianity. A more biblical ecclesiology in fact sets church planting movements free to mold their "forms" to the central "functions" of the NT church.[1]

This article proposes a flexible ecclesiology that maximizes the spiritual functions/activities of the NT church with minimal prescribed structures and organization. If the local church is especially observed through its NT functions, then our ecclesial structures should be highly adaptable to specific cultures and circumstances. In no sense does this work intend to define an entire ecclesiology. Rather, in brief strokes I will set forth two theological principles helpful to church planting.

1. *The church exists as a decentralized form of the kingdom of God.* In defining the church as the body of Christ, I argue that the church exists in some ways as the dialectic antithesis to Old Testament (OT) Israel. Whereas through Moses and David

---

1. Allison divides current ecclesiological models into three clusters: functional, teleological, and ontological ecclesiologies (he affirms the last) (2012, 50–53). During the 1970s and 80s, functional ecclesiologies were often at the forefront of missional church planting. In recent years, the functional methodologies have been overshadowed by ontological (theological) or more teleological (pragmatic) models. I suggest that we can affirm an ontological model (the divinely given nature of the church) without losing the richness of identifying early church's central activities as instructive for what the church should be.

the OT kingdom of God was *centralized* in a geography, racial lineage, Sabbath, and professional priesthood, in the NT the outward form of God's kingdom is precisely the opposite—centralized in Christ but *decentralized* geographically, organizationally, temporally, and ethnically in its expansion throughout the earth.

2. *The local church is practically defined by NT functions.* Regarding the forms and structures of the earliest local churches, Gerald Bray observes:

The evidence of the New Testament is not sufficiently detailed to allow us to re-create an authentically "biblical" church to the exclusion of any alternative. It may have been the case that individual congregations were organized along different lines but we do not have enough details to be able to compare one with another. It may also be that many of the churches lacked any fixed organization. Perhaps they operated on a fairly *ad hoc* basis, with little sense that there was only one right way of doing things. (2016, 42)

If the NT reflects ambiguity regarding organizational forms, what appears far more tangible are the God-glorifying activities of the early church. That is, in terms directly relevant to church planting, the local church is identified and measured especially through its primary activities in response to its Lord. What the church is by nature (theologically) should be reflected in the intentional, Spirit-generated functions of local churches. Thus ontology (what God has made the church) and functionality (how God's people rightly respond) are closely related. While necessarily having some organizational structure, the local church is designed to reflect its Lord through its activities of worship, teaching/disciple-forming, fellowship, and evangelism/mission. Whether in missional church planting or established local churches, the forms of a local church (excepting certain NT directives) are flexible and subordinate to the NT functions that reflect what God has ordained the church to be.

The work concludes with suggestions on how better to initiate and nurture local churches in a widely diverse world. With a theological ecclesiology in place, church planting methodology advances as creative interplay with culture as guided by the Holy Spirit. A student of the target culture, working together with believers indigenous to a particular setting, will seek to test and mold forms (organization, appearance, etc.) to that which best facilitates NT functions.

INITIAL OBSERVATIONS: TOWARD A FRAMEWORK FOR CHURCH PLANTING

From the outset, certain assumptions need to be clarified. First, the people of God should be reflective of the triune God they claim to worship (cf. John 17:18; 20:21). Within progressive revelation, the *Missio Dei* as God's creative, graceful movement toward humankind provides the metanarrative for why both OT Israel and the NT church exist (Tennent 2010, 53–101; Sanders 2010, 127–66; Horrell 2009, 13–24). That God should work in different ways throughout the history of salvation reflects the unity and diversity within the holy Trinity itself.

Second, affirming the pattern of the book of Acts and more broadly the entire NT as written to the church, a missional hermeneutic is encouraged. The overarching covenants to Adam, Noah, and Abraham point to the grace of God offered finally to all humanity (Peters 1972, 83–102; Wright, 2005, 324–29). So all the Bible, but specifically the post-Pentecost NT, informs church planting efforts in a largely Gentile world.

Third, the NT clearly does *prescribe* formal aspects for the local church, notably qualified leadership, regular gathering together as "church," and the practices of baptism and the Eucharist.

On the other hand, not everything *described* in the NT is universally mandated. NT patterns guide but are not necessarily constrictive to innovational forms for the local church.

Last, this work does not intend to criticize more highly organized ecclesiologies. Indeed, more formal denominational ecclesiologies are sometimes helpful in church multiplication. Moreover such church structures give leadership and accountability to newer church planting efforts. Rather this essay seeks to define the essential functions of the NT church as criteria for evaluating the forms and multiple activities of today's churches. A host of missional church planting books are on the market today, most of them with valuable contributions.[2] I will argue for a simple (perhaps controversial) template for the local church—one as adaptable in Tehran or rural Cameroon as in Shanghai, Paris, or Chicago. As such, the paper is designed to complement established ecclesial and missional forms by stimulating new possibilities, as well as to orient church planting efforts in situations calling for radical adaptations. In short, this proposal seeks a minimalist ecclesiology that maintains NT mandates regarding structure while emphasizing NT functions as the primary measure of the local church.

CHURCH AS A DECENTRALIZED KINGDOM

The Bible itself attests to progressive revelation with significant differences between OT Israel and the NT church.[3] Whatever one's

---

2. Works widely used in evangelical church planting include: Allen 1962; Dever 2013; Hesselgrave 2000; Hill 2012, 2016; Keller 2012; Malphurs 2004 and 2011; Ott and Wilson 2011; Payne 2009; Rainer and Geiger 2006; Stanley 2012; Stetzer and Im 2016; Warren 1995.

3. A host of works debate whether OT Israel is the church and whether the NT church is the New Israel. For a variety of views see: Brand 2015; Wellum and Parker 2016; Blaising and Bock 1992 and 1993; Carson 2016. My own view is set forth in Horrell 2004, 29–52. For more detailed

eschatology and however much similarity or dissimilarity one finds between Israel as God's theocratic kingdom and the NT church, certain distinctions are paradigmatic. Four categorical differences distinguish OT Israel and the NT church, with significant missiological implications.

GEOGRAPHY

From the earliest covenants with Abraham, central to Jewish identity is the "land"—found over 2,500 times as the fourth most common noun in the OT (Gen 12:1–3; 15:7–20; 17:8). The Promised Land figures prominently in the Exodus, Joshua's conquest, the ensuing wars up to (and after) the Davidic kingdom, the Assyrian and Babylonian exiles, subsequent returns to the land, and the Jewish tenacity to live in and defend the land even today (cf. Brueggeman 2002, esp. 1–45; McDermott 2012, 29–40 and 2016, 11–22; Bock and Glasser 2014, 71–82). Not only is the land of Israel endemic to OT theology, David's Jerusalem becomes the City of God and Zion the Mountain of God. Even more concentrically defined, Solomon's Temple and later temples were structures erected both to invite yet keep out the foreigner, women, Jewish laity, and finally everyone but the high priest from the Holy of Holies, the epicenter of God's presence on earth. The invitation to the nations was to come to Jerusalem and worship the only true God, "bring an offering and come into his courts" (Ps 96:8).

With the NT church a geographic inversion occurs. Believers are commissioned to go into all the world. For the church, finally, there is no geographic center, no Promised Land, no Jerusalem, no temple, no altar, no Rome, no houses of God. Where two or three are gathered Christ is present. Early Christians met wherever they

---

information, see Bray 2016,14–29, Ferguson 1996, 60–69, and Allison 2012, 61–122. In my understanding, the universal church is constituted by all regenerate believers in Jesus Christ beginning with the baptism of the Spirit at Pentecost, united under the headship of Christ, and present in believing local churches and fellowships throughout the world.

could in both public and private spaces. While literature mentions church buildings from the end of the second century, prior to Constantine "it is uncertain whether these were existing structures remodeled for church use…or new constructions" (Ferguson 2008). It's not that church buildings are unhelpful as local meeting places for believers; rather (unlike the temple), church buildings themselves are unessential. The local church can meet anywhere.

RACIAL LINEAGE

The children of Abraham are God's covenantal people. Not Ishmael, not Esau, but through Isaac and Jacob, the Lord God promises to multiply the patriarchs' children like the stars of the sky and the dust of the earth (Gen 15:5; 22:17; 26:4; 28:14). That Rahabs and Ruths are incorporated into the chosen people reflects a coming universality and God's grace to the world. Yet in the OT the purity of the Jewish racial lineage remains of central importance. Priests were to be wholly Hebrew. With the return from Babylon, Ezra and the leadership of Israel required all who had intermarried to send away their foreign wives with their children, then to offer guilt offerings, so that God's blessing return to his people (Ezra 9–10).

With the NT form of the kingdom, the church radically reverses racial centrality: once "excluded from citizenship in Israel and foreigners to the covenants of the promise, without hope . . . now in Christ Jesus" (Eph 2:12–13) the barrier is gone. "There is no Jew nor Gentile" (Gal 3:28). Non-Jewish believers are made coheirs of promise, children of Abraham, and participants in the New Covenant. Now in the local church, racial unity-in-diversity is encouraged.

SABBATH DAY

Contrary to what some suppose, the Sabbath (*šabbāt*) is introduced to Israel in the desert as manna fell only six of seven days

(Ex 16:23–30). Unlike circumcision, no credible evidence exists that anyone anywhere practiced a Sabbath in the known world (Hasel 1992, 5:850–51; Bacchiocchi 1991, 70–79)—this includes Noah, Abraham, and Jacob's offspring in Egypt. Only in the Fourth Commandment (Ex 20:8–11) is the Sabbath defined and related to God's own rest (*šābat*) at creation (Gen 2:4). That Sabbath ordinance—by word count longer than the Fifth through Tenth Commandments combined—apparently describes something new to the Israelites. Like circumcision, now the Sabbath serves as an explicit covenantal sign between the Lord God and Israel: "The Israelites are to observe the Sabbath, celebrating it for the generations to come as a lasting covenant. It will be a sign between me and the Israelites forever" (Ex 31:12–17; cf. Ezek 20:12, 20). As Nehemiah 9:13–14 reiterates, God made known his Sabbath at Sinai.

With Jesus's inauguration of the New Covenant at the Last Supper, there appear parallels between Israel's two covenantal signs of circumcision and Sabbath and the two ordinances given to the church—baptism and the Lord's Supper (cf. Allison 2012, 78–79). Whatever one's perspective on the age and mode of baptism, like circumcision in OT Israel, so NT baptism is the public sign of one's new identity with Christ and his body the church (cf. Col 2:11–13). Implicitly as well, the Jewish Sabbath is replaced by the regular meetings of Christians that culminate in the Lord's Supper (1 Cor 11:24, "Do this in remembrance of me"). The Jerusalem Council (Acts 15:24–29) conspicuously set aside OT commands of circumcision and Sabbath for the emerging Gentile church—a discontinuity argued forcefully by Paul (cf. Rom 14:5–6; Gal 5:1–6; Col 2:16). Whereas early Jewish believers may have also worshiped on the Sabbath, Sunday as the Lord's Day of resurrection takes precedence but without commandment. While believers are not to forsake gathering together for worship (Heb 10:25), no day is commanded. A believing community appears free to come together "as church" whenever it deems appropriate as long as it is habitual.

PROFESSIONAL PRIESTHOOD

The Pentateuch designates Aaron and his sons as the priestly lineage and it "sets apart" the entire tribe of Levi for special service to God. Heirs by bloodline (esp. the Levitical clan of Kohath), the Aaronic priests were the mediators between Israel and God. The Mosaic Law gives detailed instructions for rituals, various forms of sacrifices, even proper clothing. "The Levitical priests—indeed the whole tribe of Levi—are to have no allotment or inheritance with Israel. They shall live on the food offerings presented to the Lord, for that is their inheritance" (Deut 18:1; cf. Rehm 1992, 4.303–4). Led by the high priest, the Levitical priests of Israel were to be a professional religious caste financially sustained by the people. Only they were ordained to offer sacrifices. When King Saul offered sacrifices by himself he was irrevocably disqualified as Israel's monarch. By God's own design, the priest was to be the mediator between God and the nation of Israel.

With the New Covenant, now Jesus alone is the great High Priest (Heb 4:14) and through him every believer is declared a priest (1 Pet 2:5, 9; Rev 1:6). Indeed, the Christian is more than priest but also daughter and son of the living God. While the apostles and later leaders are given certain authority, they serve as shepherds for the purpose of equipping "his people for works of service, so that the body of Christ may be built up" (Eph 4:12). The contrast is striking between the OT priestly hierarchy and the leadership of the NT church (simple fishermen) called to strengthen others for full service to the Head of the body.[4]

---

4. Bray comments: "Following the legalization of Christianity in the Roman Empire (in 313) and its establishment as the state religion (in 380), church leaders looked to the OT for models of how a Christian society ought to be governed....The Christian clergy were organized into an order of priests on the Aaronic model and given a tithe of all produce for their maintenance, just as the ancient Levites had received....[T]he OT was allegorized to make it fit the needs of the Christian church" (2016, 14–15).

Rather than conduits of God's will for the "sheep" or mediators between God and humanity, Christian leaders function as facilitators in nurturing believers to maturity in their own obedience to Jesus Christ.

Summarily, then, in the OT the kingdom of God was *centralized* in: (1) the Promised Land, Jerusalem, and the Temple; (2) the Jewish racial lineage (Abraham's offspring) as God's covenantal people; (3) the Sabbath day that distinguished Israel from the nations; and (4) the hierarchy of priests as an exclusive professional guild.

In the kingdom of God, the NT church is the dialectic antithesis to the centralized forms of OT Israel. No one denies the continuity of many other aspects of God's kingdom through the OT and NT, however the *form* of that kingdom radically shifts with the NT church. In the condominium of God's people, different apartments function under different rules. This should not surprise us from a Trinitarian God constituted in both unity and diversity. As a spiritual entity the church is centralized in the Head Jesus Christ, unified by the indwelling Holy Spirit, sent into every part of the world, a communion for all peoples, manifest in local churches, acknowledging every day (ultimately) alike, and affirming the priesthood of every believer. Contrary to popular images, the NT local church is not defined by a building (or "temple"), Sunday Sabbath, worship service, and full-time pastor. Thinking afresh sets church planters free from conventional conceptions to focus on what is essential to the local church in the diverse contexts of a lost world.

THE LOCAL CHURCH AS PRACTICALLY DEFINED BY NT FUNCTIONS

While various lenses enrich our understanding of the church, the local NT church is especially identified both by adherence to the apostles' doctrine and its God-glorifying activities. In contrast to the carefully prescribed external forms given to ancient Israel, NT ecclesial forms exist to accomplish the primary roles prescribed for the local church. This is not to say that certain unifying forms of organization, qualified leadership, and ordinances (or sacraments) do not remain in place (such forms are established by our Lord and the apostles). Nor does creativity of ecclesial forms in any way negate firm adherence to classical Christian doctrine ("the Great Tradition"). But beyond these minimal organizational prescriptives that unite all true Christian assemblies, the church's organization, structure, liturgies, and music are to be deliberately flexible in order to accomplish the transgenerational and transcultural functions of the church. The forms of the church should maximize the congregation's spiritual vitality in ways reflective of the experiences of the early church.

Acts 2 initiates the outworking of Jesus's Great Commission (Matt 28:19–20) with Pentecost's sequence of proclamation, making disciples, baptizing, and teaching (Ferguson 1996, 14). As the first expression of the body of Christ, Acts 2:42–47 can be seen as a matrix for categorizing the primary NT functions of worship, teaching/discipleship, fellowship, and evangelism/mission—activities of the church then amplified throughout the NT.[5] While the approach might seem simplistic, this fourfold description remains heuristically useful as a blueprint for church

---

5. Van Gelder assigns the category of "functional ecclesiology" to various subgroups including seeker-sensitive, purpose-driven, small-group, and niche-market churches (2000, 21). Allison does somewhat the same (2012, 50–51). But one would have to say that almost all missional ecclesiologies are variations of functional ecclesiologies. Only the most naïve of treatments would not also affirm the importance of the ontological (theological) dimension of the church as the chosen people of God and the body of Christ. But this ontology is to be manifested in the visible activity of the local church. Note: I have not included miracles, prayer, and social outreach as specific functional categories—the first is not always evident in the NT church, and the latter two overlap with more than one category (Horrell 2004, 73–85).

planters everywhere in the world. Indeed, for many Christian workers entangled in the mechanics of church institutionalism, a return to the simple, central functions of the NT church brings perspective and generates creative, contextualized expression.

VIBRANT WORSHIP

From the beginning, the church was characterized by worshiping the Lord God and his Son Jesus Christ. Adoration and praise spilled over into everything. The believers "devoted themselves . . . to prayer" (Acts 2:42); "everyone was filled with awe" (v. 43); "they broke bread in their homes" (v. 46), "praising God" (v. 47). The early church recognized that it exists *preeminently* for the glory of God. Indeed, on certain occasions the *fear* of the Lord describes the church's reverence before the Lord (5:11; 9:31; 19:17). With the indwelling of the Holy Spirit, believers perceived themselves as the living temple of God's presence. From the very beginning, the Lord's Supper became a focal point of worship and came to function as the Christian's Holy of Holies (1 Cor 11:23–33). Collective devotion included singing, reading of Scriptures, sacrifice of one's material possessions (gifts, offerings), and prayers of adoration to God and Christ. Worship occurred not only in official assemblies but also in spontaneous occasions when believers simply met together (Acts 4:23–31; Eph 5:18–20).

As the new bride of Christ, the earliest church effervesces with creative love. To be creative means to be innovative and at the same time authentic to who we are as individuals and as believing communities. Many North Americans (myself included) have little experience in communal worship where the presence of the Lord is both openly sought and emotionally experienced. As biblical truth and self-honesty help guide us, the NT allows freedom to experiment with expressions of worship indigenous to a culture yet reflective of the NT church. While certain ecclesial traditions might be transferrable, when beginning a new congregation, a primary manifestation of the true church is genuine, heartfelt worship. Without collective honoring and experiencing of God, a church is less than what our Lord intends.

VIBRANT TEACHING/DISCIPLESHIP

"They devoted themselves to the apostles' teaching" (Acts 2:42). In light of the negativism toward "doctrine" and "theology" among millions of evangelicals around the world, it is surprising how frequently the Bible speaks of teaching, doctrine, and example. Jesus speaks of himself as teacher (John 13:13). He is called *teacher* (Heb. *Rabbi*; Gk. *didaskalos*) fifty-nine of a total of seventy-seven times the terms occur in the NT. The verb "teach" *(didaskō)* and the term *didachē* (teaching, doctrine) are repeated about another 160 times in the NT (Silva 2014, 1.710)—with generally positive connotations. Teachers such as Apollos (Acts 18:24–28) stand in high esteem in the early church. In 1 and 2 Timothy and Titus alone, we find nearly fifty references to instruction, doctrine, and teaching by example—all with a view to strengthening others in Christ-like maturity. Paul charges Timothy, "Watch your life and your doctrine closely. Persevere in them, because if you do you will save both yourself and your hearers" (1 Tim 4:16 NIV). The Bible insists teaching is foundational to the believer's life (Rom 12:2; Eph 4:11–13). In an age in which lax study, subjectivism, and prophetic "visions" rule many pulpits of the world, it is essential that those forming new congregations teach and model the biblical doctrines and principles of the faith (Jude 3). A primary function of the local church, modeled by qualified leadership, is to teach "sound doctrine" and "refute those who oppose it" (Titus 1:9; 2:1 NIV).

Neither the term *teaching* nor its intended effect of *learning* captures the breadth of NT exhortations. Christ's Great Commission specifies *"make disciples* of all nations . . . teaching them to obey everything I have commanded you" (Matt 28:19–20 NIV).

Activities involve multiple levels of discipleship, testimonies, and models of godly living. Learning is generated both by the power of the Word and by examples of faithfulness. If believers are not steadily learning truths that excite and nurture them in the Lord, then the local church, again, is failing in its God-given NT responsibility. The church planting task is to maximize faithful teaching/learning, grounded in Scripture, in contextualized patterns that fit the participants' ways of learning.

VIBRANT *KOINŌNIA*

The intra-Trinitarian love of the Father, Son, and Holy Spirit is to be reflected in believers' affections toward one another (John 17:26; 1 John 4:7–16). Recounting the birth of the church at Pentecost, Luke writes: "They devoted themselves . . . to fellowship" (Acts 2:42 NIV); "They broke bread in their homes and ate together with glad and sincere hearts" (v. 46 NIV); and "All the believers were together and had everything in common" (v. 44 NIV). The initial intensity of this sacrifice-all fellowship did not continue, but the exhortations and examples to care for one another are frequent in the epistles. In classical Greek, the term *koinōnia* denoted fellowship within a close bond, a two-sided relation—notably in marriage "closer and more comprehensive than all other forms of fellowship" (Hauck 1967, 3.798). Occurring some twenty times in the NT, the Greek term *koinōnia* refers both to our personal communion with God and more often to one believer's relationship with another (1 John 1:3,6–7).

In the twenty-first century with the collapse of human significance, perhaps the greatest apologetic for Christian faith is anthropology—our createdness in the *Imago Dei*. Our humanity, all the more reconciled to our Creator, has the richest of meaning. Christian *koinōnia* signifies the deepest of human relationships through mutual openness and heartfelt commitment around love for our Lord. Yet connectedness with other believers cannot be orchestrated. It is dependent on the Holy Spirit himself. Indeed, prayer is one of the most powerful forces that unites the local church. Incumbent upon the church planter, therefore, is the challenge to pray and think through with others in the local church how best to create conditions for strengthening genuine *koinōnia*. A primary task of the church planter and pastor/leader is to nurture deep fellowship among believers.

At the same time, the NT function of *koinōnia* is perhaps the most sensitive of a cross-cultural church planter's challenges. To be considered are issues of gender relations, ages of participants, social class, race relations, mixtures of cultural and religious backgrounds, and the boundaries of what is perceived as proper in a given socio-religious context as well as prescribed in the Bible itself. Christian fellowship will look significantly different between churches in Chennai, Cairo, and Rio de Janeiro—even as leaders are called to encourage genuine spiritual friendships. In the NT, a living church is known by the love that members have for one another.

VIBRANT OUTREACH

Fourth among these core functions of the NT church is mission itself. In his last words before ascending into heaven, Jesus commissioned his followers to spread the gospel throughout the world (Acts 1:8). At Pentecost, Peter preached the gospel and three thousand people were baptized. Luke records that these first believers enjoyed "the favor of all the people. And the Lord added to their number daily those who were being saved" (Acts 2:47 NIV). Acts records the failures as well as the zeal of the early church in spreading the good news through courageous testimony, open preaching, apologetic debate, missionary travels, and martyrdom. While outreach directly entails evangelism and mission, the NT also exhorts doing good to others (Titus 3:1–2,8,14), sharing of possessions (Heb 13:16; Jas 1:27), exemplary conduct amidst unbelievers (1 Pet 2:12), and readiness of response to those who ask about the reason for one's hope (1 Pet 3:15). Especially powerful is the infectious attraction of the communal life of the early church, even with its problems.

The church must be both attractional and missional. It is not a cruise liner, and not always a battleship—it is called to be an aircraft carrier teaching its people "to share the gospel, without the help of the pastor, in the community, and start ministries and Bible studies—even churches—in places without them. Churches must become discipleship factories, 'sending' agencies that equip their members to take the battle to the enemy" (Greear 2015, 191). Intentional proclamation, outreach, and mission are fundamental for every truly NT church, whether a congregation in formation or those established generations past.

In short, the theological ontology of the church is evidenced by the palpable, visible activity of the local church first reflected in Acts 2:24–27. The popular conceptions of the church as a building, with a Sunday Sabbath, full-time pastor, and high-octane worship program stand distant from the NT ideal. They are also distant from what underground believers experience as a persecuted church in various parts of the world today. The vivid functions of the NT church are the Spirit's invitation to simplicity and in many cases sincere, critical rethinking for ecclesial change (Schaeffer 1970, 71–77; Snyder 1975, 89–99, 105–11; Stanley 2012, 265–91).

To conclude, this work has set forth two ecclesiological principles central to the church planting endeavor.

1. *The church exists as a decentralized form of the kingdom of God.* Through Abraham, Moses, and David, the OT kingdom of God was centralized in geography, racial lineage, Sabbath, and professional priesthood. In the NT, the form of God's kingdom is precisely the opposite—spiritually centralized in Christ but decentralized in the world. Quite decidedly, the church is not constituted by

temples, a priestly caste, or Sunday performance. Rather the NT allows significant freedom to test and mold the forms of local churches to cultures, contexts, and circumstances.

2. *The local church is tangibly defined by its NT functions.* If a local church is to reflect its ontological relation to the body of Christ, then it is measured especially through its God-glorifying activities. That is, while necessarily having some organizational structure, the local church is designed to reflect its Lord through its functions of worship, teaching (disciple-forming), fellowship, and outreach (evangelism/mission). These are the pistons that move the church forward in the power of God. Many a church struggles with only three, or two, or one piston functioning. To the extent that the vital functions of the NT church are not experienced, that congregation is less than the church God intends. A retuning of the local church in light of the primary NT functions—throwing out what encumbers, cleaning out what has encrusted—can revive a congregation to new life. Missiologically speaking, in the formation of new congregations, the vibrant activities of Acts 2:24–27 serve as a basic, transferrable matrix for incentivizing, praying, organizing, and structuring the local church, all by the power of the Holy Spirit.

In everything that has been said, what is *not* being suggested is that all church planting efforts are subject to the whims of maverick founders or isolated, autonomous congregations. Churches are to seek out and nurture relations with other local churches and recognize themselves as part of the Great Tradition of orthodox doctrine and the historic, worldwide body of Christ.

New congregations must work toward and remain within NT directives for presbyters/elders and deacons, the ordinances of baptism and communion, and discipleship as well as discipline in the congregation. Most churches are related to traditions or mission orientation and should respect their greater ecclesial families. On the other hand, wise denominational and mission leadership will encourage fresh experimentation and cultural adaptation in efforts to begin new congregations—whether in unevangelized fields or in established settings closer to home. Older churches can and should parent and encourage fresh models for daughter churches.

In the end, Scripture itself allows significant diversity among the transcultural, transgenerational manifestations of Christ's followers. Recognizing NT flexibility regarding forms and the primacy of NT functions in the church planting effort, missionaries and indigenous leaders are freed to adapt forms and organize in such ways that encourage the full expression of these activities. A student of a target culture, working together with believers native to a particular setting, will seek to test and mold forms (organization, appearance, etc.) to that which best facilitates these foremost NT activities. This is the challenge of creative ecclesiology and church planting. The implications of the simple NT teachings are remarkably liberating.

REFERENCES CITED

Allen, Roland. 1962. *Missionary Methods: St. Paul's or Ours?* Grand Rapids, MI: Eerdmans.

Allison, Gregg R. 2012. *Sojourners and Strangers: The Doctrine of the Church.* Wheaton, IL: Crossway.

Bacchiocchi, Samuele. 1991. "Remembering the Sabbath: The Creation-Sabbath in Jewish and Christian History." In *The Sabbath in Jewish and Christian Traditions,* edited by Tamara C. Eskenazi, Daniel J. Harrington, and William H. Shea, 69–97. New York, NY: Crossroad.

Blaising, Craig A., and Darrell L. Bock, eds. 1992. *Dispensationalism, Israel and the Church: The Search for Definition*. Grand Rapids, MI: Zondervan.

———. 1993. *Progressive Dispensationalism*. Wheaton, IL: Victor/ Bridgepoint.

Bock, Darrell L. and Mitch Glasser, eds. 2014. *The People, the Land, and the Future of Israel: Israel and the Jewish People in the Plan of God*. Grand Rapids, MI: Kregel.

Brand, Chad Owen, ed. 2015. *Perspectives on Israel and the Church: 4 Views*. Nashville, TN: B & H.

Bray, Gerald. 2016. *The Church: A Theological and Historical Account*. Grand Rapids, MI: Baker.

Brueggeman, Walter. 2002. *The Land: Place as Gift, Promise, and Challenge in the Biblical Faith*. 2nd ed. Minneapolis, MN: Augsburg/Fortress.

Carson, D. A., ed. 1982. *From Sabbath to Lord's Day: A Biblical, Historical, and Theological Investigation*. Grand Rapids, MI: Zondervan.

———. 2016. "When Did the Church Begin?" *Themelios* 41(1):1–4.

Dever, Mark. 2013. *Nine Marks of a Healthy Church*. 3rd ed. Wheaton, IL: Crossway.

Ferguson, Everett. 1996. *The Church of Christ: A Biblical Ecclesiology for Today*. Grand Rapids, MI: Eerdmans.

———. 2008. "Why and When Did Christians Start Constructing Special Buildings for Worship?" *Christian History* (Nov. 12). http://www.christianitytoday.com /history/2008/november/why-and-when-did-christians -start-constructing-special.html.

Greear, J. D. 2015. *Gaining by Losing: Why the Future Belongs to Churches that Send*. Grand Rapids, MI: Zondervan.

Hasel, Gerhard F. 1992. "Sabbath." In *Anchor Bible Dictionary*. 6 vols., edited by David Noel Freedman, 5:849–56. New York, NY: Doubleday.

Hauck, Friedrich. 1967. "κοινός, κοινωνός, κοινωνέω, κοινωνία, συγκοινωνός, συγκοινωνέω, κοινωνικός, κοινόω." In *Theological Dictionary of the New Testament.* 10 vols., edited by Gerhard Kittel and translated by Geoffrey W. Bromiley, 3.789–809. Grand Rapids, MI: Eerdmans.

Hesselgrave, David J. 2000. *Planting Churches Cross-Culturally: North America and Beyond.* Grand Rapids, MI: Baker.

Hill, Graham. 2012. *Salt, Light, and a City: Introducing Missional Ecclesiology.* Eugene, OR: Wipf & Stock.

———. 2016. *Global Church: Reshaping Our Conversations, Renewing Our Mission, Revitalizing Our Churches.* Downers Grove, IL: IVP.

Horrell, J. Scott. 2004. *From the Ground Up: New Testament Foundations for the 21st Century Church.* Grand Rapids, MI: Kregel.

———. 2009. "The Trinity, the Imago Dei and the Nature of the Local Church: The Framework of Christian Mission." In *Connecting for Christ: Overcoming Challenges across Cultures,* edited by Florence Tan, 1–30. Singapore: F. P. L. Tan.

Keller, Timothy. 2012. *Center Church: Doing Balanced, Gospel-Centered Ministry in Your City.* Grand Rapids, MI: Zondervan.

Kivitz, Ed René. 1995. *Quebrando Paradigmas.* São Paulo: Abba.

Malphurs, Aubrey. 2004. *Planting Growing Churches for the 21st Century: A Comprehensive Guide for New Churches and Those Desiring Renewal.* 3rd ed. Grand Rapids, MI: Baker.

———. 2011. *The Nuts and Bolts of Church Planting.* Grand Rapids, MI: Baker.

McDermott, Gerald R. 2012. "Covenant, Mission, and Relating to the Other." In *Covenant and Hope: Christian and Jewish Reflections,* edited by Robert W. Jenson and Eugene B. Korn, 19–40. Grand Rapids, MI: Eerdmans.

———, ed. 2016. *The New Christian Zionism: Fresh Perspectives on Israel and the Land.* Downers Grove, IL: IVP.

Ott, Craig, and Gene Wilson. 2011. *Global Church Planting: Biblical Principles and Best Practices for Multiplication*. Grand Rapids, MI: Zondervan.

Payne, J. D. 2009. *Discovering Church Planting: An Introduction to the Whats, Whys, and Hows of Global Church Planting*. Downers Grove, IL: IVP.

Peters, George W. 1972. *A Biblical Theology of Missions*. Chicago, IL: Moody.

Rehm, Merlin D. 1992. "Levites and Priests." In *Anchor Bible Dictionary*. 6 vols., edited by David Noel Freedman, 4.279–310. New York, NY: Doubleday.

Sanders, Fred. 2010. *The Deep Things of God: How the Trinity Changes Everything*. Wheaton, IL: Crossway.

Schaeffer, Francis A. 1970. *The Church at the End of the 20th Century*. Downers Grove, IL: IVP.

Silva, Moisés. 2014. "Διδάσκω." In *New International Dictionary of New Testament Theology and Exegesis*. 2nd ed. 5 vols., edited by Moisés Silva, 1.707–17. Grand Rapids, MI: Zondervan.

Snyder, Howard A. 1975. *The Problem of Wine Skins: Church Structure in a Technological Age*. Downers Grove, IL: IVP.

Stanley, Andy. 2012. *Deep and Wide: Creating Churches Unchurched People Love to Attend*. Grand Rapids, MI: Zondervan.

Stetzer, Ed, and Daniel Im. 2016. *Planting Missional Churches: Your Guide to Starting Churches that Multiply*. 2nd ed. Nashville, TN: B & H.

Tennent, Timothy C. 2010. *Invitation to World Missions: A Trinitarian Missiology for the Twenty-first Century*. Grand Rapids, MI: Kregel.

Van Gelder, Craig. 2000. *The Essence of the Church: A Community Created by the Spirit*. Grand Rapids, MI: Baker.

Warren, Rick. 1995. *The Purpose Driven Church: Growth Without Compromising Your Message and Mission*. Grand Rapids, MI: Zondervan.

Wellum, Stephen J., and Brent A. Parker, eds. 2016. *Progressive Covenantalism: Charting the Course between Dispensational and Covenant Theologies*. Nashville, TN: B & H.

Wright, Christopher J. H. 2005. *The Mission of God: Unlocking the Bible's Grand Narrative*. Downers Grove, IL: IVP.

WHEN THE CHURCH WAS THE MISSION ORGANIZATION

RETHINKING WINTER'S TWO STRUCTURES OF REDEMPTION PARADIGM

Edward L. Smither

Critical observers of mission history remark that following the sixteenth-century Reformation in Europe, one reason for the initial inaction of Reformed Protestants in global mission was the lack of missionary sending structures. Roman Catholics on the other hand possessed a number of sending structures—most notably monastic orders (e.g., Franciscans, Augustinians, Dominicans, Cistercians, and Jesuits) that were formed in the medieval period for the purpose of sending witnesses to the world. So how did mission sending happen and what structures were in place in the early and medieval church prior to the rise of monastic missionary orders? In this article, I argue that the church itself was the key organism and catalyst for mission sending. In doing so, I offer an alternative conclusion to Ralph Winter's (Winter 1999, 220–29) popularly accepted claim that there were two structures of redemption in mission history—modalities (e.g., churches) and sodalities (e.g., monastic movements)—and argue that the church was the sole means of sending. To make the case, I will highlight the examples of five missionary-monk-bishops who served between the fourth and eighth centuries: Basil of Caesarea (fourth-century Asia Minor), Patrick (fifth-century Ireland), Augustine of Canterbury (sixth- and seventh-century England), Alopen (seventh-century China), and Boniface (eighth-century Germany). Though not exhaustive, these cases serve as representative models for early Christian and medieval Christian practice in the global church.

BASIL OF CAESAREA (AD 329–379)

Remembered in church history for being one of the Cappadocian fathers famous for their articulation of Trinitarian thought, Basil also engaged in mission in his home city of Cappadocian Caesarea in Asia Minor. Born into a wealthy and ascetically minded family, he studied rhetoric and philosophy before embracing a monastic lifestyle. After a few years of living in monastic community, Basil was set apart by the church at Caesarea as a reader, presbyter, and then finally a bishop. Though ordained, Basil remained in his monastic calling and joined a growing number of fourth-century church leaders who served as monk-bishops (Rousseau 1998, 2, 68–69, 84–85, 93; Sterk 2004, 43, 74–76).

Because of its strategic location on Roman roads that connected trading centers such as Constantinople and Syria, Caesarea was an important city and Roman administrative center in the fourth century. With diverse peoples from Asia Minor, Armenia, Syria, Persia, and the northern Gothic regions regularly passing through the city, it became a significant intercultural crossroads (Rousseau 1998, 133–134; Holman 2001, 69–70). On the other hand, due to an earthquake and famine in the region beginning around 368, many Cappadocians faced poverty and near starvation. In addition to these economic and social problems, Basil seemed to have regular political conflicts with Roman officials and theological ones with other church leaders (Smither 2011, 80–82; Holman 2001, 5, 65–69).

How did Basil approach mission in his Cappadocian context? As bishop of Caesarea, Basil's first priority was preaching—not only to train believers but also to evangelize non-believers (Basil, *Morals* 70.9–11, 31–34). Though Basil was committed to caring for humanitarian needs, his close friend and biographer Gregory of Nazianzus indicated that Basil's first concern was the spiritual needs of his hearers:

> [Basil] provided the nourishment of the Word
> and that more perfect good work and distribu-
> tion being from heaven and on high; if the bread
> of angels is the Word, whereby souls hungry for
> God are fed and given to drink, and seek after
> nourishment that neither diminishes nor fails
> but remains forever; thus [i.e., by his sermons]
> this supplier of grain and abundant riches [he
> who was] the poorest and most needy [person] I
> have known, provided, not for a famine of bread
> or a thirst for water, but a longing for the truly
> life-giving and nourishing Word, which effects
> growth to spiritual maturity in those nourished
> well on it (Gregory of Nazianzus, *Oration* 43.36 in
> Holman 2001, 65).

Basil's preaching also included a prophetic discourse against the injustices occurring in Caesarea. He confronted moneylenders who exploited the poor by charging exorbitant interest rates. He challenged the poor themselves for failing to be content and live within their means. He chastised the wealthy for refusing to be generous and for those who hoarded grain during the famine. Though most of his prophetic preaching was aimed at poverty related issues, he also preached against slavery (Smither 2011, 83–85).

In addition to speaking about poverty issues, Basil was actively involved in caring for the needs of the poor in Cappadocia. In response to the famine of 368, Basil led an effort to open the storehouses of grain and distribute food to the poor and hungry. Gregory of Nazianzus wrote:

> By his word and advice [Basil] opened the stores
> of those who possessed them, and so, according to
> the Scripture, dealt food to the hungry and satis-
> fied the poor with bread . . . and in what way? . . .

He gathered together the victims of the famine with some who were but slightly recovering from it, men and women, infants, old men . . . and obtaining contributions of all sorts of food which can relieve famine, set before them basins of soup and such meat as was found preserved among us, on which the poor live. (Gregory of Nazianzus, *Oration* 43.34-36 in Holman 2001, 65–66)

The most concrete expression of Basil's ministry to the poor in Caesarea was the establishment of the *basileas* ("new city")— "a complex of buildings constructed at the edge of Caesarea during the early years of Basil's episcopate" (Sterk 2004, 69). Constructed on land that was either owned by Basil's family or donated by the emperor, the complex included a home for the poor, a hospital, an early version of a job training center, and storehouses from which food supplies were distributed. Also, given Caesarea's position on the crossroads between Asia Minor, Syria, Armenia, and the Gothic regions, the *basileas* included a hospice so that hospitality could be shown to travelers (Smither 2011, 88–90).

Reflecting upon Basil's Cappadocian mission, we note that his entire ministry was carried out under the auspices of the church at Caesarea. Basil served as a cross-cultural and urban missionary from his platform as bishop of the church at Caesarea. In addition to preaching, leading the sacraments, and generally administrating the church, he made cross-cultural mission work a part of his job description as bishop. In this sense, he followed in the footsteps of earlier missionary-bishops Irenaeus of Lyons in second- and third- century Gaul and Gregory Thaumaturgus in third-century Asia Minor (Smither 2014, 34).

In addition to self-deploying in mission as part of his role as bishop, Basil also directed a community of monks and clergy in this same work in Cappadocia. A monk-bishop, Basil lived in community with other monks and clergy literally on the outskirts of Caesarea. These coenobitic (communal) urban-dwelling monks carried out the noted ministries of the *basileas* (Smither 2011, 88–90).

Finally, Basil served as a metropolitan bishop for Asia Minor, meaning he oversaw and influenced the ministries of some fifty other bishops in the region. He stayed in contact with these leaders through regular pastoral correspondence as well as an annual church council in the region. Basil's letters indicate that he expected bishops to care for the poor in their communities, and other church leaders launched projects similar to the *basileas* because of Basil's influence (Basil 1962, 70.19–20; Basil 1951 141–144; Sterk 2004, 69–74; Smither 2011, 88–90).

PATRICK OF IRELAND (CA. 389–CA. 461)

Mostly likely British, Patrick served as a pioneer missionary-bishop among the Irish in the fifth century. Taken captive by the Irish as a teenager, Patrick spent six years among this Celtic people as a slave, clarifying his own commitment to Christ and learning the Irish language and culture. After escaping captivity and returning home to Roman Britain, Patrick wrote in his *Confessions* that he received a vision calling him back to the Irish. Interpreting this later in his life, he wrote: "The one and only purpose I had in going back to the people from whom I had earlier escaped was the gospel and the promises of God" (O'Loughlin 1999, 89; McNeill 1974, 56–59; O'Loughlin 2005, 37–42).

Though traditional sources claim that Patrick prepared for ministry under Bishop Germanus of Auxerre in Gaul, it is more likely that local clergy in Britain supervised his pre-mission training. Eventually, Patrick was set apart as a missionary-bishop by Bishop Celestine of Rome. Unlike the bishops in the fourth and fifth centuries who were appointed as organizers of established Christian communities, Patrick's "missionary work is explicitly aimed at those Irish who are not Christians" and he saw himself as "the final missionary to Ireland, the one who went to mop up the last pockets of paganism so that Ireland could be wholly Christian" (O'Loughlin 2005, 58–59; Freeman 2005, 62–63).

Though Patrick encountered some Irish Christians when he arrived, the majority were still adherents to Celtic paganism and worshiped as many as four hundred gods while also venerating certain animals, sacred places, and sacred dates. A priestly class known as the Druids facilitated their teaching and rituals (Olsen 2003, 28). In terms of social structure, fifth-century Ireland was organized along tribal networks and no actual towns or cities existed.

Believing that he was ministering in the last days and literally at the ends of the earth, Patrick's first step in the Irish mission was to approach tribal leaders, seek their protection and favor, and ask permission to proclaim the gospel among their people (Wilken 2012, 271). Patrick was one of the earliest missionaries in church history to reference Matthew 28:18–20 as a central mission text, so it is not surprising that itinerant preaching characterized his ministry. Leading teams of monks and clergy, Patrick expected that they would encounter suffering and hardship in the work. Despite this, he also preached prophetically against injustice and slavery in Irish society. After thirty years of ministry (ca. 432–ca. 461), Patrick saw much of Ireland evangelized to the point that the Irish church was becoming a hub for reaching other parts of Europe (Patrick, *Confessions* 1, 9, 12, 23, 34, 39, 43, 48; O'Loughlin 2005, 65–68, 72–77).

Patrick's mission work was also based in the church and had churches as its most visible outcome. Ordained by the bishop of Rome and likely trained by British church leaders, Patrick's sending authority was effectively the churches of Britain and Rome. His evangelism and preaching were organically related to catechesis (a thorough period of instruction prior to baptism) and baptism itself. O'Loughlin points out that the confession of faith in the opening paragraphs of Patrick's *Confessions,* which surely informed his catechesis, was based on a creed that greatly resembled that of Nicaea (Patrick, *Confessions* 4 in O'Loughlin 1999, 54–55). Reflecting on the fruit of his ministry, Patrick spoke of the "many thousands, my brothers and sisters, sons and daughters, I have baptized in the Lord" (Patrick, *Confessions* 14). He further rejoiced that he had raised up new church leaders who shared those values—"clergy everywhere to baptize and preach to a people who are in want and need" (Patrick, *Confessions* 40 in O'Loughlin 1999, 75–76).

Patrick was also a monk-bishop who planted new churches around Ireland and deliberately "sought to establish monasteries in the regions of his missionary labors" (Irvin and Sunquist 2001, 236). Patrick's monastic convictions also influenced the leadership structure of the developing Irish church. With no towns to speak of in Ireland prior to Patrick's mission, the monastic communities (and their structures) filled that void and became the first towns. Though bishops existed in the Irish church, monastic abbots became the primary leaders. This monastic form of church polity certainly made the Irish church distinct from the broader church in the world (McNeill 1974, 69–70).

AUGUSTINE OF CANTERBURY (D. 604)

According to an eighth-century biography of Bishop Gregory I (540–604) of Rome, one day while walking through the Roman markets Gregory observed boys "with fair complexions, handsome faces, and lovely hair" being sold as slaves. Inquiring about their identity and background, he learned that they were *Angli* (Anglo or English). Employing a play on words, he responded, "they have the face of angels [*angeli*] and such men should be fellow-heirs with the angels in heaven" (Bede, *Ecclesiastical History* 2.1). Though most scholars doubt the accuracy of this particular story, what is undeniable is that around 596, several years after becoming bishop of Rome, Gregory sent Augustine of Canterbury and a group of about forty monks on a mission to evangelize the English. It was the first cross-cultural mission effort in church history initiated by a Roman bishop. (Mayr-Harting 2001, 57–59; Markus 1997, 177–78).

The English mission was a mission of obedience. While Venerable Bede's account presents Gregory as a strong and assertive bishop and Augustine as a rather weak and uncertain monk, we might wonder why Gregory chose Augustine to lead the effort. The most likely reason was that since Augustine was already serving as the abbot of Gregory's St. Andrew's monastery, Gregory had a great deal of confidence in him. In addition, the monks in his charge on the English mission had made a vow of obedience to Augustine and, of course, Augustine had made the same vow to Bishop Gregory. Obedience to spiritual authority was a strong value in this missionary effort, especially as the monks faced difficulties that came with cross-cultural ministry among a pagan people (Mayr-Harting 2001, 61).

After traveling over land through Gaul, the monks were greeted by King Ethelbert of Kent upon their arrival in England. Having been married to a Christian wife for thirty years and apparently remaining unmoved by the gospel, it comes as no surprise that Ethelbert did not respond immediately to the monks' message. However, the king allowed them to build a church and establish a mission base at Canterbury and gave them freedom to preach among his subjects. According to Gregory, in the first year of their ministry, over ten thousand Anglo-Saxons believed the gospel and were baptized. Though it is difficult to know exactly when Ethelbert converted, the king eventually embraced the gospel for himself (Bede, *Ecclesiastical History* 1.25–26; Mayr-Harting 2001, 62–64; Markus 1963, 19–24).

In terms of Augustine and the team's mission strategies, like Patrick and others, they began by approaching a political leader, preaching the gospel to him, seeking his favor, and receiving permission to minister to his subjects. Second, their preaching received credibility because of the monks' holy examples and also through their apparent working of miracles. Finally, they were sensitive to contextualize the gospel in English forms. In particular, they transformed existing pagan temples into houses of Christian worship and adapted a pagan cattle festival into a thanksgiving feast (Bede, *Ecclesiastical History* 1.25–26, 30–31).

The English mission was very much a church-driven mission. First, as shown, the visionary behind the effort was the Roman Bishop Gregory. Called out of the monastery to serve as a deacon and later bishop, Gregory wrestled with the tension between the contemplative (prayer, fasting, devotion to Scripture) and active (service, ministry, mission) aspects of monastic living (Demacopoulos 2015, 21, 26, 28–30). For Gregory, service to others always trumped contemplation and this value surely undergirded his passion for mission. This was evident in his work as a deacon distributing material aid to the poor in Rome, and also in his vision to see the unbelieving English hear the gospel. Gregory seemed particularly burdened for the English because they represented the last vestiges of paganism within the Roman Empire (Mayr-Harting 2001, 13–16, 22–30; Markus 1997, 80–82).

Second, once Augustine and the monks had departed for England, they remained under Gregory's authority and pastoral care. Sometime after the journey began, the community of monks either experienced dissension or became overwhelmed by the hardship of the journey and the task before them. Bede writes, "They began to contemplate returning home rather than going to a barbarous, fierce, and unbelieving nation" (Bede *Ecclesiastical History* 1.23). Augustine apparently left the group for a time and returned to Rome to convince Gregory that the mission should be abandoned. The strong-willed bishop demonstrated pastoral care for his struggling abbot; however, he refused to allow the monks to return. Instead he sent Augustine back with a brief letter to encourage the group:

You must, most beloved sons, fulfill the good work
. . . with the help of the Lord, you have begun.
Let, then, neither the toil of the journey nor
the tongues of evil-speaking men deter you; but
with all [urgency] and all fervor go on with what
under God's guidance you have commenced,
knowing that great toil is followed by the
glory of an eternal reward. Obey in all things
humbly Augustine your provost (*præposito*), who
is returning to you, whom we also appoint your
abbot, knowing that whatever may be fulfilled in
you through his admonition will in all ways profit
your souls. May Almighty God protect you with
His grace, and grant to me to see the fruit of your
labor in the eternal country; that so, even though
I cannot labor with you, I may be found together
with you in the joy of the reward; for in truth I
desire to labor. God keep you safe, most beloved
sons (Gregory, *Letter* 6.51).

Third, once King Ethelbert granted the monks space to live
and work, one of the first things they did was establish a church as
a base of ministry. As the English work developed, more churches
were started and Augustine and at least two other monks were
set apart as bishops (Bede 2008, 1.27, 2.3; Markus 1997, 180–81).
Though they were not indigenous leaders and the church structures that were adopted were clearly Roman, one clear outcome
of the English mission was the establishment of churches. In short,
the mission to England was the vision of the bishop of the church
at Rome and its outcomes included new churches and church
leaders in England.

ALOPEN AND THE CHURCH OF THE EAST MONKS (SEVENTH CENTURY)

While missionary monks were proclaiming the gospel to English kings in the seventh century, others were sharing the same message in the Far East. The often-overlooked reality in mission history is that during the medieval period, the gospel traveled much farther east than it ever did west. Our understanding of the Church of the East's story was greatly enhanced in 1623 with the discovery of the so-called Nestorian monument in X'ian in Central China—a large black stone monument measuring three meters tall and one meter wide and that dated to 781. The monument's inscription claimed that, among other things, in 635 a certain mission-ary-monk named Alopen arrived in the region and was welcomed by the Emperor Taizong (唐太宗 ; T'ai Tsung) to preach Jingjiao (景教 ; Jiang Jiao), the "luminous religion of Syria" (Neill 1990, 82; Irvin and Sunquist 2001, 316; Lieu and Parry 2014, 159–164). Alopen's mission captures part of the story of the Church of the East and a movement of missionary monks who spread the gospel from Syria and Persia eastward through Central Asia and into China by the mid-seventh century.

Often incorrectly referred to as Nestorians because of a supposed connection to the embattled fifth-century Bishop Nesto-rius of Constantinople (ca. 386–451), the Church of the East was a key movement among the ancient Christian communities of Syria and the Middle East. For our purposes, the Church of the East refers to Syrian and Persian Christians who lived between Edessa and Nisibis in the border region between the Roman and Persian Empires and who related to the Patriarch of Seleucia-Ctesiphon (Lieu and Parry 2014, 147; Moffett 1998, xiv; Baum and Winkler 2000, 3–9).

The Church of the East originated as the gospel spread east-ward from Antioch to Edessa, which was a city on the Old Silk Road connecting traveling merchants between Rome, Armenia,

Persia, and Arabia. Because of Edessa's strategic position on the route, the gospel quickly moved east toward the Persian regions largely through the witness of business people. Following the emergence of the Sassanid Empire in Persia in 225, the Church of the East took on much more of a Persian identity. The church was based at the Persian capital of Seleucia-Ctesiphon and its theological school was at Nisibis. Christians in Persia suffered much discrimination and, at times, persecution from the Zoroastrian government, which caused many to leave their homeland and immigrate to places like Arabia and other places along the Silk Road (Moffett 1998, 92, 112, 117, 137–45, 157–61; Irvin and Sunquist 2001, 199–203).

From a very early point, the Church of the East was known for its strong ascetic tendencies and a related commitment to mission. In fourth-century Persia, monasticism seems to have developed in part as a means for Christians to pursue safe communities given the discrimination they experienced from the Zoroastrian majority. In addition to training monks and others in theology and pastoral ministry, Persian monasteries also gave instruction in medicine and often integrated the study of theology and medicine.

Because Seleucia-Ctesiphon was located on a crossroads to the East, "the expansion of the Christian movement east of Persia after the year 600 was primarily the work of East Syrian monks, priests, and merchants who traveled the trade routes across Asia" (Irvin and Sunquist 2001, 305; Atiya 2010, 257). Lieu and Parry add that these eastern believers "took Christianity to the oasis towns of Central Asia and, eventually, by the seventh century, to China" and that they "were the most evangelical of the Christians trading on the overland Silk Road," witnessing among Zoroastrian, Manichean, Buddhist, and Muslim peoples (Lieu and Parry, 2014, 149).

Alopen arrived in 635 preaching the "luminous religion" and a faith in the "Triune mysterious Person, the unbegotten and true Lord" (Irvin and Sunquist 2001, 316). He and his team of largely Persian monks had been set apart for the mission by Bishop Ishoyahb II of Balad (modern Iraq) (Baum and Winkler 2000, 40–41; Moffett, 1998, 298). The Chinese emperor T'ai Tsung welcomed the monks and apparently began to study the Christian faith himself. After three years, the emperor issued an edict giving Alopen and his group freedom to proclaim the gospel in China while effectively sponsoring their work by giving land in the imperial capital on which to build a monastery (Lieu and Parry 2014, 164; Baum and Winkler, 47).

Within the first century of the monks' arrival, they apparently enjoyed much freedom to continue their ministry though they experienced some backlash from their Buddhist counterparts. In 823, a certain David was consecrated by Timothy of Baghdad as the first bishop, overseeing the church in all of China. However, in 845 the Emperor Wu Tsung, a committed Taoist, led a campaign to suppress Buddhism and Buddhist monasticism throughout the country. Though they were Christian monks, the Church of the East missionary monks were also implicated in these measures and the emperor ordered the closure of their monasteries. Over three thousand monks were ordered to renounce their monastic callings and ministries. When a monastic envoy visited China in 987, he reported no visible evidence of Christianity in the country. Though the church probably did not completely die out, the churches and monasteries failed to recover fully and sustain a viable Christian movement (Baum and Winkler 2000, 47, 50; Moffett 1998, 294; Lieu and Parry 2014, 151).

This eastern missionary movement was very much driven by the authority of the local church. As shown, Alopen and his team were set apart for the Chinese mission by Bishop Ishoyahb II of Balad. This Persian bishop was also responsible for sending missionaries and setting apart new church leaders in Hulwan (modern Iran), Herat (Afghanistan), Samarkand (Uzbekistan), India, and other regions of China. Timothy of Baghdad, who served as bishop in a city that was also the base for the Muslim Abbassid Caliphate, was responsible for sending out over one hundred missionaries to other parts of Asia. In one case, he responded to the request of a Turkish king for Christian missionaries to come to his territory. Timothy also set apart leaders for new churches in China, Tibet, and among the Turks. Further, the Church of the East missionary monks remained accountable to the bishops who sent them, and they regularly sent back letters and updates to their sending churches. At the same time, some eastern bishops sent emissaries every few years to visit deployed missionaries and to check up on them (Irvin and Sunquist 2001, 307, 313; Baum and Winkler 2000, 40–41, 53, 61–62; Lieu and Parry 2014, 149–53).

While Church of the East missionaries valued the church as their sending structure, they also prioritized church planting, and it was an evident outcome of their ministries. As monasteries were started along the Silk Road between Sogdiana (Persia) and China, new churches were also started and these two structures continued to be organically integrated. The missionary-monk Alopen was also set apart as a bishop so he could give leadership to Chinese churches once they were planted. This custom of setting apart new bishops—both Persian and Chinese—continued as new Chinese churches were started (Irvin and Sunquist 2001, 307, 319–20).

BONIFACE (CA. 680–754)

Boniface was the most well-known eighth-century Christian missionary and, arguably, the most influential English Christian on European Christianity in the medieval period. Originally named Wynfrith, he spent the first forty years of his life in monasteries at Exeter and Nursling. While living in the monastery at Nursling and probably inspired by the accounts of the Celtic monks, Boniface felt the initial urge to leave and move out among pagans for the purpose of pilgrimage and mission. Though initially resistant to Boniface's vision, his monastic abbot eventually released him to go. This initiative for mission seemed to rest squarely on Boniface's vision as no monastic or ecclesiastical sending initiative was in place (Willibald 2000, 1–2; Talbot 1970, 45–46).

Boniface's missionary career began around 719 when he joined the missionary Willibrord's work among the Frisians, a Germanic people who lived in what is now Holland and Germany. After a year of ministry, Boniface journeyed to Rome where he was set apart by Bishop Gregory II as a missionary envoy to the Frisians and was given the name Boniface (Talbot 1970, 48). After another season of ministering with Willibrord, Boniface returned to Rome in 722, and Gregory II set him apart as a missionary-bishop for all of Germany. Boniface took a vow of allegiance to the pope and committed to propagating a Roman form of Christianity among the Germanic peoples. Boniface's episcopal appointment resembled Patrick's as both men were charged to lead churches in areas where they had not yet been established (Talbot 1970, 49).

The most celebrated account of Boniface's ministry among the Germans came in 724 when he confronted pagan ritual and belief head on by cutting down the sacred oak tree of Jupiter in the town of Geismar. Boniface's biographer Willibald writes:

> With the counsel and advice of the latter persons, Boniface in their presence attempted to cut down, at a place called Geismar, a certain oak of extraordinary size called in the old tongue of the pagans the Oak of Jupiter. Taking his courage in his hands (for a great crowd of pagans stood by watching and bitterly cursing in their hearts the enemy of the gods), he cut the first notch. But when he had made a superficial cut, suddenly, the oak's vast bulk, shaken by a mighty blast of wind from above crashed to the ground shivering its topmost branches into fragments in its fall. As if by the express will of God (for the brethren

> present had done nothing to cause it) the oak burst asunder into four parts, each part having a trunk of equal length. At the sight of this extraordinary spectacle the heathens who had been cursing ceased to revile and began, on the contrary, to believe and bless the Lord. Thereupon the holy bishop took counsel with the brethren, built an oratory from the timber of the oak and dedicated it to Saint Peter the Apostle (2000, 6).

As his mission work continued and particularly as he saw churches established, Boniface's gifts as an administrator began to be recognized. In 737 and 738, following another trip to Rome, he was given authority over all the churches of Bavaria, and he organized several new churches and appointed bishops in the region. Though he wanted to move away from administration and presumably back toward more pioneering mission efforts, Gregory III of Rome ordered Boniface to stay in this role. Between 741 and 747, his administrative tasks only grew as he was tasked with reforming the already established Frankish churches and dealing with immoral clergy and financial abuses among other issues (Boniface *Letters* 23–24, 27–29, 35; Talbot 1970, 53–55).

Neill writes, "As Boniface grew older, he withdrew more and more from the field of administration; at the end the spirit of the missionary prevailed, and drove him out again into the lands where Christ had not been named" (1991, 66). In 753, and well into his seventies, Boniface headed back out to a part of Frisia where there were still unbaptized pagans. In the midst of this new work of preaching, baptizing, and teaching, Boniface and his companions were attacked by an angry mob and martyred in 754.

In terms of his mission practice, Boniface first made contact with German leaders and preached Christ to them, while also seeking their favor to preach among their people. Boniface was also in contact with Frankish Christian political leaders—including Charles Martel, Carloman, Griffo, and Pepin—who provided military protection as he preached among the Frisians (Willibald 2000, 5; Talbot 1970, 45). Second, despite this protection, Boniface's mission work was centered on building relationships and preaching. As shown in the account at Geismar, a key part of his preaching included confronting paganism. Boniface followed up the evangelistic work among the Frisians through teaching, catechesis, and the establishment of new churches (Willibald 2000, 5; Boniface *Letters* 3, 11–12; Mayr-Harting 2001, 263). Third, Boniface was an innovator in team ministry by recruiting monks and nuns to serve among the Frisians. In fact, he is one of the earliest missionaries to involve women in the work of mission (Willibald 2000, 8; Boniface *Letter* 6; Talbot 1970, 51).

Boniface's ministry was also characterized by a strong connection to the church. Though not sent out by his monastery or the English church, he aligned himself with the bishop of Rome and became ordained as a bishop for missionary work in the Germanic regions. Effectively, he was sent out for mission by the bishop of Rome.

As Frisians embraced the gospel, Boniface catechized and baptized new believers and established new churches. As shown, part of Boniface's work as a bishop was serving as an administrator of existing German churches and bringing reform to the Frankish churches.

Like Augustine of Canterbury, Boniface's mission work also had a distinct Roman-ness about it. Boniface demonstrated a strong loyalty to the bishop of Rome, and he consistently worked to align the German churches with Rome's authority, teaching, and practices. In Gregory II's initial letter to Boniface, the bishop encouraged him to assimilate German believers into the church according to Roman customs (Boniface *Letters* 5, 23, 25, 37, 46–47). As the Roman bishop gave Boniface further direction on questions related to ordinations, marriage, and the liturgy among other things, Roman theology and approaches to church certainly prevailed (Boniface *Letters* 14, 16; Talbot 1970, 51–52;

Mayr-Harting 2001, 269). Though this influence hindered local Germanic Christianity from developing, Boniface's regard for the authority of the Roman church and his commitment to begin new Roman style churches are without question.

CONCLUSION

In this essay, I have endeavored to narrate representative accounts in five contexts (Asia Minor, East Asia, Ireland, England, and Germany) from the fourth to eighth centuries in which the church functioned as the sending structure for missionaries. Though the circumstances, strategies, and contexts differ, a constant value was that mission flowed from the church and resulted in churches.

In the case of Basil of Caesarea, he self-identified as a bishop and not as a missionary; however, a clear part of his job description was serving as an intercultural, urban missionary in the multicultural context of Cappadocia. A monk-bishop and leader of the church and the monastery in his region of Asia Minor, Basil recognized only one structure for ministry and mission—the church.

Patrick of Ireland also viewed himself first and foremost as a bishop (cf. O'Loughlin 1999, 48). Though not set apart to serve an existing congregation as Basil and other early Christian bishops were, he was appointed as a missionary-bishop for the sake of non-believers. Patrick was, of course, set apart under the authority of the bishop of Rome, and he most likely apprenticed for the Irish ministry under British church leaders. When the Irish embraced the gospel, Patrick planted churches and started monasteries, and church leadership structures followed monastic structures, which resulted in an organic relationship between the two. Though later Celtic missionary monasticism flourished because of Patrick's legacy, in his day we cannot really separate the monastic and ecclesiastical structures for mission.

The bishop of Rome initiated Augustine of Canterbury's mission to England, while Boniface petitioned the bishop of Rome to send him to Germany. However, both men were clearly sent by and ministered under the authority of the Roman church. Though they established monasteries on their fields of service, these communities were accountable to the church. If there were two structures in these contexts, then the monastic structure was so subservient to the ecclesiastical one that the former was engulfed in the latter. Finally, as Augustine and Boniface received pretty specific directions from the Roman leadership, the most visible outcome of their work was theologically and culturally Roman churches.

From the fourth to eighth centuries and prior to the rise of monastic missionary orders, it was the church that sent missionaries, trained them, kept them accountable, provided authority, and often gave specific direction for ministry. One may reasonably ask: in the examples surveyed, were missionaries sent by the local church or the universal church? The simple answer is both. In the period of our study, there is an organic relationship between the universal church (*catholica*) and local congregations. Basil of Caesarea certainly regarded his local work in Asia Minor in light of the whole church in the whole world. Patrick and Boniface traveled to Rome to receive blessing and sponsorship from the Roman church, which was increasingly moving to the center of Western Christianity. Their church planting efforts in Ireland and in Germany respectively were local contextual efforts that certainly related to Rome. Augustine's mission to England was the vision of Gregory the Great, the leader of both the local church at Rome and also the developing Roman *catholica*. Church of the East missionary monks in Asia were sent by local bishops such as Timothy and Ishoyahb and continually functioned under their authority. In short, the missionary-monk-bishops surveyed did not draw a great distinction between the local church and the universal church.

In summary, although Winter's paradigm for two structures of redemption may be more evident in later periods in church history, I suggest that it does find adequate support from the narrative of early and medieval mission history through the eighth century. Rather, in the period of our study—the first eight centuries—the church alone functioned as the sending structure for mission to the nations.

REFERENCES CITED

Atiya, Aziz S. 2010. *History of Eastern Christianity*. Piscataway, NJ: Gorgias Press.

Basil of Caesarea. 1951. *Letters. Volume 1* (1–185). Fathers of the Church 13. Translated by Agnes Clare Way. Washington, DC: Catholic University Press.

———. 1962. *Ascetical Works. Fathers of the Church 9*. Translated by M. Monica Wagner. Washington, DC: Catholic University Press.

Baum, Wilhelm, and Dietmar W. Winkler. 2000. *The Church of the East: A Concise History*. London: Routledge.

Bede. 2008. *The Ecclesiastical History of the English People*. Edited by Judith McClure and Roger Collins. Oxford: Oxford University Press.

Boniface. *Letters. Medieval Sourcebook*. http://sourcebooks.fordham .edu/Halsall/basis/boniface-letters.asp

Demacopoulos, George E. 2015. *Gregory the Great: Ascetic, Pastor, and First Man of Rome*. Notre Dame, IN: University of Notre Dame Press.

Freeman, Philip. 2005. *St. Patrick of Ireland: A Biography*. New York, NY: Simon and Schuster.

Gregory. *Letters. Nicene and Post-Nicene Fathers* 2.12. Christian Classics Ethereal Library. http://www.ccel.org/ccel /schaff/npnf212.iii.v.vi.xxxii.html.

Holman, Susan R. 2001. *The Hungry are Dying: Beggars and Bishops in Roman Cappadocia.* Oxford: Oxford University Press.

———, ed. 2008. *Wealth and Poverty in Early Church and Society.* Grand Rapids, MI: Baker Academic.

Irvin, Dale T., and Scott W. Sunquist. 2001. *History of the World Christian Movement: Volume 1, Earliest Christianity to 1453.* Maryknoll, NY: Orbis.

Lieu, Samuel N.C., and Ken Parry. 2014. "Deep into Asia." In *Early Christianity in Contexts: An Exploration across Cultures and Continents,* edited by William Tabbernee, 143–80. Grand Rapids, MI: Baker Academic.

Markus, Robert A. 1963. "The Chronology of the Gregorian Mission to England: Bede's Narrative and Gregory's Correspondence." *Journal of Ecclesiastical History* 14:16–30.

———. 1997. *Gregory the Great and His World.* Cambridge: Cambridge University Press.

Mayr-Harting, Henry. 2001. *The Coming of Christianity to Anglo-Saxon England.* State College, PA: Penn State University Press.

McNeill, John T. 1974. *The Celtics Churches: A History A.D. 200–1200.* Chicago, IL: University of Chicago Press.

Moffett, Samuel H. 1998. *A History of Christianity in Asia, Volume I: Beginnings to 1500.* Maryknoll, NY: Orbis.

Neill, Stephen. 1990. *A History of Christian Missions.* London: Penguin.

O'Loughlin, Thomas. 1999. *Saint Patrick: The Man and His Works.* London: SPCK.

———. 2005. *Discovering Saint Patrick.* Mahwah, NJ: Paulist Press.

Olsen, Ted. 2003. *Christianity and the Celts.* Downers Grove, IL: Intervarsity Press.

Rousseau, Philip. 1998. *Basil of Caesarea.* Berkeley, CA: University of California Press.

Smither, Edward L. 2011. "Basil of Caesarea: An Early Christian Model of Urban Mission." In *Reaching the City: Reflections* on *Urban Mission for the 21st Century*, edited by Gary Fujino, Timothy R. Sisk, and Tereso C. Casino, 59–75. Pasadena, CA: William Carey Library.

———. 2014. *Mission in the Early Church: Themes and Reflections*. Eugene, OR: Cascade Books.

Sterk, Andrea. 2004. *Renouncing the World Yet Leading the Church: The Monk-Bishop in Late Antiquity*. Cambridge, MA: Harvard University Press.

Talbot, C. H. 1970. "St. Boniface and the German Mission." In *The Mission of the Church and the Propagation of the Faith*, edited by C.J. Cumming, 45–58, Cambridge: Cambridge University Press.

Wilken, Robert L. 2012. *The First Thousand Years: A Global History of Christianity*. New Haven, CT: Yale University Press.

Willibald. 2000. "The Life of Boniface." Fordham University. http://legacy.fordham.edu/halsall/basis/willibald-boniface.asp.

Winter, Ralph D. 1999. "The Two Structures of God's Redemptive Mission." In *Perspectives on the World Christian Movement: A Reader, edited by Ralph D. Winter and Steven C. Hawthorne, 220–29. 3rd ed*. Pasadena, CA: William Carey Library.

FROM SOLIDARITY TO SODALITY

COMPASSIONATE MISSION, LOCAL CHURCHES, AND THE FOSTERING OF CROSS-CULTURAL MISSIONARY BANDS

Jerry M. Ireland

A colleague recently shared with me a disturbing story. As leader of a group of missionaries working among Unreached People Groups (UPGs), he recounted how his team had gathered to plan and strategize on evangelism and church planting. After sitting silently for most of the meeting, one team member spoke up and declared, "I don't need to be here. I'm here to do social justice work, not church planting." The rest of the team sat back in disbelief. Where did this person get the idea that mission, and mission among UPGs no less, could consist of social justice and *not* church planting and evangelism?

My own conversations with members of the missiology committee within Assemblies of God World Missions (AGWM) suggest that this sort of thinking is increasingly the norm rather than the exception among new missionary candidates. Other evidence suggests a growing trend toward compassion work among mission-sending churches. In the United States, mission giving to evangelism and church planting declined by roughly 10 percent between 1998 and 2008 while giving to relief and development work increased by about 5 percent during the same period (Weber 2010, 52). This raises the important question of whether there is a way to better connect those who feel called and gifted in the area of compassion to serve in mission in a way that more directly connects to church planting and evangelism. In this essay I suggest that compassion can serve the primary goal in mission of taking the gospel to the unreached and thereby overcome some of the compartmentalized thinking seen in the story above. My thesis is that solidarity, defined as an essential feature of corporate holiness according to the New Testament, constitutes a vital ingredient in the emergence of indigenous mission movements. Missionaries can facilitate this vital solidarity by removing themselves as the primary doers of compassion and by focusing on discipleship.

WINTER'S MODALITY AND SODALITY STRUCTURES

In a series of essays and articles in the 1970s, Ralph Winter articulated what he at one point labeled "the two structures of God's redemptive mission" (1974, 121). Winter distinguished between what he considered the two redemptive structures of Christianity, "modalities" and "sodalities," wherein the denomination and local church both constitute a modality and the missionary band or mission agency a sodality. According to Winter, it is sodalities that have historically broken through to take the gospel to new frontiers, and that they have often been the source of renewal within the church. Winter also argues that where sodalities were absent, the church has often lapsed into a dangerous nominalism (1974, 131).

Winter's purpose in making this distinction was to guard the church's missionary mandate by distinguishing between the purpose and function of the mission organization and that of the local church or denomination. Central to this distinction was Winter's belief that church structures (modalities) were too inclusive and democratic for sustained mission to the unreached (1971a, 198–99; 1974, 135; cf. Fields 2011, 49–54).

According to these designations, "a modality is a structured fellowship in which there is no distinction of sex or age" (Winter 1974, 127). That is to say, participation is open to all comers. A sodality, on the other hand, restricts participation based on an adult second decision beyond modality membership. Thus, a sodality can be understood as a more specific structure in function that moves beyond the larger structure and function of the local church. Sodalities by definition have a more limited participation and scope. The primary criterion for Winter regarding sodalities is that of a second-level commitment (Winter 1974, 123; Camp 1995, 199; Wallis 1991, 187). Also, sodalities tend to be task oriented and modalities people oriented (Guder 2000, 182–83).

It is important to also note that Winter believed that modalities and sodalities together form the fabric of the *ecclesia* of the New Testament. He therefore resists any effort to make one structure more normative—or "more church"—than the other as is implied in the distinction between "church" and "para-church" (1979, 143). He asks, "Why not call churches para-missions?" (1979, 143). Winter intends this to mean that neither can be properly understood apart from the other. "The two are indeed interdependent and the evidences of history do not allow us to understand either of them as complete without the other" (1979, 144). In fact, one of Winter's concerns regarding modalities and sodalities lies in the Protestant tendency to foster a "schism" between these two structures (1979, 143). Winter's understanding of the relationship between modalities and sodalities, between churches and mission bands, can be seen in the idea that sodalities "nourish" modalities and thereby breathe life into what otherwise tends toward nominalism due to its broadly inclusive nature (1974, 127; Wallis 1991, 186–87).

Following these definitions, Winter argues on historical grounds that modalities and sodalities defined the diocesan and monastic movements up through the Middle Ages, noting that monastic sodalities functioned as a renewing force for the diocesan modality (1974, 124–27). Winter also argues that early Protestants lost sight of the necessity of sodalities, with Luther explicitly rejecting the idea (1974, 131). Protestantism recovered the importance of sodalities though only as it rediscovered its missions mandate through individuals such as William Carey (1974, 132). The key to understanding Winter's proposal is that "the New Testament is trying to show us *how to borrow effective patterns*" (1974, 123).

By this he means that early Christians borrowed patterns from the surrounding culture, whether Jewish or pagan, and gave them new meaning and significance. What is required then is faithfulness to the functions of these patterns or structures, but not necessarily to the forms (Camp 1995, 201).

EVALUATING THE MODALITY/SODALITY DISTINCTION

C. Peter Wagner says that while Winter was not the first to observe the modality-sodality distinction, his "unique contribution has been to legitimize the two structures biblically, and to show how they are both needed for God's purposes in the world to be carried out effectively" (1981, 186). Whether Wagner is correct and Winter has successfully accomplished this is a matter of some debate (Camp 1995; Fields 2011, 55–56).

As Bruce Camp has observed, Roland Allen, Harry Boer, and George Peters are among those who denied that the concept of mission agencies (sodalities) finds support in Scripture (Camp 1995, 197). Boer, for example, calls them a "blessed abnormality" and Peters argues that the issue is not clear enough in Scripture to be dogmatic (cited in Camp 1995, 197–98; Boer 1964, 214; Peters 1972, 224). Camp himself takes issue with the idea that the church and missionary band should both be considered equal expressions of the universal church (1995, 201). In defense, he points out that Paul's missionary bands were never called the "church" (1995, 201). He also takes issue with the notion of limiting participation in sodalities, saying that to do so "violates both scriptural teaching (1 Cor 12:21) and early church practice (Acts 1–2)" (1995, 203).

To resolve these questions, some discussion of the biblical marks of the church is needed in order to understand more precisely those things that define the church and those that define the mission band. As Stephen Van Zanen has said, much of the disagreement between Winter and Camp likely reflects differing ecclesiologies (2014, 14–17). Unfortunately, neither Winter nor

Camp proves very helpful, because neither identifies the marks of the universal church that they believe should be reflected in local churches or in mission bands.

Other critics of the modality-sodality distinction fear that the two-structure system minimizes or negates the obligation of local churches to be involved in mission. Costas for example, claims "there is no ground in the New Testament for a concept of mission apart from the church, just as there is no concept of the church apart from mission" (1974, 168). This raises the important question as to whether local churches can and should do missions or if that task should be relegated to sodality-type organizations. I will address that momentarily, but first it is necessary to determine whether the two-structure system can be defended biblically.

Because Winter's argument is primarily historical, it would be easy to assume that the biblical basis is thin. Fortunately, several others have picked up the argument where Winter left off and have shown that a solid scriptural case can be made. Paramount is Acts 13:2 (NASB) which says, "While they were ministering to the Lord and fasting, the Holy Spirit said, 'Set apart for Me Barnabas and Saul for the work to which I have called them.'" Edward Murphy refers to this verse and the launching of missionary sodalities using Winston Churchill's famous phrase, "a hinge of history" (1976, 113). Importantly, this passage is portrayed by Luke as partial fulfillment of the mandate of Acts 1:8 (Keener 2013, under Part 5, Section II: "The Spirit's Call (13:2)"). Given the context of prayer and fasting and the consequent move of the Spirit, Arthur Glasser says in reference to this passage, "From this, we cannot but conclude that both the congregational parish structure and the mobile missionary band are equally valid in God's sight" (1992, A-127–28). Indeed, it takes considerable effort to interpret the words "set apart" as anything other than a narrower, task-oriented role for the missionary band of Saul and Barnabas. Furthermore, this role can be equated with what today is referred to as cross-cultural mission (Bruce 1988, 246;

Glasser 1992, A-128; Tennent 2010, 454). Beyond this, Murphy has helpfully shown that similar missionary (sodality) structures that functioned differently from church structures soon dominated in carrying out the Great Commission in the remaining chapters of Acts (13:13; 15:22–34; 15:40; 15:37–39; 16:1–9; 16:10; 18:2–23; 19; 20:4; Murphy 1976, 113).

But what about the claim that the mission band was born out of church negligence? Costas, arguing along these lines, claims that the formation of missionary sodalities represents only the permissive will of God (not the perfect will) as well as the failure of modalities to be faithful to their calling. He fears that the modality-sodality paradigm unbiblically separates church from mission (1974, 169). In this, he appears to have overlooked the symbiotic relationship that Winter upheld between modalities and sodalities. Winter never suggests that they can function apart from each other. On the contrary, Winter is quite clear. "It is our attempt here to help church leaders and others to understand the legitimacy of both structures, and the necessity for both structures not only to exist but to work together harmoniously for the fulfillment of the Great Commission" (1974, 136). To say that both structures work together harmoniously regarding the Great Commission implies that mission is the prerogative of both modalities and sodalities, but perhaps in different ways. I will elaborate more on that below. For now, nothing in Acts 13:2 implies anything other than that the formation of a mission sodality was by design on the part of God. The church prayed, the Spirit moved, and a new structure for cross-cultural witness was born. One looks to the text in vain for any indication that God was less than pleased with this development.

That said, I agree with Camp on the problematic claim by Winter that both modalities and sodalities are equal expression of the universal church. Without a doubt, the modality-sodality structure becomes especially complex at the point of clarifying scripturally the nature of the church and that of the mission band

and how they differ. If a sodality, for example, is defined as "task oriented" as Winter says, and that task relates solely to cross-cultural frontier mission, how can Winter claim that both structures are equally "the church"? A church may not do less than mission, but surely it does more.

Some resolution to this tension may be found by looking more closely at Winter's argument. Winter's desire to hold together modalities and sodalities as the fabric of the *ecclesia* constitutes the context for his asking "why should a parachurch be less church than a local church." The main issue for Winter is interdependence and only secondarily whether one structure is more "church" than the other. Winter's main interest, in other words, lies directly in the passage Camp cites in 1 Corinthians 12:21 (Winter 1979, 143–45). The body of Christ needs all of its many parts to function properly.

Winter himself seems to define modalities and sodalities differently in terms of their "church-ness" in his well-known E-0 to E-3 evangelism paradigm. Here he rightfully points out that local churches are best suited for E-0 to E-1 evangelism because of cultural proximity. But E-2 and E-3 evangelism require a degree of specialization and commitment that local congregations often lack and of which they are perhaps incapable (1992, B-169). Mission bands, because they are not bound to be everything the local church must be, are free to focus on the most urgent task of E-2 and E-3 evangelism and not become bogged down in the many other things that occupy the life of the local church. Given Winter's argument here, it seems wholly unnecessary to the legitimacy of Winter's modality-sodality structure to claim that both the local church and mission band are equal expressions of the universal church. Rather, it is sufficient to simply note that the New Testament supports the idea that cross-cultural mission requires a more specifically mission-oriented structure than what one finds in the local church, as illustrated in sending of Saul and Barnabas in Acts 13. This does not mean that local churches are excused from the Great Commission, for the church at Antioch plays a vital part, as do many other local congregations with which Paul is associated. Church and mission go inextricably together (Carriker 1993, 45; Little 2005, 119–30; Ott and Strauss 2010, 192–93). In Antioch, it was that church's fasting and praying that led to the missionary call and sending of Saul and Barnabas in the first place. The church at Antioch thus plays a very different role in mission, though no less important, than those who make up the sodality and are the ones sent to engage in the cross-cultural, church planting task.

Some may object to this on the grounds that missionaries who go to unreached peoples are the local church in that area, at least until an indigenous church is established. Perhaps so. But the very notion of indigeneity requires that missionaries step out of central roles as soon as possible (Ott and Strauss 2010, 115). To the extent that the missionary band considers itself the local church, then it ought to do and be all that a biblical local church should do and be. That would include at least the four marks of the church described by Charles Van Engen in his work *God's Missionary People: Rethinking the Purpose of the Local Church* (1991). He describes the "many-sided" nature of the local church according to the New Testament: *koinōnia* (community); *kerygma* (proclamation); *diakonia* (service); and *martyria* (witness) (1991, 89). It is my contention that the missionary band (sodality) should work to disciple in all of these areas, but has no mandate to embody all of these, especially long-term. To the extent that it does, the forward momentum of mission grinds to a halt. The goal of the mission band is not ultimately to be the church, but to foster the emergence of an indigenous local congregation. Once this happens, the missionary band ought to either move on or shift its focus to helping foster the emergence of indigenous mission movements. This relates precisely to the value in the modality-sodality distinction. Again, Winter himself also seems to recognize this when he says:

It is a tragic perversion of Jesus' strategy if we
continue to send missionaries to do the job that
local Christians can do better. There is no excuse
for a missionary in the pulpit when a national
can do the job better. There is no excuse for a
missionary to be doing evangelism on an E-3
basis, at an E-3 distance from people, where
there are local Christians who are effectively
winning the same people as part of their E-1
sphere. (1992, B-164)

MODALITIES, SODALITIES, AND INDIGENOUS MISSION MOVEMENTS

While affirming compassionate mission, or what Winter refers
to as mission "service agencies" that engage in "medical work,
orphan work, or radio work, or whatever" (1974, 135), he also
argues that these "must be aware of, and concerned about, the
interface between that activity and the church-planting function"
(1974, 135). This interface is what was absent in the story I shared
at the beginning of this essay and what I hope to recover by the
conclusion. Winter argues that there must be, by mission agencies, an intentional effort to plant mission sodalities, by which
Winter means non-Western mission efforts (1974, 135). He
points out that "The concept of 'the indigenous church' is widely
emphasized today. But how much do we hear about the indigenous mission agency? The task of church planting is fairly well
known. But what about the art and science of mission planting?"
(1971a, 193). The distinction between modalities and sodalities for
Winter was not only to advance mission among the unreached,
but also to see mission efforts by sending nations lead to indigenous mission movements. Winter illustrates this point with the
following scenario:

Suppose a mission agency goes to Nigeria and establishes fifty indigenous churches among the Yoruba, and those churches then plant even more Yoruba churches. In that case, the initial "missiological breakthrough" would be called mission while the further church planting expansion by the Yoruba churches would be considered evangelism. But if now the Yoruba send missionaries to break through to a cultural group where there is not yet an indigenous church movement, then you can say that the Yoruba believers are not only involved in ordinary evangelism but also in cross-cultural work, in the creation of a new worshipping tradition of Jesus followers. Such efforts classify as a [sic] mission activities.

We can further say that if the initial mission agency is not involved in that further outreach but is content to continue to work with the Yoruba church, then it ceases to be a mission agency but becomes merely what could be called a "foreign evangelism" agency. (2002, 7)

In relation to this, Costas has argued regarding indigenous sodalities that "even when they exist apart from modalities, [they] cannot be fabricated from the outside. They emerge naturally and spontaneously as part of concrete historical situations" (1974, 172). I agree, but would add that the way in which missionaries go about their work, particularly in the area of compassion, can either help or hinder the emergence of indigenous churches and mission movements.

SECOND STAGE MISSIONS

In establishing a means by which to evaluate Protestant mission structures or sodalities such as mission agencies and parachurch organizations, Winter proposed five general questions as a rubric. Of those, the fifth question is particularly relevant for our present discussion: "For what function is the agency designed?" Here "agency" refers to the sodality, whether a mission agency or missionary band. In response, Winter lists the distinction of First Stage Missions, Second Stage Missions, and Consolidation Missions. Winter only clarifies the meaning of the first two of these, stating that First Stage Missions consists in crossing geographic borders to plant the church where it does not exist. Second Stage Missions refers to mission partnerships that ideally strengthen the capacity of established churches through "interchurch aid" (1979, 173). More specifically, this aid or partnership should endeavor to especially strengthen the capacity of indigenous churches toward their own missionary enterprises (1979, 173). Lesslie Newbigin has argued similarly in distinguishing between "fraternal workers"— or those who are merely sent from one church to another—and those rightly called "missionaries" who either directly work to plant the church where no Christian witness is present, or those who "assist another church in its specifically missionary tasks" (1977, 216). Winter argues that compassionate service, or social concern, bridges First Stage Mission and Second Stage Mission.

As it concerns the expression of compassion in cross-cultural work, this notion of both modalities and sodalities, along with Second Stage Missions, becomes vital. Missionaries who go to work with other national churches in the area of compassionate ministry must understand their role as not only strengthening the capacity of local churches, but of doing so with a specific mission agenda in mind. That agenda should be to foster cross-cultural mission bands (sodalities) among the mission-receiving churches (modalities). The ultimate goal in Second Stage Mission, if it is to remain mission, must be to see mission-receiving churches become mission-sending churches. Compassion constitutes a key link in achieving this objective.

The ability to accomplish this will depend on the manner in which Second Stage Mission proceeds and the ways in which missionaries engage in compassionate work. If missionaries act as the primary "doers" of compassion, then often the result is that local congregations become robbed of their role as salt and light in the community (Matt 5:13–14). It is instructive in this regard to consider Acts 11 and the pattern we find there regarding the ministry of Barnabas and Saul at Antioch. In 11:26 we read that Barnabas and Saul spend a whole year teaching the church. It is also noteworthy that Barnabas and Saul in this passage function as a sodality even before they are sent out in Acts 13. Barnabas was sent from the more mature church in Jerusalem to Antioch, and he in turn went to Tarsus to recruit Saul. Thus, they were not the local church in Antioch, but an extension of the church in Jerusalem sent to aid a fledgling congregation and help it mature. A key point is that Barnabas and Saul were not supposed to be the local church in Antioch but were there to equip that church. It is also noteworthy that between chapters eleven and thirteen of Acts, the Antioch church moves from being a mission-receiving church to becoming a mission-sending church. When their work is finished at Antioch, Barnabas and Saul are called by the Holy Spirit and commissioned by the church to continue moving on toward unreached areas (13:2–3).

What is particularly important in the way Luke has presented the story in Acts 11 is that the teaching/equipping ministry of Barnabas and Saul (v. 26) leads directly to the indigenous compassionate response of the local church. In 11:27 we read that a prophet arrives in Antioch proclaiming a coming famine. Acts 11:29 states, "And in the proportion that any of the disciples had means, each of them determined to send a contribution for the relief of the brethren living in Judea." It was not Barnabas and Saul who spearheaded the response. Rather each of the disciples determined, according to their own means, how to respond. In fact, this appears to be a consistent pattern in the New Testament.

We read in 2 Corinthians 8:3 (NASB) concerning the Macedonian church that "according to their ability, and beyond their ability, they gave of their own accord." In both cases, the emphasis is on the indigenous compassionate response of the local church to freely and voluntarily give according to their means.

Christopher Little has warned, "when the church engaged in cross-cultural mission ignores Pauline orthopraxy, especially in relation to the proper use of finances, it places unnecessary obstacles in the path of the *missio Dei*" (2005, 3). This essay examines precisely this question in relation to compassionate mission. If Barnabas and Saul were part of many mission organizations today, one wonders if any room at all would be given for an indigenous response. It seems to me that the modern tendency would be to start a project—perhaps "The Judean Famine Fund"— commission foreign missionaries to head it up, print up some nice JFF tee-shirts, and launch a fundraising campaign among supporting churches. But such actions become highly problematic precisely because they fundamentally confuse the role of the sodality, in this case the missions band or agency, with that of the local church, the modality. Arguably, this same problem lies at the center of the story I shared in the beginning. This in fact underscores the need for Winter's two-structure approach. What ultimately gets neglected in the process of missionaries doing compassion that should be (and could be) done by local believers is the important biblical concept of solidarity. In what follows I will explain this concept further to show that solidarity is the key to fostering local expressions of missions—or, indigenous sodalities.

SOLIDARITY IN THE PAULINE EPISTLES

David Horrell in his monograph on Pauline ethics, *Solidarity and Difference* (2015), has argued that Pauline ethics consists of two foundational "metanorms"—namely, corporate solidarity in Christ regarding the Christian community and "other-regard" modeled on Christ's own selfless compassion. Corporate solidarity regarding those in Christ focuses on the formation of moral virtue among the believing community, and thereby on an observable distinction between the church and the world. Solidarity therefore refers essentially to oneness in Christ. This oneness though, as Horrell's title suggests, does not obliterate differences within the community, but fosters mutual love and concern for one another. That is, differences are allowed for, even celebrated, so long as they do not impinge upon the solidarity of the community.

According to Horrell, Paul's ethics is concerned not so much with providing specific ethical instructions, though those are present, but rather with declaring the values necessary for the formation of a moral community (Horrell 2015, chapter 9.1.1). The *summum bonum* for Paul is that which contributes to the flourishing of the community and avoids the creation of divisions. This intra-communitarian ethic, however, is not limited to the church but overflows from the church into the world, as believers seek to "do good to all people, but especially to those who are of the household of faith" (Gal 6:10; see Horrell, chapter 4.5 and 9). Furthermore, Paul understands the achievement of this solidarity to depend on the rites of baptism and the Lord's Supper, on the important use of familial language among believers (especially "brothers"), and through the imagery of the church as the body of Christ (Horrell, chapter 4).

BAPTISM

Regarding baptism, Horrell notes that Paul refers to the baptism of believers as incorporation into Christ. Referring especially to 1 Corinthians 12:13 and Galatians 3:26, he notes the emphasis in both passages on baptism resulting in a profound revaluation of various ethno-social distinctions that existed prior to baptism. As Paul says in 1 Corinthians 12:13 (NASB), "For by one Spirit we were all baptized into one body, whether Jews or Greeks, whether slaves or free, and we were all made to drink of one Spirit."

In Galatians 3:26–29 (NASB), Paul states the issue even more strongly: "For you are all sons of God through faith in Christ Jesus. For all of you who were baptized into Christ have clothed yourselves with Christ. There is neither Jew nor Greek, there is neither slave nor free man, there is neither male nor female; for you are all one in Christ Jesus." Thus the rite of baptism "constructs a new form of human solidarity which transcends the lines of previous distinctions" (Horrell 2015, chapter 4.1).

THE LORD'S SUPPER

The Lord's Supper also constitutes another important Pauline understanding of corporate solidarity. According to Horrell, "While baptism may be defined as a rite of initiation concerned with boundary-crossing and status transformation, the Lord's Supper is clearly a ceremony, practiced regularly, which confirms and celebrates the status and identity of community members" (2015, chapter 4.1.2). Furthermore, the Lord's Supper functions to "confirm and consolidate" the solidarity of oneness in Christ (2015, chapter 4.1.2). As Horrell observes, it is important also to note that the primary criticism Paul has against the Corinthians relates to their fractious quarrelling that stands in direct violation of this supreme value of corporate solidarity, as a violation of having been made one body in Christ (2015, chapter 4.1.2).

BROTHERS

Paul's use of *adelphoi* (or brothers) to refer to fellow believers in several texts is intended "to impress an ethical demand" (Rom 14:10–21; 1 Cor 6:5–8; 1 Cor 8:11–12; Horrell 2015, chapter 4.2). The designation functions for Paul not merely as a nicety, but as a constant reminder that believers are in a real sense incorporated into a new family. Paul uses this term or some form of it over seventy-five times in his letters, and it is his preferred term for fellow believers. Furthermore, as James Thompson points out, Paul's use of *adelphoi* could refer to men, women, and children and, as such, represented a highly inclusive concept of family that crossed both gender and social stratifications in a way unknown in that day (2014, 44). Paul's preference for *adelphoi* and his efforts to engender a sense of family belonging and responsibility among believers is buttressed by his use of "one another." This would include the instructions to be "devoted to one another" and "give preference to one another" (Rom 12:10 NASB), to be "of the same mind with one another" (Rom 12:16 NASB), to "love one another" (Rom 13:8 NASB), to "build one another up" (Rom 14:19 NASB), to "accept one another" (Rom 15:7 NASB), and so on (Thompson 2014, 44). As Thompson says, "Paul's frequent use of 'one another' reflects the family relationship and the solidarity of the community" (2014, 44). The significance of this is that those in Christ are to understand their relationship to one another according to obligations such as love and support that are characteristic of obligations toward the members of one's own family. Thus:

> . . . the reason why believers should show generous concern for one another is precisely because the other is an *adelphos* and as such belongs with them to the same family group. The mutual love that should characterize the congregations is the love of siblings, a *philadelphia* (Rom. 12:10; 1 Thess. 4:9). This solidarity, we should note, is explicitly seen to reach beyond the confines of the local congregation to encompass believers everywhere, who also share this family identity (1 Thess. 4:10). (Horrell 2015, chapter 4.2)

THE BODY OF CHRIST

Regarding the church as the body of Christ, Horrell observes that "there are two significant texts where Paul presents the notion of the community as a body to engender the idea of a diversity-in-unity, or solidarity and difference: Rom 12.4–8 and

1 Cor. 12.12–31" (2015, chapter 4.4). Paul's primary point in these references is to foster mutual care and support among the members of local churches and to regard one another as equally valuable.

Horrell argues that for Paul the concept of solidarity functions as the key to community formation, and that Paul's ethics is especially concerned with this above all else. The people of God are to be a transformed people, living in harmonious unity with each other and overcoming former social divisions. This is furthermore meant to stand as a testimony to their participation in Christ. "The basis for solidarity, for the construction of community, as the central Christian rituals show, is found in Paul's Christology: as believers make the story of Christ their own, participating in his death and new life, so they leave behind the old world, and become members of one body, in Christ" (Horrell 2015, chapter 4 under "Conclusion").

SOLIDARITY AND "OTHER-REGARD"

Though much of Paul's ethics is devoted to community formation, he also speaks frequently about the broader role of the church in the community. Furthermore, the nature of concern for others in the larger community stems from the essential character of the community, modeled on the life of Christ who gave himself as a ransom for all. In the same way, the Christian community is to be "for all" in a number of compassionate ways. This compassionate stance of the church should not be conceived as a means to an end, even though there are missional implications that follow, most importantly the removal of hindrances to gospel proclamation (Horrell 2015, chapter 8.4). Rather, the responsibility to be "for others" is a gospel-worthy pursuit in its own right.

A number of important passages in Paul provide a basis for the movement of Christian compassion from the community of faith to the outside world. Among these are three passages in 1 Thessalonians (3:12; 4:12; 5:15). First Thessalonians 3:12 (NASB) states "may the Lord cause you to increase and abound in love for one another, and *for all people*, just as we also do for you" (emphasis added). Richard Hays rightly points out that this represents not a command by Paul, but rather a prayer (1996, 22). Even so, it shows clearly that Paul expected the Thessalonian church to embody *agapē* for one another and for all those whom its members encountered in everyday life. Plus, a few chapters later, Paul does express nearly an identical idea in more of a command form. In 1 Thessalonians 5:15 (NASB) he instructs, "See that no one repays another with evil for evil, but always seek after that which is good for one another *and for all people*" (emphasis added). Paul employs strikingly similar language in Galatians 6:10 (NASB) where he states, "while we have opportunity, let us do good *to all people*, and especially to those who are of the household of the faith" (emphasis added). Other Pauline texts that present a variation on this theme include Philippians 4:8, Romans 12:14–21, and 2 Corinthians 8:21. In each of these passages Paul expresses in various ways a concern for how local believers are perceived by the larger community. Their witness in the community is to be both in word and deed, and there is an inherent expectation that outsiders will take notice. The practice of solidarity within the community was to result in radically transformed lives that stood apart from the world and caused believers to "shine like stars in the universe" (Phil 2:15 MOUNCE; cf. Horrell 2015, chapter 8.4).

SOLIDARITY AND THE SPIRIT

Lesslie Newbigin has said that "the agent of mission is the Holy Spirit who is the living presence of the Kingdom in foretaste" (1977, 218). The primary function of the notion of solidarity in both Luke and Acts is the cultivation of the presence of the Holy Spirit among the people of God. Solidarity leads to holiness, that is, to the people of God being "a people set apart." It is the Spirit's

dynamic presence and empowerment that Luke especially highlights as the primary agent in missions.

Whereas it is Paul's Christology that primarily forms the
theological basis for believers' oneness in Christ (solidarity), it is
his pneumatology that serves especially as the basis to bring about
this reality. The Spirit functions "primarily in the role of motivator
and enabler of conduct" as it relates to Christian ethics (Horrell
2015, see "*Solidarity and Difference*, Ten Years On, II"). When Paul
talks about the oneness of believers in Christ (solidarity), he has in
mind the cultivation of the Spirit's presence as the ultimate goal.
Solidarity is about more than merely treating one another well.
Rather, the entire concept is rooted in holiness, and it is holiness
that generates the kind of community that makes room for the
operation and dynamic presence of the Spirit.

Paul's ethics is concerned not with individual transformation, as we are so inclined to conceive of spiritual formation in
the West. Instead, he is especially focused on the corporate function of the gathered saints to be conformed to Christ as a body
and not merely as a collection of individuals (Thompson 2014,
104). As Thompson has explained, Paul's goal in ministry "is a
community that will be his boast at the day of Christ (2 Cor. 1:14;
Phil. 2:16; 1 Thess. 2:19; cf. 2 Cor. 11:3)" (2014, 104; emphasis
added). Throughout his letters Paul describes his labors as related
to primarily the formation of communities whose spiritual progress continues until Christ's coming and who are increasingly
conformed to the image of Christ (Rom 8:29; 1 Cor 15:49; 2 Cor
3:18). Furthermore, this community-oriented spiritual formation
is a function of the Holy Spirit. As Paul says, "For by one Spirit we
were all baptized into one body, whether Jews or Greeks, whether
slaves or free, and we were all made to drink of one Spirit" (1 Cor
12:13 NASB). Paul's consistent emphasis on the transformation
of believers by the Spirit puts the onus on the work of the Spirit
among the churches, and not on the will of the individual. For
example, Paul asserts, "If by the Spirit you are putting to death

the deeds of the body, you will live" (Rom 8:13 NASB). Thus, Thompson is right in declaring that "ethical transformation is a gift of the Spirit" (2014, 124).

It is significant to observe in the book of Acts that there is a dual emphasis both on the role of the Spirit regarding solidarity among the members of the fledgling Jesus movement and the unfolding missionary impulse of church. We see this from the disciples in Acts being described as "with one mind" (1:14; 2:46), which certainly bears resemblance to the Pauline notion of solidarity outlined above. But the clearest show of solidarity appears in Acts 4:

> And the congregation of those who believed were of one heart and soul; and not one of them claimed that anything belonging to him was his own, but all things were common property to them. And with great power the apostles were giving testimony to the resurrection of the Lord Jesus, and abundant grace was upon them all. For there was not a needy person among them, for all who were owners of land or houses would sell them and bring the proceeds of the sales and lay them at the apostles' feet, and they would be distributed to each as any had need (vv. 32–35 NASB).

Later, Ananias and Sapphira are presented as the repudiation of this solidarity, and as such, are accused of having "lied to the Holy Spirit" (5:3 NIV), whom as we have argued, provides the motivation and power that makes solidarity possible. Thus, not only does the Ananias and Sapphira incident represent a break down in solidarity, but also a hindrance to the working of the Holy Spirit within the community. The grievousness of their sins stands on the detrimental nature their actions have toward the whole community and the interference with the vital notion of corporate solidarity, much like in the story of Achan in Joshua 7.

It is therefore not incidental to the themes of Luke-Acts that when we come to Acts 13 and the sending of Barnabas and Saul, the context of this sending is the corporate worship of the church. "While they were praying and fasting, the Holy Spirit said, 'Set apart for Me Barnabas and Saul for the work to which I have called them'" (Acts 13:2 NASB). Their expression of solidarity and the resulting *koinōnia* in which they participate are vital to the proper functioning of the church according to the missional mandate of Acts 1:8. We see this idea of solidarity and community connected to the presence of the Spirit and missions explicitly declared in Acts 9:31 NASB: "So the church throughout all Judea and Galilee and Samaria enjoyed peace, being built up; and going on in the fear of the Lord and in the comfort of the Holy Spirit, it continued to increase."

CONCLUSION

The great challenge in modern missions, in my view, concerns the need for Western missionaries to increasingly step into the background and allow local churches to flourish both in solidarity with one another and in loving their neighbors in the way that Paul envisioned. This means, if we return to Acts 11 as our paradigm, that we follow the model of Barnabas and Saul, and disciple for compassion rather than engaging in direct acts of compassion ourselves. For when we are the primary doers, we interrupt this vital concept of solidarity as believers show love for one another and concern for the broader needs of the community.

Without this "metanorm" in Pauline ethics, the important biblical concept of *koinōnia* mutates into what Wagner calls *koinōnitis*, that is, a church whose entire activity and attention becomes so inwardly focused that the church no longer functions as it was intended, as a radiant expression of the present and coming kingdom of God (1979, 78). When missionaries engage in compassion in a way that robs local congregations of their role as salt and light in the community, the result will always be churches whose spiritual growth is stunted and whose missionary impulse is dampened. The remedy is therefore to ensure that missionaries maintain a concern for Second Stage Mission in which compassion is seen as an essential ingredient in the formation of local missionary sodalities. By stepping away from a central role in compassionate mission, and by instead focusing on teaching and equipping, cross-cultural workers can remove their own self-imposed hindrances to the expression of solidarity between local church members and between churches and the communities in which they reside. Because of the broad missional implications for local churches, a focus on discipling for compassion is not only the most compassionate thing that a missionary can do but also the most fruitful.

REFERENCES CITED

Bruce, F. F. 1988. *New International Commentary on the New Testament: The Book of the Acts*. Accordance electronic ed. Grand Rapids, MI: Eerdmans.

Boer, Harry R. 1964. *Pentecost and Missions*. Grand Rapids, MI: Eerdmans.

Camp, Bruce K. 1995. "A Theological Examination of the Two-Structure Theory." *Missiology* 23(2):197–209.

Carriker, Timothy C. 1993. "Missiological Hermeneutic and Pauline Apocalyptic Eschatology." In *The Good News of the Coming Kingdom*, edited by Charles Van Engen, et al. Eugene, OR: Wipf and Stock.

Costas, Orlando. 1974. *The Church and its Mission: A Shattering Critique from the Third World*. Wheaton, IL: Tyndale House.

Fields, Mark I. 2011. "Contours of Local Congregation-Based Mission in the Vineyard Movement, 1982 to 2007." PhD diss., Fuller Theological Seminary.

Glasser, Arthur. 1992. "The Apostle Paul and the Missionary Task." In *Perspectives on the World Christian Movement: A Reader*, edited by. Ralph Winter and Stephen Hawthorne, A-121–33. Rev. ed. Pasadena, CA: William Carey Library.

Guder, Darrell L. 2000. *The Continuing Conversion of the Church*. Grand Rapids, MI: Eerdmans.

Hays, Richard. 1996. *The Moral Vision of the New Testament: A Contemporary Introduction to New Testament Ethics*. New York, NY: Harper One.

Horrell, David G. 2015. *Solidarity and Difference: A Contemporary Reading of Paul's Ethics*. 2nd ed. London: Bloomsbury. Kindle edition.

Keener, Craig. 2013. *Acts: An Exegetical Commentary*. 2 vols. Grand Rapids, MI: Baker.

Little, Christopher R. 2005. *Mission in the Way of Paul: Biblical Mission for the Church in the 21st Century*. New York, NY: Peter Lang.

Murphy, Edward F. 1976. The Missionary Society as an Apostolic Team. *Practical Anthropology* 4(1):103–18.

Newbigin, Lesslie. 1977. "Future of Missions and Missionaries." *Review & Expositor* 74(2):209–18.

Ott, Craig, and Stephen J. Strauss. 2010. *Encountering Theology of Mission*. Grand Rapids, MI: Baker Academic.

Peters, George W. 1972. *A Biblical Theology of Missions*. Chicago, IL: Moody.

Tennent, Timothy. 2010. *Invitation to World Missions*. Grand Rapids, MI: Kregel.

Thompson, James W. 2014. *The Church According to Paul: Rediscovering the Community Conformed to Christ*. Grand Rapids, MI: Baker Academic.

Van Engen, Charles. 1991. *God's Missionary People: Rethinking the Purpose of the Local Church*. Grand Rapids, MI: Baker Academic.

Van Zanen, Stephen J. 2014. "Local Churches in Global Missions: Developing a Strategic Plan to Help Christian Reformed Churches to Engage in International Missions." DMin project, Trinity International University.

Wagner, C. Peter. 1979. *Your Church Can Be Healthy*. Nashville, TN: Abingdon.

———. 1981. *Church Growth and the Whole Gospel: A Biblical Mandate*. San Francisco, CA: Harper and Row.

Wallis, Joe L. 1991. "Church Ministry and the Free Rider Problem: Religious Liberty and Disestablishment." *The American Journal of Economics and Sociology* 50(2):183–96.

Weber, Linda J. 2010. *Mission Handbook: U.S. and Canadian Protestant Ministries Overseas*, 21st Edition. Wheaton, IL: EMIS.

Winter, Ralph D. 1971. "Churches Need Missions Because Modalities Need Sodalities." *Evangelical Missions Quarterly* (1971):193–200.

———. 1974. "Two Structures of God's Redemptive Mission." *Missiology* 2(1):121–39.

———. 1979. "Protestant Mission Societies: The American Experience." *Missiology* 7(2):139–78.

———. 1992. "The New Macedonia: A Revolutionary New Era in Mission Begins." In *Perspectives on the World Christian Movement: A Reader, edited by* Ralph D. Winter and Stephen C. Hawthorne, B-157–175. Pasadena, CA: William Carey Library.

———. 2002. "From Mission to Evangelism to Mission." *International Journal of Frontier Mission* 19(4):6–8.

Part Two

CHURCH ON MISSION IN GLOBAL PERSPECTIVE

MISSIONS AND THE LOCAL CHURCH
ONE PERSPECTIVE
Boris Sarlabous

More than one hundred years after the first groups of missionaries from the United States entered Cuba, and after those missionaries founded the first serious and long-lived Protestant churches (during which those missionaries came to dominate, among other things, the theological thought of the churches), an event took place that would change not just the course of Cuban politics, but likewise, to a significant degree, the religious life of the nation. That event was the triumph of the Communist Revolution of 1959. Churches that had previously been founded by primarily North American missionaries and led, up until that moment, by those same missionaries witnessed a massive departure as those missionaries left, some sooner and some later, for their own country. They left the religious reins of all denominations in the hands of the few Cuban pastors that existed at that moment. You could say that necessity led each and every denomination to resign itself to the idea of continuing the kingdom of God on the island through the efforts of the Cuban Christian community.

Years later the church began to experience what would be, in my judgment, the challenge to live, expand, and think rightly of itself in the midst of a society that had openly declared itself to be Communist. In the light of this reality, the Cuban church could face its circumstances through one of two means:

> Create an authentic theology which would defend the interests of the kingdom of God; which would seek to offer all people, rich or poor, salvation as

found in the Bible and made available by Christ on
the cross to all who believe in Him (John 3:16), or
Submit itself to a system of thought antagonistic
to the biblical task, designing a syncretistic means
of survival within that same antagonistic system,
sacrificing the interests of the kingdom of God and
replacing those with the interests of a social idol.

The post-revolution Cuban church encountered three significant stages. The first was related to survival. This stage took place immediately after the triumph of the revolution and was above all marked by the growing acceptance of Marx-Lenin ideology in which there is no room for religion beyond empty rites and conditioned on the self-development of society. The Cuban church in this stage ceased to be a living, viable church and became instead fearful. The church was a poor representative of the Lord and his universal church.

So that you might have an idea, in its first fifty years the Cuban evangelical church came to have a strong presence in Cuba's society from any point of view: educational, missionary, economic, etc. As we said previously, many North American missionaries had a strong presence on the island and carried the weight of developing missionary and evangelistic programs. Denominations like the Free Will Baptist Church would come to experience faster growth than other churches. In only eighteen years it grew to more than fifty churches with approximately three thousand members as well as a theological seminary to train Cuban leaders to pastor those churches. Stories like this one were repeated across the island until the year 1959.[1]

We could say that during this stage, missions were promoted from the United States, the origin of the majority of missionaries who served in Cuba. This situation changed dramatically during

---

1. Adolfo Pandiello recalls this period in the biography of Free Will Baptist missionary Thomas Willey (1898-1968).

the first steps of the newly triumphant Cuban Revolution which many believers saw as a social expression of Christianity, even viewing socialism as the model that could best define Christians. All would have been good were it not for the break in relations between the Cuban regime and the United States, leading then to the alliance between Cuba and the USSR. The alliance with the USSR resulted in a thought system ideologically opposed to Christian faith.

At that point the Cuban church began what we will call the eclipse of the evangelical church in Cuba—a church that fifty years before had represented the whole island but in just a few years nearly disappeared. Why do I say "nearly" disappeared? Because even though church worship centers and buildings remained intact, all that identifies a church as a living church had disappeared (missions, evangelism, etc.). Many seminaries were expropriated, and others were closed and prohibited from functioning. The church operated in a timid manner within its community and for the most part fought simply to survive.

This kind of situation tends to create changes in lifestyle, and the Cuban evangelical church's reaction was no different. There were two significant sorts of reaction which defined these lifestyle postures. First, one segment of the church corrupted its message so that its people could escape persecution. It created a kind of philosophical/theological syncretism between the Marx-Lenin postulates and European liberal theology as reflected, among others, in the work of Karl Barth, Emil Brunner, and Dietrich Bonhoeffer. This school of thought placed aspects of liberation theology and sociology above theology. This "church" *called itself a revolutionary church, and specifically a Cuban-revolutionary church.*[2] Biblical principles were no longer normative for this segment.

---

2. Arce-Martinez presents this idea in his book—La Misión de la Iglesia en una Sociedad Socialista (The Mission of the Church in a Socialist Society.)

The second segment of the church became a persecuted church, suffering to maintain itself faithful to the Bible, obedience, and worship of God. Accordingly, this church developed a strong sense of Christian fellowship but failed to see itself as an instrument of God to reach the lost. It became what I call the evangelical ghetto of Cuba.

Pastors were persecuted in many ways. Some were imprisoned and obligated to work in forced labor camps; others were exiled or oppressed nearly to the point of renouncing their faith. I had a seminary professor who, because of a shortage of pastors, had responsibility for three churches separated by enormous distances. These were difficult days for the Cuban church.

Now we might ask ourselves, why this overview of the history of the Cuban church from the beginning of the 1970s through the end of the 1980s? It is because before we consider where we are now, it is good to consider where we have come from, where we were before, and the process of struggle and development that the Cuban church had to confront.

THE UNEXPECTED REVIVAL

As we have noted, in the midst of its own problems the Cuban church involuntarily wrapped itself in tasks of simple survival and continued fellowship among the few remaining Christians. Mission efforts fell into a sort of lethargy, waiting to be awoken. That awakening would arrive some ten years later. It is worth mentioning that there were isolated examples of evangelistic intentions, but nothing as serious as a missionary movement or church planting effort, etc.

When we consider revivals across the years and in many parts of the world, they were preceded by events and people who had upset their world with new ideas, inventions, and calls for change. As an example, we can consider the Protestant Reformation of the sixteenth century led by Martin Luther during a time of political tension which included the invention of the printing press. In the case of Cuba, there were factors that preceded the Cuban revival which cultivated that revival. First of all, we have to remember the sovereign work of God and how, in the midst of the most difficult days of persecution, there were men and women of God who were willing to continue extending the kingdom of God. One of the most representative was the now deceased President of the Cuban Evangelical League, Alejandro Nieto Selles. In 1984 he began to advance a vision called, "Cuba for Christ" which sought to unite the Cuban evangelical church and promote evangelism of the island with an interdenominational effort. Those endeavors took shape under the name "Full Life," supplying evangelistic materials to the pastors and church leaders across denominational lines. It was a representative movement because it supported evangelistic ministries in all denominations and equipped those groups with many resources like Bibles, gospel tracts, and cassette recordings with gospel sermons. This may be seen as "pre-revival" of the Cuban church; we say "pre-revival" because the church remained submerged in the lethargy of fear, fighting for survival.

In that social and political environment, changes were evolving in Cuba which would have repercussions later in the development of the church. In the words of journalist Yoe Suarez in his book, *Tú No Te Llamas Desierto,* which traced the history of the of the Evangelical League denomination of Cuba alongside the Cuban evangelical church in general:

> The 90s are the years of the fall of the socialist camp. Cuba is alone. Many are betting that the social project of the revolution will go under in a few months. A bitter economic crisis began which was euphemistically called "the Special Period." The government would take measures which would overturn the country's history. It understood that to save Cuba would require all Cubans; even those previously excluded. (Suarez 2015, 143)

During this time, there were significant structural changes taking place in the highest levels of the revolution to permit the existence of a plurality of concepts and thought, something that the revolution had feared and prohibited previously. It is for that reason that in the fourth Congress of the Communist Party of Cuba, significant modifications to the constitution were approved. As an example that directly affected us as Christians, Cuba ceased to be an atheist state and came to be called a secular state. Granted there is not much difference, but this anticipated significant changes regarding the evangelical churches (León 2003, 56).

Another event that marked a change in the mindset of the leaders of the revolution with regard to the church, was the meeting in 1991 called between Fidel Castro, the seventy-four members of the Ecumenical Council of Cuba, and evangelical denominations from across Cuba. This was an extraordinary event that became the basis of changes that were beginning to take place.

There was another key event that affected the church in Cuba—the profound economic crisis that threatened the country. This moved the hearts of Cubans to look to God, and the churches would become one of the focal points for these masses of people. It was for this reason that many people did not know how to respond to the crisis which was happening among them. In the beginning some churches that received help from outside the country tried to help by providing food for those in need, others began to develop evangelistic programs to address their spiritual needs. What is certain is that the Cuban church began to take an active stand once again in Cuban society; there was a general awakening that began to extend the kingdom of God across the island, and nothing would again be able to detain that extension.

TOWARDS A MATURE MISSIONARY CHURCH

After many years of inactivity in terms of evangelistic work, the Cuban church took a turn towards church planting. A Law of

Associations was passed that permitted groups of the faithful to meet in homes for Bible study and prayer, returning to a biblical model of church. There were no permits for construction of new church buildings, only for remodeling those that existed before the revolution. However, the simple act of meeting in homes loosed a church planting movement that has not slowed. The church planting movement within Cuba is based on this model. All denominations use some variation of home meetings. There are various names: some go by home worship, others by house church, houses of peace, source of light, etc. These groups have clear limitations imposed by the government. They must be at least two kilometers from any other home group, they may not use microphones or musical instruments, and they may not gather more than twenty people. For the most part these restrictions are not honored. Many groups meet within a kilometer or less from another group. Some have a hundred members and others up to twenty thousand. This is a church model that is not limited by a building but rather attracts many families; it is a living organism in constant growth. According to some statistics, every twelve to eighteen months a new church is born in Cuba.[3]

Missions work in Cuba has been centered in rural parts of the island for years, but in these recent times various denominations have begun to develop programs that seek to reach urban centers of the cities. This is because of the increasing growth of urban populations. Rural areas are disappearing and with them many of the rural churches, but that which has been planted in urban centers has been strengthened.

---

3. This statistic is taken from various mission institutions in Cuba. It is likely that these numbers have changed.

CHARACTERISTICS OF CUBAN CHURCH PLANTING

First, these denominations work in general with local mission-aries[4], prepared in mission-focused Bible institutes whose specialty is to prepare workers for the mission field. These missionaries have all of the necessary authority of pastors; some denominations present them with special licenses so they can baptize, serve the sacraments, etc.

Generally these groups do not function as traditional churches but rather as groups of families. The liturgy is often informal although reverential. Preaching does not have an academic feel, but more like Bible studies for small groups in which the pastor, besides being preacher, might be a sort of moderator for various topics. The primary objective of these groups is multiplication, reaching nearby communities within a short amount of time. Generally there are monthly meetings in a central church building or at the mother church. Many have begun to refer to these meetings as church planting conferences. I know churches that have around two hundred of these groups with an average of twenty members or more in each group. A question that we often hear with respect to finances is: How is it that these missionaries and their families are supported financially? In some cases, the missionary has a job and is bi-vocational, others receive a minimum of ten CUC[5] each month to a maximum of twenty CUC per month as a form of assistance, provided irregularly by brothers from outside the country who wish to help support this work. Another alternative is the national micro-business movement. One example of this is raising hogs. The sale of the hogs contributes to the missionary's salary. Others have sewing workshops or some other business that can provide the salary of a missionary. It is worth mentioning that others work without any kind of remuneration.

---

4. Cubans refer to church planters as "local missionaries."
5. Cuban Convertible Peso.

Chaplaincy programs in Cuban prisons and hospitals are also contributing to the growth of the Cuban church. About three years ago I met with an official of the Council of Churches in Cuba in my province. He told me how the government had been seeking the help of the evangelical churches to solve growing problems within the incarcerated population in Cuba. He spoke of the positive impact of the gospel in the lives of many communities, and how the levels of divorce, violence, addiction, and other negative social indicators had diminished. For that reason, he had authorized the church to train leaders and pastors for ministry in the prisons and hospitals, a privilege that previously had been reserved for the Catholic Church. The opening was such that today one can teach the Bible openly and hold regular Christian worship services in the prisons. For this reason, we speak of the "Church Behind Bars"—men who, though incarcerated, are free because of the gospel of Christ. There is similar work being done with families of prisoners, and today there are thousands of members of these churches. Results like these have also been observed throughout the hospitals.

The Cuban church in recent years has employed a system to encourage church multiplication. Each church member has a principle assignment of making disciples of all nations, though we are aware that to achieve this, we must, first of all, reach our own people through daughter churches, granddaughter churches, great-granddaughter churches, etc. This must happen in a spontaneous way without external forces that initiate the process (Acts 13:1–3; Patterson 2014, 102).

Within these growing groups of new churches, the majority belong to Pentecostal and charismatic churches, although these churches do not have any relationship with hyper-charismatic groups that are filling Latin America and the Caribbean.

CHALLENGES AND METHODS OF CHURCH PLANTING AND THE SPONTANEOUS EXPANSION OF CHURCHES

One of the great challenges of this system is the need for constant training of new missionaries so that they might pastor the small flocks. The best way to do this has been to train them in the mission field. Many seminaries, including ours, have developed distance education programs in their Bible institutes to provide doctrinal and mission teaching to these pastors within their own communities. This became a problem for us in that our students were taking nearly four years to complete a seminary program and in this time four to six new churches were being formed, needing someone to guide them. That is the reason why these Bible institutes now work directly with local churches and missionaries to reduce the time required to prepare them. Now, they are able to study while also continuing to work in their mission field.

Some seminaries accelerate the educational process of these missionaries but consequentially lower the standards of doctrinal quality in such a way that though achieving the rapid birth of new churches through a church planting movement, many of them fall victim to false doctrines due largely to the poor preparation of their pastors and leaders. For that reason, solid preparation of leaders and local missionaries has been found to be necessary in a program that combines solid teaching with efficient use of time.

What has happened in Cuba is very similar to what George Patterson shared in his article, "Spontaneous Multiplication of Churches":

> There are four simple things that can be done in order to have a successful mission movement in any culture or place. To see this, we need to distinguish between general principles and applications for a specific culture. Biblical principles themselves, if carried out with culturally appropriate methods, should permit that churches

reproduce themselves wherever there is sufficient good soil. Speaking theologically, the fertile soil necessary for the gospel to put down roots and multiply is lots and lots of bad people. (Patterson 2014, Section 102)

It does not matter if one is a missionary or not, one can multiply disciples by doing these four simple things:

1. Know and love the people you disciple.
2. Mobilize your disciples so that they might immediately edify those they are discipling.
3. Teach and practice obedience to the basic commands of Jesus in love, over any other thing.
4. Create relationships that hold one another accountable in love between the disciples and the churches so that churches might reproduce themselves.

THE CUBAN CHURCH AND CROSS-CULTURAL MISSION

The Cuban church now has a mission agency for sending cross-cultural workers to the nations (Agencia Cubana de Cuba a las Naciones). Years ago this would have been unbelievable but now, thanks to God, it is a tangible reality. This Cuban international missions agency is an interdenominational reality, formed by gathering missionaries from various denominations. Its normal way of working is to seek available people from different churches so that they might be trained and sent to the nations. At present the majority of these brothers work in Latin American or Caribbean countries, but the hope is to send them to non-Spanish speaking nations.

At this point, I'd like to speak about the challenges for the Cuban church engaging in cross-cultural missions work. Though we rejoice that we are making an effort to send Cubans to the nations—a sign of the maturing of the Cuban church—this step does not come without its significant challenges:

- We experience the challenge of emigration. The majority of Cubans who have left with the intention of cross-cultural missions have instead, upon completing their work, not returned to their country. This has negative consequences if we look at it from the perspective that these missionaries are the faculty who will teach new generations of Cuban missionaries. Because of that, when they emigrate we lose a valuable resource. A second concern due to emigration is the economic welfare of the family members who are left behind.

- We experience the challenge of inadequate formal training for cross-cultural missionaries. We do not have solid programs that can prepare Cuban missionaries for the challenges they will encounter with other cultures. In some cases, far from being a blessing, these under-prepared missionaries turn out to be a curse.

- Another challenge we have is the poor theological preparation of many missionaries. Generally, missionaries require professional preparation as doctors or teachers so they might enter closed countries. This doesn't leave time for formal theological education.

The Cuban church has previously done cross-cultural missions in a variety of ways, perhaps the most well-known being through the Cuban diaspora in the United States where there is a significant group of pastors who emigrated from Cuba and have developed ministries among the Hispanic population throughout the nation.

Another way that Cuba has participated in intercultural missions has been through medicine, education, sports, etc.

Promoted by the Cuban government, which has sent many professionals to different countries, these people are often ordained by their churches as missionaries to the world.

Another interesting way that Cuba has participated in world missions is through the many churches that have developed evangelistic programs to reach international students who study in Cuban universities. I know one brother who began a ministry to reach Chinese who study Spanish in Cuba.

These are some of the various ways that the local Cuban church is extending itself and contributing to the growth of the kingdom of God in Cuba and the world.

HOW CAN THE NORTH AMERICAN CHURCH HELP THE CUBAN CHURCH?

Cuban churches and missions ministries have many needs and limitations, which the North American church could help to meet, but this has not impeded the ongoing labor and work of God in Cuba.

We mentioned previously that the method of using local missions to extend the kingdom of God through house churches is a rapid and effective plan that does not require the time and money to build large buildings. We normally buy houses into which a pastoral family or missionary family moves. From that house, they begin missionary work in the community to which they have been sent. The houses we buy are inexpensive compared to the price in the USA or any other nation. The price of a house fluctuates between one thousand to five thousand dollars. We avoid buying any houses that cost more than that. The funds to help buy these houses that we convert into new churches would be a great help from the USA. On the other hand, one of the biggest challenges of missions in Cuba are the salaries of pastors and missionaries, though this does not deter many of them who work without a salary, simply out of love. My family and I were among this kind of Christian worker for at least two and a half years. Currently many missionaries work for ten dollars a month; these are normally singles or married couples without children. If it is a married couple with children, their salary is twenty dollars a month which, though it seems to be nothing, is actually a lot; and again if one were to help in this way it would be very good for us.

We have the experience among many local churches of beginning micro-businesses which generate salaries for a few missionaries. In Cuba it is not easy to hold private property, and even more difficult to undertake some kind of large business. But we have seen results from raising hogs or driving a "bicycle taxi" (a means of transportation in Cuba), which generate funds for the support of missions. Help in establishing micro-businesses would also be very good.

On the other hand we need teachers who can help us equip missionaries. For example, in our seminary we are forming a program in missions with the objective of training for all levels of mission work in Cuba. We need professors, tutors, literature, audiovisuals such as computers, televisions, etc. Our seminary charges no tuition because the Cuban pastors and missionaries cannot pay for the cost of their studies. Additionally, students need support for housing and food expenses while they study. Up to now, individual believers and institutions have supported us, but it is a continuous challenge to keep this kind of institution open in Cuba. Our seminary spends approximately one thousand dollars each month, which is to say that a full year of maintaining the seminary would cost some twelve thousand dollars. We are making plans to diminish the costs by producing food from the land, which would also permit some cash crops. This would somewhat break the dependence on outside funding, but in order to start this production we need outside investment, and we, as yet, do not have a source for that.

CONCLUSION

This overview of recent church planting and missions work in Cuba, by the grace of God, is not the conclusion of the work that God is doing in Cuba. The church in Cuba has much to contribute to the work of God in the world. It has many important experiences, acquired over years of persecution, that would be useful for the development of God's work in countries that are difficult to access with the gospel. Christianity in Cuba has grown much faster than in other countries with much more freedom. It is one of the few countries in the world where, without the presence of a large number of foreign missionaries, the church works in an organized manner. This contradicts the idea that without funding and foreign monitoring, the national church can't successfully develop a missions mindset. The only factor essential to do missions from the local church is God, and we have never lacked his presence.

The church hopes to face challenges in this new century in the same way, focused on spreading the kingdom of God in Cuba and in the rest of the world. To successfully do this, we need to develop formal missionary training programs, ranging across the local, national, and international levels. In addition to this, we must learn to carefully evaluate the challenges that the new times offer, without the church isolating itself as in the past.

REFERENCES CITED

Arce-Martínez, Sergio Samuel. 2004. *La Misión de la Iglesia en una Sociedad Socialista*. La Habana: Editorial Caminos.

León, Arnaldo Silva. 2003. *Breve História de la Revolución Cubana*. Editorial Ciencias Sociales. La Habana: Instituto Cubano del Libro.

Pandiello, Adolfo. 2010. *Un Fiel Mensajero: Sermones y Conferencias del Misionero Thomas H. Willey*. Miami, FL: Eagle Lithographers.

Patterson, George. 2014. "Multiplicación Espontaneo de Iglesias"
    in *Perspectivas del Movimiento Misionero Mundial—Libro 2*.
    Pasadena, CA: William Carey Library.
Suarez, Yoe. 2015. *Tú no Te Llamas Desierto*. La Habana: Ediciones

THE BRAZILIAN NEOCHARISMATIC MOVEMENT AND INTERNATIONAL EXPANSION

Murilo R. Melo

One of the most remarkable characteristics of Brazilian neo-Pentecostalism is its transnational nature. Paul Freston (2001) argues that we must overcome the parochialism of certain perspectives on religion in an era of globalization, such as the disregard by the academia of significant movements of Pentecostalism simply because they occurred independently of religious initiatives in the North Atlantic. While recognition of this phenomenon of rapid indigenous movement has become more frequent in the last decade, there is still a tendency toward broad generalizations. The thesis of this paper is that evangelicals should study and selectively learn from the international expansion of Brazilian Neocharismatic churches, and help them to correct some practices. We will initially provide a brief overview of Protestantism in Brazil before we discuss the particularities of the international expansion of Brazilian Neocharismatic churches.

Brazil is the largest country in Latin America in terms of population, GDP, and landmass, and the only country that has Portuguese as the official language. In 1940, only 2.5 percent of the population claimed Protestant faith, while in 2010 over 42 million (21 percent) affirmed Protestantism (evangelicalism[1]) in the census (IBGE 2010). With thirty-four thousand Brazilian missionaries in 2010, it is the second largest sending country in the world (Center for the Study of Global Christianity—Gordon-Conwell

---

1. Owing to the significant German Lutheran population in the southern states, the Portuguese term *evangélico* is often equated with all *protestantismo* (a term relatively unused).

Theological Seminary 2013). Thus a dramatic change in little more than a half-century has occurred in the religious scenario in Brazil, and this exceptional growth is mostly due to the rise of Brazilian Pentecostalism which accounts for more than 60 percent of all Protestants (IBGE 2010).

Traditionally, the rise of Pentecostalism in Brazil is explained in three waves. The first wave (1910–1950) is marked by churches being founded by foreign missions—the so-called "traditional" Pentecostal churches. In 1909, Luis (Luigi) Francescón (an Italian missionary with training from Chicago) established the Christian Congregation of Brazil (Burgess and Van der Maas 2002, 39). In 1911, Daniel Berg and Gunnar Vingren (Swedish missionaries) founded "The Apostolic Faith" which later became the Assemblies of God in the state of Pará (Burgess and Van der Maas 2002, 39). Edwin Williams (USA) and Jesus Ramos (Peru) started crusades in 1951 which formed the Four Square Gospel movement (Burgess and Van der Maas 2002, 39). The second wave (1950s–1970s) is marked by the development of indigenous Brazilian churches, with little or no involvement of foreign missionaries. The rapid growth of the second wave movement coincides with Brazil's period of urbanization and the widespread accessibility of mass media. Within the Charismatic movement, churches like Brazil for Christ (founded in 1955) became the pioneers in using public and secular spaces such as cinemas and theaters or communication tools like radio and TV for church services and meetings. Founded in 1960 by Canadian Robert McAlister, the relatively small New Life Church (Conselho Nova Vida) downplayed the traditional Pentecostal emphases on legalism and asceticism and emphasized radio programs which influenced other churches to follow this more popular approach for outreach (Kramer 2002). God is Love (1962), House of Blessing (1964; Casa da Benção) and Maranatha (1968; Igreja Cristã Maranata) are some of the largest churches during this period. Continuing a populist philosophy of public ministry, the Third Wave movement (1970s to today) emphasizes the power of the Holy Spirit in healing the sick, casting out demons, and use of prophecies. In general, these churches abandon the conservative ethics (customs) and aesthetics (worship style) of traditional Pentecostalism (Freston 1999, 151). The explosive numerical growth gives these churches the assurance that the Holy Spirit is blessing them, their efforts are being rewarded, and they have visible fruit because they represent Christ in the world. Moreover, such tangible growth encourages their boldness to reach other countries.

The New International Dictionary of Pentecostal and Charismatic Movements opted for a new classification defining Neocharismatics as Christian bodies characterized by "Pentecostal-like experiences with no traditional Pentecostal or charismatic denominational connection (and sometimes only slender—if any—historical connections)" (Burgess and Van der Maas 2002, 928). Such a classification defines some of the second-wave and all third-wave Pentecostals—totaling at least 9 million in Brazilian Neocharismatic churches in 2010, although others estimate as high as 18 million (Grim 2009, 487). There is a wide range of practices in place, and many belong to the New Apostolic Reformation.[2] Most Neocharismatic churches, and all churches with international expansion mentioned in this paper, seem to hold to an orthodox view of the Trinity, the person of Christ, the inerrancy of Scriptures, and salvation by grace through faith. In this paper, I will explore the distinctiveness of Brazilian Neocharismatics, focusing on the common growth approach these churches adopt, their strong focus on proselytizing, and more specifically their assimilation of native cultural and religious expressions. We will also address its sacrificial requirements for liberation from both economic and spiritual oppression and the use of tangible expressions of faith, as well as the anticipation of ritual expressions.

---

2. This will be explained later in the text.

DISTINCT BELIEFS

We will narrow the focus of this discussion to the following churches:

1. Igreja Universal do Reino de Deus (UCKG; Universal Church of the Kingdom of God) is the most researched of the group, and is also the most representative of the Third Wave Pentecostalism. By some accounts, it might have as many as 4,700 churches in 172 countries (Mafra, Swatowiski, and Sampaio 2013).

2. Deus é Amor (God is Love Church), founded by David Miranda in 1962, is now present in seventy-eight countries.

3. Igreja Mundial do Poder de Deus (WCGP, World Church of God's Power) was founded in 1998 (after Apostle Valdemiro Santiago left UCKG) and is now present in seventeen countries.

4. Igreja Internacional da Graça de Deus (IGGC, International Grace of God Church) was founded by R.R. Soares (brother-in-law of UCKG's Edir Macedo), and is present in eleven countries (História).

5. Sara Nossa Terra (Heal Our Land Church) was founded in 1994 by physicist Bishop Robson Rodovalho with his wife Bishop Lucia, and is already present in thirteen countries, reaching 1.3 million believers (História da Sara).

The main characteristic that distinguishes these churches from traditional Protestant churches is experiencing the power of the Holy Spirit in healing the sick, casting out demons, prophecy, and exercise of other spiritual gifts. These Third Wave ministries further distinguish themselves from traditional Pentecostal churches as they have less emphasis on glossolalia as the sign of baptism in the Spirit (some emphasize simply being filled with the Spirit). All of them are part of the New Apostolic Reformation in which leadership, spiritual direction, and vision-casting are centered in the founding pastor (whether formally called "apostle" or not), with minimal or no role for a board of elders, or other forms of accountability (Wagner 2002, 930). This autocratic, apostolic element is so strong that even after a year since David Miranda passed away, the website of God is Love Church still does not mention a successor.[3]

It is also a prominent teaching that believers, as children of God, deserve blessings in this life. The emphasis on prosperity varies widely, with R. R. Soares (2006) believing the blessings are "not to be rich, but to clean your name, to pay all debts and never more incur them" while Valdemiro Santiago (2012) exhorting believers to "tithe what you will choose, not based on what you earn, but what you would like to earn."[4] On another occasion, as Brazilians receive a thirteenth monthly salary in December, Apostle Valdemiro, as he is usually called, suggested that believers "give 30% representing the Holy Trinity: Father, Son and Holy Spirit, to this work, and the 70 (%) that you will keep, you will do things that you have never done in your life, and you will see the year flowing, your life blasting in success, your projects succeeding, and the work of God with these resources will accomplish many things. . ."[5]

Brazilian Neocharismatics emphasize that both God and the devil are actively involved in the world, with a real spiritual battle in which all believers are warriors. The strong emphasis on evangelism is not only a consequence of obeying the Great

---

3. David Martins Miranda had a heart attack and died on February 21, 2015. His successor is not mentioned in the History of IPDA: Igreja Pentecostal Deus é Amor

4. Author's translation in both quotes (trying to replicate their respective styles).

5. Author's translation of Santiago (2010).

Commission but also because believers are part of this cosmic battle for souls (Corten and Marshall-Fratani 2001, 9). In this context, many churches become involved in an international expansion, as conquerors for God (Droogers 2001, 56). As they see it, their growing numbers are a clear indication that God is on their side in this cosmic battle.

These churches are able to listen globally, engaging believers with God's work in the whole world and encouraging them to participate in the globalization of the faith. Heal Our Land Church (Sara Nossa Terra 2009, 2012) brought bishops Nnaji and Gift Chuks from Nigeria to Brazil, teaching about spiritual deliverance and performing miracles. Brazilian R.R. Soares records miracles in South Africa (2014a), Portugal (2014c), and the USA (2014b), showing them to his Brazilian audience in quite attractive videos. Through their public testimonies, believers become part of this worldwide spiritual movement—able to see and communicate what God is doing all over the world. Considering that most members are poor and excluded from the economic benefits of globalization, they can now play a powerful spiritual role in the international scenario as part of these globally expanding churches.

THE ROLE IN THE SOCIOCULTURAL CONTEXTS

As these churches grew in other countries, they provided rich soil for sociocultural studies and religious contextualization. Being relatively newer churches, they had freedom to innovate and adapt to recent changes in society and culture, especially among the growing number of working women and the aspirations of social mobility in a globalized world. Neocharismatic discourses and practices persuade believers to take control of their lives and of society by challenging cultural norms through the power of the Holy Spirit. Often, this more individualistic worldview involves breaking with the family power structure (including ancestor worship but also regarding live family members), destabilizing its network and the security it may provide in places where the State is more fragile and less supportive (van de Kamp 2012b). Unfortunately, one observes that the Neocharismatic churches only partially compensate for this change, as there is a weaker congregationalism with fewer moments for fellowship beyond the services (Oro and Semán 2001).

Brazilian Neocharismatic churches also show boldness in interacting with each country's original religious traditions in order to communicate its message effectively, sometimes even to the point of confronting traditional religious beliefs and practices. In 1995, on national television, a UCKG pastor brazenly kicked off the stage a statue of the Brazilian Virgin Mary—Our Lady Aparecida (the Brazilian National Basilica is in her honor).[6] After the massive public outcry because of this event, confrontation became less aggressive, yet still firm. Such confrontation is manifested both physically and spiritually. Physically, huge churches are built in areas of oppression. For example in South Africa, the UCKG built an eight-thousand-seat temple near Soweto's beer halls that once stood for resistance during the apartheid (Vásquez 2009). Spiritually, as they forcefully declare that other religions and practices are demonic, they boldly touch witchcraft objects without being harmed (Kamp 2015). Spiritual confrontation is understood as an intentional application of power from God to overcome. By faith one should be "the head and not the tail" according to Deuteronomy 28:13 (Bronsztein 2014, 133).

Liberation Theology opted for the poor, but the poor opted for the Neocharismatic movement.[7] Yet, some charismatic movements

---

6. This was part of a message that was aired during the national holiday of Our Lady of Aparecida, Brazil's patron saint, October 12th (Universal 1995).

7. The saying goes that the poor opted for the Pentecostals, but Neocharismatic churches grew even more than traditional Pentecostal churches. This is now such a popular saying in Latin America that tracing

like Reborn in Christ and Heal Our Land targeted and achieved success with the middle-class. The attraction was a holistic gospel that did not recognize the guilt of being rich as preached by liberation theologians and instead rewarded present material blessings for the faithful. These blessings can also be understood on a national scope, as attested by the key verse that gives the name to the church "Heal Our Land" (2 Chr 7:14). As previously mentioned, breaking with traditional Pentecostalism's legalism and moving toward the acceptance of makeup and common dress also resulted in less emphasis on ethical behavior, including work ethics. The churches that adapted well to the middle-class have a distinct aesthetic, with modern forms of worship and audiovisual features (Freston 1999, 150).

Media and marketing are powerful tools and are well-used by these churches. The God is Love Church has programs on seventeen international radio stations. Ironically, while this church prohibits the use of TV due to morality concerns, they have been able to make good use of the internet (Rivera 2013). UCKG has television shows in many countries, including the US. The history of Heal Our Land Church is narrated in a video clip with language and intonation similar to political TV commercials. Media is particularly useful as professions of faith become more public, especially when Brazilian soccer players wear evangelistic T-shirts and publically pray together during the Confederations Cup matches (Rial 2012, 134). In urban settings the strategic use of public spaces is intentional either by using physical proximity as in the case of the UCKG in Maputo, which built a church across the street from the Mozambican capital's oldest and largest mosque, or by targeting cultural icons—such as the theater Cine Estrella in Lima, now home of the God is Love Church—to declare spiritual conquest of physical spaces (Mary 2002). The Neocharismatic movement's ability to coordinate

---

its origins is complicated, but perhaps Samuel Escobar was the first to use it.

beliefs, intentional action, and a coherent and attractive narrative is commendable.

Internationally, the same factors that helped growth in Brazil were also explored, namely the aspiration for social mobility in contrast with the current exclusion of the poor from globalization and wealth-creation. For instance, women represent up to 75 percent of believers in "Brazilian" churches in Africa. Seeking autonomy from the bondage imposed by traditional religions and Islam, the church helps women reformulate their worldview and empowers them to work toward financial independence— something almost unknown among their ancestors (van de Kamp 2012a). In Europe and in the USA, growth is especially directed toward minorities. The UCKG church in London is 90 percent "non-white," with Indians, Africans, and all kinds of non-European believers gathering at the Rainbow theater (Freston 2001, 209). In London, they created a "Victory Youth Group" that was responsible for UCKG expansion to Manchester, Luton, Nottingham, Swindon, and Birmingham. This group explains that "music, drama and dance added a 'wow factor' to serious messages about facing up to life's challenges and achieving greater fulfillment for young people." (UCKG-UK 2013). In the US, the Latino community is the largest group reached by these churches, but growth has also been observed among African Americans. In Japan and elsewhere, Brazilian migrants are the major target group. The international expansion of the UCKG is directed by a commission that investigates the probability of success, the most appropriate discourse, and the best location for churches, besides carrying out rental or purchase of property (Freston 2001, 199). However, the local pastors can and do adapt the message, as well as the language, as they work in the field (both adding services in other languages and altering the use of expressions for the demonic, etc.). So, while there is a strong central coordination, there is also relative autonomy for the local pastor.

Political involvement has generally been more pragmatic than ideological, building alliances to help the churches' interests in media, taxes, etc. The Assemblies of God was highly effective among Protestants in the political arena, electing thirteen congressmen in Brazil's first open election after the military regime in 1986 (Corten 1999). In that country, one of the largest voting blocs is the Evangelical Parliamentary Front (Frente Parlamentar Evangélica 2014), with eighty-two of the 513 congressional seats. The UCKG was able to use these connections in Brazil to buy and keep the State concessions of forty radio stations and twenty-three TV broadcast relay stations, becoming one of the largest media empires in the country in its three decades of existence (Souza 2011, 20). Unfortunately, ethical problems are frequent among these political leaders (Reich and dos Santos 2013): even the former chair of Congress Eduardo Cunha, a member of Heal Our Land Church, has been involved in scandals and is banned from politics (Magalhães 2015). The UCKG also tried, unsuccessfully so far, to found a political party in Portugal (Freston 2001) and has maintained cordial ties to the President of Mozambique[8] and enjoyed the presence of the Minister of Youth and Sports in one of its events in that country (Universal 2015).

THEOLOGICAL METHOD, HERMENEUTIC, AND PRAXIS

Many Brazilian Neocharismatic churches share what Vásquez (2009, 276) proposed as "Pneumatic Materialism." The Holy Spirit is central to the experience of the sacred yet there is a rejection of the Cartesian dichotomy between spirit and matter, creating a new "spirit-matter" nexus and a holistic re-articulation of self and society. This pneumatic materialism

---

8. After the grand opening of a temple in Maputo, with seating for 12,500 people, with seventy thousand people waiting for it, Bishop Macedo was received by the President of Mozambique with a big smile (Universal 2007).

bridges the tension between the seen and unseen. The relatively high functional illiteracy of some groups promoted the growth of a visual and oral religious culture, with concern for the message-sending and correct decoding of the message (Bellotti 2010). Many churches use physical objects to depict spiritual realities, as tangible reminders of the faith, promises, battle, and commitment. While there are ancient examples of this practice like the blessings of palms for Palm Sunday since the eighth century and the use of ashes on Ash Wednesday since the tenth century (Cross and Livingstone 2005, 115), these churches offer a creative ecclesiology focusing on objects of daily use as reminders of God's provision and power. In Portugal, the UCKG (Centro de Ajuda Universal 2015) offered handkerchiefs anointed with sacred oil to address the spiritual problems related to sickness and quality and joy of life. Grace of God International Church (Igreja Internacional da Graça de Deus 2016) offered soap to wash a believer's family clothes (cleansing a "heavy environment," discord, addictions, etc.) because Jesus's second coming will be like a launderer's soap (Mal 3:2), thoroughly cleaning and leaving no spots. A bishop from Heal Our Land Church developed a company to sell the "aroma of blessing," an oil spray from Israel (Gnoticias 2010). These are merely samples of a vast universe of objects being used to represent spiritual realities. While Grace of God International Church tries to connect the object somewhat more tightly with the work of Jesus Christ, unfortunately on many occasions this connection is either weak or even nonexistent. Instead, the spiritual reality is rather grounded in pastor's prayers, the Promised Land (e.g. sand, oil, rocks from Israel), the church, or somewhat vaguely the power of God. Finally, the use of photographs of family members while presenting them in prayer to the Lord is often widely practiced (Oro and Semán 2001, 190).

This pneumatic materialism is linked in practice with an economy of sacrificial giving. Believers are encouraged to participate in campaigns of offerings, as the services build up to a ritualized climax of sacrificial giving in which people fulfill their pledges of support (Kramer 2002, 30). The distributions of material items are framed as exchanges that people need "to give in order to receive," using biblical texts such as 2 Samuel 24:24 when David refuses to make a sacrifice that costs him nothing. At the World Church of God's Power (Igreja Mundial do Poder de Deus 2013), believers' testimonies after using the blessed "Pillowcase of Dreams" and contributing monthly to the campaigns entitled "Multiplication" and "Great Conquests" are used to validate these physical-spiritual realities. The UCKG's Bishop Edir Macedo explains, "Sacrifice is the materialization of faith in God" as believers deny themselves and follow Christ; only then can they demand the "fulfillment of the benefits afforded by His presence. It's give and take! . . . What is unacceptable is to want to enjoy the benefits of faith without paying the price, which is, without sacrificing. There is no other way to profit from the benefits of faith!" (Macedo 2013, loc: 988). The UCKG's British website even cites Winston Churchill, "We make a living by what we get, but we make a life by what we give." (UCKG-UK 2016b).

With an emphasis on the continuity between OT and NT, the blessings in this world are available just as were promised to the nation of Israel. These national blessings stimulate churches to direct political involvement. Moreover, by appropriating rich Jewish imagery (i.e., the Temple of Solomon, Ark of the Covenant, menorah, etc.), a nation's success and prosperity are interpreted as direct blessings from God with no reference to Protestant ethics. Individual blessings are a result of the believer's position as a child of God. Churches like the IGGC (Igreja Internacional da Graça de Deus 2008) instruct the believers to act in faith in order to take possession of blessings like healing which are already available to them in the Bible by using Kenneth Hagin's teaching that "to ask" (αἰτέω, John 14:13) means "to ordain" (Soares 2002, 10). Through such prayer, blessings will become available once the demonic opposition is removed. Soares explains further,

"From now on you will not have to pray and ask for healing, prosperity or to have victory over your temptations; you will ordain or demand that all evil leave your life." (2002, 10–11). He illustrates his point with a story of a farmer whose livestock were dying and who heard Soares' teaching on TV. The farmer

> went out into the yard and exclaimed with his hand raised, 'Not one more chicken or pig will die here, in the name of Jesus.' Three months after he declared this, he met me in a meeting I was holding in Catanduva. With tears streaming down his face, he told me that since then not a single animal had died on his farm. It is not difficult. This can and should happen to you. The Lord Himself has so declared. (Soares 2002, 11)

However, if someone lives in a way that his or her income does not last until the end of the month, it is also necessary to be faithful in tithes and offerings, the requisites for God to "rebuke the devourer," as a UCKG pastor explained using Malachi 3:11.

Valdemiro Santiago popularized the motto "God's hand is here" for his church (WCGP, World Church of God's Power). He boldly confronted other Neocharismatic churches by declaring that "believers do not have to demand here," a direct challenge against R. R. Soares. Opposing Edir Macedo's teaching he also declared, "If you don't have faith, come here and use mine to be blessed" (Bitun 2010, 14). Other pastors in the WCGP imitate Santiago's simple style of communication from the pulpit with strong preference on the use of dialogue, interviewing believers, and occasionally reading the Scriptures. There is also an almost mythological aura among church members and pastors of his church regarding Santiago's instrumentality as a healer from God, which is why his image is now displayed in churches all over the world (Sousa 2014, 3). Competition among these churches is intense, and there is a contingent of believers that tends to oscillate among them as they seek the most visible power of God manifested in miracles. While Macedo explains the importance of serving Jesus and not the UCKG, he concludes one book with the statement

> Throughout the history of the Universal Church of the Kingdom of God, not even one of the many who rebelled has managed to survive. Not because someone cursed them . . . but because they cursed themselves when they rebelled against the authority established by the Holy Spirit. . . . And all those who rebel against the authorities established by God have been inspired and led by the same spirit of Satan. (2013, loc:1031)

Spiritual warfare is heavily emphasized in the movement. While in Brazil and in Africa pastors cast out demons using the names of Afro-Brazilian deities ("orixás"), in other regions of the world pastors contextualize differently. As Manuel Silva, a pastor of UCKG in New York, explained, the UCKG

> is the reflection of a peculiar society that has been permeated by the belief and fear of the spirits and, consequently, exorcism is the most frequent practice of this church . . . We will have to wait and see how the Igreja Universal adapts to new cultures in which the people do not have the same fear of spirits as they do in Brazil. Most likely the church will continue dealing with the same spirits and with as much success as it has had in Brazil, but, following Jacques Ellul's ideas, they may find that new demons are lurking in the big cities of the world and in other different cultures. (1991, 161)

In the twenty-six years since this prediction, UCKG was able to not only focus on Latin Americans, Africans, and African Americans who already share the same worldview but also to contextualize its message in other places. The terminology changed in Argentina, Portugal, and Italy, where more general categories of deliverance were used, i.e., from witchcraft and psychologized figures of suffering (Oro and Semán 2001, 185). In practice, Corten, Dozen, and Oro (2003, 139) see pastors engaging with spiritual warfare use expressions like, "Out! Evil spirit of sexual abuse, of depression, of alcoholism! Out! Demons of unemployment, of spouses addicted to drugs!" In the UK (UCKG-UK 2016a), the focus is on substance abuse. There is flexibility and adaptation in countries where belief in the devil is less prevalent, where pastors need to teach about the demonic reality and influences before focusing on teaching deliverance, which occurs with varied success. Even physical manifestations vary, as observed by Oro and Semán, "in Brazil demon possession parallels Umbanda's 'terreiros' (small steps, *sui generis* body contortions, different voice), whereas in Argentina shouts and insults are more frequent, and need to be explained as demon activity" (2001, 189). The pursuit of holiness is also influenced by the warfare narrative, as Macedo explains, "A minor sin today, another tomorrow, and then suddenly faith gets cold and the fear of God disappears, thus giving room to doubt. And doubt is what makes one weak before the armies of hell" (2013). Personal sanctification, then, occurs before angels and impacts a believer's influence over them.

Sermon themes of liberation, conquest, and dominion are emphasized, together with faith and financial fidelity as major expectations of believers. Yet, the gospel is preached in a holistic way, often emphasizing the spiritual liberation. It is always transformational. God is said to vomit out the indifferent, so believers come to worship with the expectation not only to hear the Word, but to experience God and his transforming power in their lives. R. R. Soares teaches that:

God expects us to accept our redemption and begin to act as redeemed people. The devil knows he has to obey all those who discover this truth. The Bible declares: "For you were bought at a price; therefore glorify God in your body and in your spirit, which are God's" (1 Cor. 6:20). We must demand all disease to leave our bodies. If we are not free from all maladies, how will we be able to glorify God in our bodies? We must also demand that all sinfulness leave our spirit, otherwise it will be impossible to glorify God in our hearts. (2002, 74)

The UCKG offers a new framework for contextualizing human brokenness with its motto "Stop Suffering." It is a remarkable theodicy, reconciling the omnipotent and omnibenevolent God with the presence of evil through its exorcisms and prosperity gospel (Corten, Dozon, and Oro 2003, 140). There is hope for this life, even for the poor, uneducated, and oppressed. In his book *Rational Faith*, Edir Macedo argues that "In these end times, the Spirit of God has revealed the faith-benefit. This type of faith materializes divine promises in the lives of those who practice it" (2010, 1).[9] This leads believers to a simple and deep faith that has practical consequences in all aspects of life.

Despite the frequent emphasis on prosperity in the UCKG's preaching, Macedo elsewhere teaches about what is to be born again and that the one born of the Spirit has objectives "aligned with the Spirit of God, including: a passion for the presence of God, a passion for souls, and a passion to do the will of God" (2013, 283). He said, "Unfortunately, Christianity today is more committed to itself than to others" much like Simon the sorcerer who yearned for economic profits (2013, 77). While a number of participants go to the UCKG simply seeking urgent solutions for

9. Author's translation.

their particular problems, there is also a group of *obreiros* (workers), laypeople highly engaged in the church's activities (Oro and Semán 2001, 191). This latter group is frequently active in vigils and prayer meetings and assists with ministries of the church. While most *obreiros* have menial "secular" jobs, they are proud to be UCKG workers—and the ones we know have a sincere love for the Lord.

UCKG celebrates religious meetings on each day of the week with its particular focus: financial success for Monday meetings, healing for Tuesday, faith for Wednesday, family and marriage for Thursday, spiritual cleansing for Friday, therapy of love for Saturday, and general worship for Sunday. The UCKG maintains this agenda in all countries, with some adaptation of terminology. Church meetings have ample time for testimonies usually consisting of a story of hardship, defeat, and failure—typically the believer is asked "How were you before arriving here?"— followed by what occurred through the ministry of UCKG and their improved status. While some testimonies demonstrate the attitude of surrendering to God, often the focus is participation in an activity or campaign of the church. One example is a convert receiving a phenomenal job offer after participating in the "Nation of 318," which is a meeting of 318 pastors praying for believers-entrepreneurs, based on Genesis 14:14. The story ends with detailed descriptions of many material blessings received by the believer like new car, home, etc. The detail of the material blessings in the testimonies is seen as legitimate and acceptable because desiring a life full of the earthly signs of success, with products of high commercial value is viewed as an answer to the ideal of happiness (Bronsztein 2014, 140).

In 1993, the Evangelical Alliance of Portugal (AEP) had to concede that UCKG's body of doctrines "is very close to the doctrinal principles of the AEP, but its 'guiding ideas' . . . as well as some of its practices, put it outside the traditional universe of the Portuguese evangelical churches." (Freston 2001, 207).

Apparently, none of the Brazilian Neocharismatic churches present in Portugal were allowed membership in the Evangelical Alliance.[10] Concerned with the scandals present in many of these churches, the broader evangelical church considers it the so-called "vampirization" of believers and has distanced itself from the Brazilian Neocharismatic movement and practices (Mary 2002, 465). Unfortunately, given the attention that Neocharismatic churches gather in the media, non-believers cannot clearly understand this difference.

CONCLUSION

I agree with Paul Freston (2013, 69) as he sees a future numerical stabilization of the growth of Protestantism in Brazil, with an increased percentage of members through birth and older converts. There will be stronger demands for teaching and for different types of church leadership and greater expectations in the field of social actions. As the Brazilian Neocharismatic movement is increasingly criticized by the secular media and historical churches for its involvement in scandals and manipulations, growth seems to be shifting to the broader Protestant community (Freston 2013, 73). However, people who leave these Neocharismatic churches are facing the reality that there are only a handful of churches with Spirit-filled dynamics and solid biblical teaching. Most Protestant churches have solid doctrine, but without the power and the concern for daily problems that characterize the Neocharismatic movement. It seems that the international expansion of Brazilian Neocharismatic churches may sustain its current momentum, which further forces the larger body of Christ to learn from the experience of these churches and continue engaging with them.

---

10. The author tried to find in the Alliance's website the churches known to be present in Portugal. The search is by district and council, not by name (Evangelical Alliance of Portugal 2016).

Despite the issues that may rightly cause division, there seems to be much more in common, including the fundamentals of the faith and much more to learn from one another. The Brazilian Neocharismatic movement exposes the need for a biblical teaching that confronts the problems experienced by the marginalized. Further, they realized the need for supernatural intervention to overcome these problems and demonstrated a hands-on approach to the frequent crises of their flock. The sincere attempt to embrace the dreams of the poor to be liberated is crucial to the success of this movement. A mutual challenge for traditional Protestants and Neocharismatics is how to incorporate and practice a more nuanced biblical worldview while firmly addressing the needs of such a large population.

REFERENCES CITED

Bitun, Ricardo. 2010. "Continuidade nas Cissiparidades: Neopentecostalismo Brasileiro." *Ciências da Religião—História e Sociedade* 8 (2):122–54.

Bronsztein, Karla Regina M.P.P. 2014. "Nação dos 318: a Religião do Consumo na Igreja Universal do Reino de Deus." *PPGCOM —ESPM, Comunicação, Mídia e Consumo* 2 (30):125–42.

Burgess, Stanley M. and Eduard M. van der Maas, eds. 2002. *The New International Dictionary of Pentecostal and Charismatic Movements.* Grand Rapids, MI: Zondervan.

Casa da Benção. "História." http://cb.org.br/inicio/historia/ (accessed Feb 25, 2016).

Center for the Study of Global Christianity—Gordon-Conwell Theological Seminary. 2013. *Christianity in its Global Context, 1970–2020: Society, Religion, and Mission.* South Hamilton, MA: Center for the Study of Global Christianity. www.globalchristianity.org/globalcontext.

Centro de Ajuda Universal. 2015. "Cura: Lenço Ungido." https://
     youtu.be/RtUolJJirAw (accessed March 2, 2016).
Conselho   Nova   Vida.   "Nossa   história."   http://www
     .conselhonovavida.com.br/nossa-historia/ (accessed Feb
     25, 2016).
Corten, André. 1999. "Pentecôtisme et 'néo-pentecôtisme' au
     Brésil." *Archives de sciences sociales des religions* 44 (105):163–83.
Corten, André, Jean Pierre Dozon, and Ari Pedro Oro. 2003.
     "Les Nouveaux Conquérants de la Foi: L'église Universelle
     du Royaume de Dieu (Brésil)." In *Hommes et sociétés*. Paris:
     Karthala.
Corten, André, and Ruth Marshall-Fratani. 2001. "Introduction."
     In *Between Babel and Pentecost: Transnational Pentecostalism in
     Africa and Latin America*, edited by André Corten and Ruth
     Marshall-Fratani. Bloomington, IN: Indiana University
     Press.
Cross, F. L., and Elizabeth A. Livingstone. 2005. *The Oxford
     Dictionary of the Christian Church*. Oxford: Oxford University
     Press.
Droogers, André. 2001. "Globalisation and Pentecostal Success."
     In *Between Babel and Pentecost: Transnational Pentecostalism in
     Africa and Latin America, edited by* André Corten and Ruth
     Marshall-Fratani. Bloomington, IN: Indiana University
     Press.
Evangelical Alliance of Portugal. "Onde Estamos." http://www
     .aliancaevangelica.pt/areareservada/onde_estamos.php.
Frente Parlamentar Evangélica. Noticias. http://www.fpebrasil
     .com.br/portal/index.php/noticias (accessed March 26,
     2016).
Freston, Paul. 1999. "Neo-Pentecostalism in Brazil: Problems of
     Definition and the Struggle for Hegemony." *Archives de
     Sciences Sociales des Religions* 44 (105):145–62.
———. 2001. "The Transnationalisation of Brazilian
     Pentecostalism: The Universal Church of the Kingdom

of God." In *Between Babel and Pentecost: Transnational Pentecostalism in Africa and Latin America,* edited by André Corten and Ruth Marshall-Fratani, 196–215. Bloomington, IN: Indiana University Press.

———. 2013. "The Future of Pentecostalism in Brazil." In *Global Pentecostalism in the 21st Century,* edited by Robert W. Hefner. Bloomington, IN: Indiana University Press.

Gnoticias. 2010. "Pastora Alda Célia e Bispa da Sara Nossa Terra Lançam o Aroma Gospel, a Unção em Spray." http:// wp.me/p1YZt-31Q (accessed March 2, 2016).

Grim, Brian. 2009. "Pentecostalism's Growth in Religiously Restricted Environments." *Society* 46 (6):484–95.

IBGE - Instituto Brasileiro de Geografia e Estatística. 2010. *Censo Demográfico 2010—Características Gerais da População, Religião e Pessoas com Deficiência.* Rio de Janeiro: IBGE.

Igreja Cristã Maranata. "Quem Somos." http://www .igrejacristamaranata.org.br/?p=4110 (accessed Feb 25, 2016).

Igreja Internacional da Graça de Deus. "História." http://www .ongrace.com/portal/?page_id=7 (accessed Feb 25, 2016).

———. 2008. Missionario Responde—Determinação. http://www.ongrace.com/portal/?missionario_ responde=determinao-15402 (accessed Mach 4, 2016).

———. Quarta-feira do Sabão do Lavandeiro—IIGD Madureira. https://youtu.be/rSOAdP03SZQ (accessed March 2, 2016).

Igreja Mundial do Poder de Deus. "Quem Somos." https://www .impd.org.br/institucional (accessed Feb 25, 2016).

———. "O carnê da Prosperidade Econômica e Financeira da Igreja Mundial do Poder de Deus (IMPD)." https:// youtu.be/28VfuVgXYVA (accessed March 4, 2016).

Igreja Pentecostal Deus é Amor. "Endereços das Igrejas Deus é Amor pelo Mundo." http://www.ipda.com.br/ipda/ipda /endereco_ipda_pelo_mundo.php (accessed Feb 25, 2016).

———. "História da Igreja Pentecostal Deus é Amor." http://
www.ipda.com.br/ipda/ipda/historico_ipda.php
(accessed Feb 25, 2016).

Kramer, Eric. 2002. "Making Global Faith Universal: Media and
a Brazilian Prosperity Movement." *Culture and Religion* 3
(1):21–47.

Macedo, Edir. 2010. *Fé Racional*. Rio de Janeiro: Editora Grafica
Universal.

———. 2013. *How to do the work of God [Kindle Edition]*. Rio de
Janeiro: Unipro Editora.

Mafra, Clara, Claudia Swatowiski, and Camila Sampaio. 2013.
"Edir Macedo's Pastoral Project: A Globally Integrated
Pentecostal Network." In *The Diaspora of Brazilian Religions*,
edited by Cristina Rocha and Manuel A. Vásquez.
Boston, MA: Brill.

Magalhães, Jeane. 2015. "Bispo Rodovalho fala em entrevista
sobre o presidente da Câmara dos Deputados Eduardo
Cunha." http://www.saranossaterra.com.br/noticias/bispo
-rodovalho-fala-em-entrevista-sobre-o-presidente-da
-camara-dos-deputados-eduardo-cunha/ (accessed March 2,
2016).

Mary, André. 2002. "Le Pentecôtisme Brésilien en Terre
Africaine L'Universel Abstrait du Royaume de Dieu."
Cahiers d'études africaines 167 (3):463–78.

Oro, Ari Pedro, and Pablo Semán. 2001. "Brazilian
Pentecostalism Crosses National Borders." In *Between
Babel and Pentecost: Transnational Pentecostalism in Africa and
Latin America*, edited by André Corten and Ruth Marshall-
Fratani. Bloomington, IN: Indiana University Press.

Reich, Gary, and Pedro dos Santos. 2013. "The Rise (and
Frequent Fall) of Evangelical Politicians: Organization,
Theology, and Church Politics." *Latin American Politics &
Society* 55 (4):1–22.

Rial, Carmen. 2012. "Banal Religiosity: Brazilian Athletes as New Missionaries of the Neo-Pentecostal Diaspora." *Vibrant: Virtual Brazilian Anthropology* 9 (2):128–59.

Rivera, Dario Paulo Barrera. 2013. "Brazilian Pentecostalism in Peru: Affinities between the Social and Cultural Conditions of Andean Migrants and the Religious Worldview of the Pentecostal Church God is Love." In *The Diaspora of Brazilian Religions*, edited by Cristina Rocha. Boston, MA: Brill.

Santiago, Valdemiro. 2010. "Trizimo—Apostolo Valdemiro Santiago." https://youtu.be/0LgjL6VMEO8 (accessed March 2, 2016).

———. 2012 "Sermon on TV." http://youtu.be/3Sp65-mTNxI (accessed Feb 25, 2016).

Sara Nossa Terra. "História da Sara." http://www.saranossaterra .com.br/historia-da-sara/ (accessed Feb 25, 2016).

———. 2009. "Culto de Libertação—Bispo Nnaji- Parte 01." https://youtu.be/UarIe7Ekp68 (accessed March 2, 2016).

———. 2012. "Bispo Gift Opera Milagres na Igreja Sara Nossa Terra em Vila Velha/ES." https://youtu .be/8jlwQz7ZMu8 (accessed March 2, 2016).

Silva, Manuel. 1991. "A Brazilian Church Comes to New York." *Pneuma* 13 (2):161–65.

Soares, R. R. 2002. *Faith Course*. Rio de Janeiro: Graca.

———. 2006. "Missionário Responde: Capitalismo nas Igrejas." http://www.ongrace.com/portal/?missionario_ responde=capitalismo-nas-igrejas-14500 (accessed Feb 25, 2016).

———. 2014. "Milagres na África do Sul." https://youtu.be /_nvrAmsliKw (accessed March 2, 2016).

———. 2014. "Flórida (EUA), 22 de janeiro de 2014 - Ano da Volta da Vitória." https://youtu.be/slz_7-orBwo (accessed March 2, 2016).

————. 2014. "Veja o que Deus Fez Durante Reunião em Parede, Portugal." https://youtu.be/ijU8CwUNzvc (accessed March 2, 2016).

Sousa, Bertone de Oliveira. 2014. As Igrejas Neopentecostais e a Redefinição do Protestantismo no Brasil: Um Estudo de Caso em Imperatriz-MA e Araguaína-TO (1990-2013). Federal University of Goias.

Souza, André Ricardo de. 2011. "O Empreendedorismo Neopentecostal no Brasil." *Ciencias Sociales y Religión/ Ciências Sociais e Religião* 15:13–34.

UCKG-UK. 2013. "'Where U Going?' VYG has the Answers." http://www.uckg.org/?p=2942 (accessed March 26, 2016).

————. 2016a. "Get Clean Event." http://www.uckg.org/?p=7079 (accessed March 26, 2016).

————. 2016b. "Why is giving the key to receiving?" http://www.uckg.org/?p=7060 (accessed March 25, 2016).

Universal. 1995. "Video Completo do Pastor da Universal que chutou a Santa Nossa Senhora de Aparecida." https://youtu.be/vG963djYzno (accessed March 2, 2016).

————. 2007. "Igreja Universal: Inauguração do Templo em Moçambique." https://youtu.be/mE5QX8zB4GE (accessed March 2, 2016).

————. 2015. "Resumo do Evento Saiba Dizer Não 2015." http://www.universal.co.mz/2015/11/resumo-do-evento-saiba-dizer-nao-2015/ (accessed March 2, 2016).

Van de Kamp, Linda. 2012a. "Afro-Brazilian Pentecostal Re-formations of Relationships Across Two Generations of Mozambican Women." *Journal of Religion in Africa* 42(4):433–52.

————. 2012b. "Violent Conversion: Brazilian Pentecostalism and the Urban Pioneering of Women in Mozambique." *Compare* 42 (3):559–60.

————. 2015. "Pentecostalismo Brasileiro em Moçambique: Produção de Conhecimento Espiritual e Cultural em um Espaço Transnacional." *Sociedade e Estado* 30, no. 2:389–414.

Vásquez, Manuel A. 2009. The Global Portability of Pneumatic Christianity: Comparing African and Latin American Pentecostalisms. *African Studies* 68 (2):273–86.

Wagner, C. Peter. 2002. "New Apostolic Reformation." In *The New International Dictionary of Pentecostal and Charismatic Movements, edited by* Stanley M. Burgess and Eduard M. Van der Maas. Grand Rapids, MI: Zondervan.

A TALE OF THREE URBAN CHURCHES
THE LOCAL CHURCHES' ROLE OF MISSION IN CONTEMPORARY CHINA
Zhiqiu Xu

CHURCH GROWTH IN THE RAPIDLY URBANIZING CHINA

It was a known fact that the Protestant population in China has been expanding rapidly, and the speed of growth has accelerated quite fast in the last two decades (Sun 2015). According to reports from *Telegraph News,* Professor Fenggang Yang, a sociologist from Purdue University, predicted, ". . . by 2030 China's total Christian population, including Catholics, would exceed 247 million, placing it above Mexico, Brazil and the United States as the largest Christian congregation in the world" (Phillips and Liushi, 2014). Along with the rapid growth of Christian population, China also shows an increased level of urbanization at a pace that is unprecedented in the history of humanity. According to Professor Lu Dadao, president of the Geographical Society of China (GSC), "China's urbanization took 22 years to increase from 17.9% to 39.1%. It took 120 years for Great Britain, 80 years for the United States, and more than 30 years for Japan to accomplish this level of urbanization" (Xu 2012, 14).

When reviewing the statistics of Christian population growth and the rapid increase of urbanization, one would naturally ask whether these two historical phenomena happened independently or if they are internally related, influencing each other. What kind of opportunities or challenges does urbanization create for evangelism and church planting in China? How well do the churches survive and thrive in the fast-evolving society of China? Do many urban churches emerge as a result of urbanization? What kind of role did the urban churches in China play in the growth of China's Christian population? These are all important research topics that require a substantial amount of empirical data and field interviews, as well as critical analysis. For the convenience of data collection, I limited my research to the ten years between 2005 and 2015. The specific focus of my research is on the urban churches' role of evangelizing their communities in their neighborhood within that time period.

Before diving into the details of specific local church samples, let me first introduce Chinese Pastors Fellowship (CPF), which may give us a general picture of this urban church movement in China. CPF was initially started by a group of pastors in the United States. All of its first members came from mainland China and were committed to pastoral ministries among the Chinese diaspora in America. The group conducted training programs for churches that strongly identify with their cultural heritage from mainland China. In 2006, CPF moved its ministerial base to Hong Kong, which connects the overseas diaspora with mainland China. Since then, the group has attracted mainland Chinese church leaders who are predominantly ministering in urban settings. CPF's annual training sessions are often attended by about one thousand urban church leaders from all over China and provide good samplings for the current urban church movement research. Rev. Paul Huang from the city of Wuhan conducted a survey based on the information collected from 148 urban churches in 2014.[1] Survey statistics indicate that since 2000, the urban churches started to grow rapidly, becoming a massive movement that continues even today. It is fair to say that, before 2000, house churches in rural areas dominated the scene of church growth in China. However, after 2000 the urban churches started to become the leaders among the major forces of church growth. It is against this general background that we

---

1. Please refer to the attached Appendix for more details of this survey.

can now begin our discussion about the three urban churches located in the cities of Hangzhou, Zhuhai, and Xinyang.[2] The Hangzhou church is characterized by the evangelistic efforts in densely populated business districts in metropolitan settings. The Zhuhai church reflects the migration of blue collar labor workers from rural areas, who settled on the outskirts of a big city. The Xinyang church is situated in a third tier inland city, expanding its influences into nearby towns and villages. Both Hangzhou and Zhuhai churches were founded in 1999. The Xinyang church, though originally established by Norwegian missionaries in 1906, did not experience noticeable growth until the 1990s. All three churches illustrate the contour of a massive urban church movement, extending from north to south and from the coastal region to inland.

THREE LOCAL URBAN CHURCHES IN CHINA AND THE MOVEMENTS THEY REPRESENT

The purpose of this article is to study the role that the urban churches played in the growth of Christian population in contemporary China. With that goal in mind, the author collected a large amount of data by conducting interviews with leaders of three urban churches. Special attention was given to understand their external condition and internal vitality, along with the factors that stimulated or hindered the growths of these local churches. For the convenience of further analysis, the collected data will be organized according to the following categories: 1) brief history of each local church; 2) their relationship with government; 3) their evangelistic outreach program; 4) their training program; 5) their plans for global mission. I will introduce each church according to the five categories. I will then offer some analysis,

---

2. For safety reasons, the names of both the cities and the people are all deliberately altered.

critiques, and a brief conclusion from a missiological perspective. It is my desire that this study may help to identify the factors that facilitate the growth of Christian churches in contemporary China. It may also provide an opportunity for self-reflection, or even self-critique so as to find ways that may guide the growth in the future.

THE HANGZHOU CHURCH

A BRIEF SKETCH OF HISTORY

The Hangzhou church is located in a typical metropolitan setting. Rev. Piao, the founder of this church, suffered major persecution in 2009. The local government forced the church to scale down due to its ever-growing membership and social impact in the city. After forty days of fasting and prayer, Rev. Piao decided to change the ministry strategy of the church. Rather than aim at building up a mega church, he realized the best way for the church to survive and thrive is to develop numerous small-size branch churches with fewer than fifty participants. The model eventually worked very well. Seven years later, the church managed to establish twelve branches, scattering from suburban to the central business districts of Hangzhou. Pastor Hsu, who serves as a staff member in one of the braches, informed us about the multiple stages in the historical development of the church. The initial stage dated back to 1999, when seventeen members started the church as "Hangzhou Korean Church" because both the founding pastor and most of its members were all ethnically Koreans. Shortly after, they settled in the West District (West side of the main river) of the city. The church soon grew to one hundred members. In 2003, due to zoning adjustments, the church was relocated and managed to construct a building. Since then, the attendance stayed around three hundred. In 2005, the church started its Mandarin services. Meanwhile, the Korean section reorganized, adopting the small group ministry model.

However, the church soon had to relocate again due to pressures from the landlord. In October of 2006, the church was able to move into a spacious building, which resulted in rapid growth. By the summer of 2009, the Sunday attendance reached 1,500—Korean and Mandarin services included. At its heyday, more than three thousand members attended service regularly. Severe rounds of persecution broke out in the November of 2009, as the government decided to issue a crackdown on the church. The building was confiscated, and Sunday attendance dropped. After that, the church had to adjust its strategy by intentionally dividing into multiple parishes and worshiping centers. The church managed to stabilize itself gradually, and started to grow with its project of branch multiplication. Currently, as Pastor Hsu told us, the church has twelve parishes/worship centers, with the total Sunday attendance stabilized around five hundred people.

RELATIONSHIP WITH LOCAL GOVERNMENT

This church suffered several rounds of persecution. In 2004, the local government ordered the senior pastor to stop the worship service. The church responded with a period of fasting and prayer by all members. The unity and determination of the entire church prevented the execution of the administrative order. Another large scale persecution happened in 2009. About two thousand members of this church were warned or threatened, which resulted in the church's severe loss in membership. The church's full-time staff members were also interrogated. Many church members believed that the local authority intended to suppress the development of the church, because they did not want to see a growing church with great social impact in their city. Neither did they want the church to become publically influential. Thus, the government's unsuccessful attempt to censor the senior pastor's pulpit ministry suggested that there are still unspoken boundaries within which the church might not find space to survive and, even more, to thrive. The political pressure enabled the church to launch several revival programs, and to become even more serious about the Great Commission. Overall, according to Pastor Hsu, the environment was not totally negative against them, even though it did put on them a straitjacket by limiting their numerical growth. Under political pressure, the church was able to witness some breakthrough in its discipleship program, bringing up members with good spiritual quality. The hostile environment, as Pastor Hsu stated, also forced the church to focus more on the Lord for protection and become even more committed to its original vision. By and large, the church and its operational activities are all subject to government monitoring.

EVANGELISTIC OUTREACH PROGRAM

The Hangzhou church conducted various outreach activities, such as public hymn singing, gospel concerts in parks and on the streets, charity bazaars, benevolence for the needy, Christmas dinner parties, etc. The outcome of these activities showed that evangelism on the streets or at parks brings little significant results as people tend to be suspicious of soliciting activities. However, one evangelistic program known as "Happy Day Gospel Harvest Campaign" stood out as the most fruitful method for evangelism. The campaign consisted of a series of activities including identifying the targeted seekers, praying for the targets individually, initial contact, more praying for the targeted group, sharing the gospel, etc. The campaign extended for a period of three months, which ended in a series of intensive evangelistic efforts such as inviting the target seeker to come to the church, confirming their faith, and inviting them to commit to the church. Due to persecution from the local authorities, the church did this only once. The result turned out to be very encouraging. About two hundred people came to the Lord, and most of them gradually integrated into the congregation.

TRAINING PROGRAM

The Hangzhou church concentrates on training their members to become good and faithful servants, with the hope that these trained servants will eventually train more servants for the kingdom of God. The trainees need to enroll in the disciple-training system of the church, and go through two preparatory training sessions. Upon finishing the training, the trainees need to display the following three qualities before being commissioned and sent out by the church: 1) clear calling and vision; 2) basic theological training; 3) mature spiritual life. All training programs are supported by the church budget with a small additional amount of individual donations. The training curriculum was designed by the senior pastors, with special emphasis placed upon the church's vision and biblical knowledge. So far, about three hundred members have gone through the training system, of which about 140 are still active in ministry. The reasons some trainees drop out of full-time ministry varies from spiritual weakness to job relocation.

PLANS FOR GLOBAL MISSION

The Hangzhou church's senior pastor, Rev. Piao, is one of the founders of the Mission China 2030 movement (Zylstra 2016). The church integrates discipleship training with calling and kingdom vision. There is a built-in mission orientation in the church's training program. As a matter of fact, the church was named "All Nations Mission Church." The passion for mission lies at the core vision of this church. The Bible verses that the church quoted most frequently for promoting mission are Matthew 28:18–20, and Acts 1:8. The church is currently engaging in cross-cultural mission and church planting ministry. Their goals are to establish five thousand branches in China, to lead the nations back to God, to send out missionaries into other countries, and to build up indigenous churches on mission fields.

THE ZHUHAI CHURCH

A BRIEF SKETCH OF HISTORY

The Zhuhai church can be viewed as a direct result of urbanization when migrant workers flocked from rural areas to major cities like Zhuhai. The traditional house church networks, known as the Five Large Families (五大家), sent out mission teams among those migrant workers with the vision of establishing urban churches in their midst. Rev. Dai and his family were among the church planting program launched by the China Gospel Fellowship (one of the Five Large Families). They were sent to Zhuhai as missionaries to plant new churches for migrant workers in their vicinities. As of this point, Rev. Dai and his colleagues have established more than thirty branch churches in Guangdong province. The total number of church members is around three thousand. As peasants being relocated into urban settings, Rev. Dai and his wife went through unimaginable difficulties. Their initial missionary attempt in Zhuhai ended in a total failure even though they labored very hard for about two years. At that time, they had no financial support, and their son was having difficulties in the mission field. It was through tearful prayers and many struggles that they went back to the mission field for a second time. The door was opened this time. They happened to have the opportunity of rescuing a gang leader, who later repented and became a Christian. This gave them a foothold to effectively unfold the mission strategies. Rev. Dai now supervises migrant churches in Guangdong and Guangxi provinces.

RELATIONSHIP WITH LOCAL GOVERNMENT

According to Rev. Dai, persecutions from the local authorities have always been there. The majority of the coworkers had the experiences of being arrested, interrogated, and even incarcerated. Some of them were physically tortured, yet they consider persecution an alternative to seminary training because it helps strengthen their passion for Christ. The local government knows about the existence of these migrant churches. From time to time, they harass the churches' worship services and evangelistic gatherings. However, since this church movement devotes themselves to the migrant workers—a vulnerable group with many social and psychological problems—the government tends to tolerate their existence for their social values. The hostile political environment, hence, did not hinder the church's growth.

EVANGELISTIC OUTREACH PROGRAM

The Zhuhai church has been searching for effective strategies for evangelism for some time. Over the years, evangelism took the form of gospel tract distribution and evangelistic crusade meetings, yet neither was very effective, although one-on-one gospel sharing opportunities through personal relationship did yield some minor results. The church is currently considering using social services as a means for evangelism. The church encourages members who have a passion for missionary outreach to pursue vocational training to become barbers, auto repair technicians, massage therapists, etc. These professional trainings will allow the missionaries to be financially self-supporting, to establish connections with customers in more natural settings, and to witness to their Christian faith by providing services with high quality and a positive atmosphere. Since this approach was launched, there is no sufficient data yet to evaluate the effectiveness of this method.

TRAINING PROGRAM

The Zhuhai church does not require any special training for members to distribute gospel tracts. For those who are interested in evangelism through social services, they need to be well trained in EE—Evangelism Explosion III. In addition, they need to go through rigorous vocational training in order to be eligible for a government license for their technical skills. The trainees must display a willingness and passion for evangelism, maturity in his/ her Christian life and a strong desire to learn. In the past ten years, all branch churches have conducted evangelistic training sessions, though session numbers vary from branch to branch. In Guangdong and Guangxi, the two provinces under Rev. Dai's supervision, about 20–25 percent of all church members went through some level of evangelism training. Most of those who went through training are serving in full-time capacity. Rev. Dai considered 30 percent of them being "successfully" trained because they were able to demonstrate effectiveness in their future ministry. About 10–20 percent of those who received training gradually withdrew from full-time ministry. The reasons include insufficient or lack of general education since a certain percentage of the church members had no secondary education, family and financial pressures, and job relocations.

PLANS FOR GLOBAL MISSION

The Zhuhai church believes that the Great Commission consists of a series of actions, namely, to be dispatched to other places, to preach the gospel, to baptize, and to teach. The essence of this series of actions, according to Rev. Dai, lies with the training of all believers to become disciples. The most frequently quoted Bible verse for mission mobilization, in addition to Mathew 28:18–20, is Isaiah 6:8. The national headquarter of this massive church network has already sent missionaries to Egypt, Myanmar, Nigeria, Pakistan, and Thailand. Currently, the total number of missionaries in the mission field is about twenty to thirty. The southern branch, of which Rev. Dai serves as its leader, is charged with the responsibility of fundraising to support those missionaries. Their vision for future missionary work is aimed at the Southeast Asian countries, especially those with predominant Buddhist population, such as Myanmar. The plan is to establish schools in Myanmar, to recruit students from local communities, and to use the Bible as the educational foundation to reach the next generation in those countries.

THE XINYANG CHURCH

A BRIEF SKETCH OF HISTORY

The Xinyang church in the province of Henan represents the urban church movement in the third tier cities in China. Unlike metropolitan Hangzhou and Zhuhai with a population of more than 15 million, Xinyang represents smaller inland cities with moderate population size of about half a million, and with a relatively stable social structure. Rev. Liu, the senior pastor of the church, told me that even though the church was started by Norwegian missionaries in 1906, rapid growth didn't happen until the 1990s. According to Rev. Liu, many people in the city, after many years of being brainwashed with atheistic ideology, started to show some signs of spiritual hunger and thirst. The work of the Spirit, too, has been obvious and marvelous. During the heyday of revival, miracles happened all the time. The city is close to the hometown of Brother Yun, who wrote about his miraculous escape from severe persecution in *Heavenly Man* (Hattaway and Yun 2002). Many of the stories in that book, according to Rev. Liu, were just examples of the mighty work of the Spirit. Several aged sisters of the church displayed gifts of healing and the ability to cast out demons. These sisters traveled around the different neighboring communities, and led many to Christ. Currently, the church has grown from one location to fifteen branches, spreading all over the city. Adding all these fifteen branches together, there are approximately twelve thousand active members who practice their faith regularly in ninety-seven fellowship groups.

RELATIONSHIP WITH LOCAL GOVERNMENT

The government, according to Rev. Liu, does not support the church movement. However, this Xinyang church managed to maintain a positive relationship with the local authority. The local government officials would not object to the church planting projects as long as they were notified in advance. The government has been impressed by the scope and results of the church's social services in four major areas:

1. The church engaged in charitable activities towards AIDS patients since a certain percentage of the population in the region was affected with AIDS through contaminated needles during a blood drive (Watts 2006). The church sent out teams of volunteers to take care of the AIDS patients. They visited them, supported them financially, prayed for them, and shared the gospel of Jesus with them.

2. The church took care of the orphans and children from single parent families. Church members with businesses raised funds, along with support from the church's general budget, to provide monthly support for these children.

3. The church maintained an orphanage with new clothes, monetary support, air conditioning, etc.

4. The church sent out voluntary teams to local hospitals. They did such a wonderful job that the leaders of the hospital took the initiative to request additional support. They even granted the Christian volunteers the privilege of sharing the gospel among the patients.

However, tensions with the government do exist, and they are mainly focused on two activities: children's Sunday school class and college student ministry. Several times, the government sent policemen to force the closure of the church's children's Sunday school program. It was done under the name of the Chinese Constitution, which prohibits theistic teaching to anyone under eighteen years old. There were seasons, facing increasing government pressure, that the church had to stop using the Bible curriculum and replace it with activities of arts and crafts.

They could only resume the biblical teaching when pressure subsided. Despite the fact that pressures remain from time to time, the church's children's ministry continues to thrive. As for the college ministry, the student fellowship grew so much that it caught the attention of local officers, who threatened to shut down the program. They have also asked for a list of the attendees of this fellowship. Although Rev. Liu was very firm that he would not want the ministry to stop, neither was he willing to submit the list. The persistency and bravery of the pastoral team eventually paid off. The request for the list of names was eventually dropped. The college fellowship has been growing steadily. It has now developed into a full-fledged worship service.

EVANGELISTIC OUTREACH PROGRAM

The Xinyang church was originally considered part of the official Three-Self Church. As a result of such an affiliation, evangelism and mission activities were discouraged, if not prohibited. After the 1980s, the church managed to gradually break away from the official system, and became independent. Since then, evangelistic activities have thrived. Evangelism in the Xinyang church mostly takes the form of gospel tract distribution, evangelistic meetings, gospel concerts, and hospital visitations. Rev. Liu pointed out the church's "Numbers" project, which encourages church members to share the gospel with at least one person each day. About 60 percent of the members are actively following such a practice. Some members of the church went as far as setting up a goal of reaching one thousand people per year. The combined efforts of these evangelistic practices resulted in the church's expansion into all districts of the city, not only with fifteen branch churches, but also with numerous fellowship groups scattered throughout the city.

TRAINING PROGRAM

The Xinyang church provides training sessions from two weeks to one month. Only those who were trained may participate in local evangelism. Training materials include EE, the Bridge of Life, etc. The church organizes summer short-term mission teams, by recruiting college students for local ministries in the surrounding communities. The participating college students must go through a three-day intensive training. For those who are interested in long-term mission and ministry, the church provides training sessions extending from one to three years. The church leadership selects individual college students with high potential and sends them out for seminary education. The church also operates a training center, which offers a joint program that began with Dallas Theological Seminary and, since 2012, with the Philippines Bible College, from which Rev. Liu received his theological education. Since its beginning, the training center has already graduated seven classes with about 150 students in total. Among these graduates, more than 90 percent are actively involved in ministry. Ten of these graduates are working on the mission field in GanSu, ShaanXi, and XinJiang. There are two main reasons for the 10 percent drop out from active full-time ministry: the local church stopped supporting them financially or family issues, such as problems with children or other urgent family needs.

PLANS FOR GLOBAL MISSION

The Xinyang church uses Bible verses with strong eschatological rhetoric to promote world mission. Those verses, as Rev. Liu explained, gave us a sense of urgency to rescue souls because the end is near. They also preach mission sermons from the parable about the rich man and Lazarus, as well as Jesus's and Paul's teaching on the second coming of the Lord. The *parousia* of our Lord, Rev. Liu states, is like the thief during the night, because He could arrive at any time. The Great Commission is usually emphasized alongside the Great Commandment of love.

The central message of the Great Commission, as Rev. Liu understands, is disciple-training on a global scale. For the purpose of church planting and world mission, the church has been running a Bible school, training and maturing Christian disciples in order to send them into mission fields.

Looking into the future, the church is very committed to taking up the baton of the "Back to Jerusalem" Movement. They are determined to carry the gospel westward, push through the Muslim world in Central Asia, and bring it back to Jerusalem. The first tangible step towards this magnificent goal is to plant a branch church in LanZhou, the capital city of GanSu province. Rev. Liu will lead a team of four members, marching westward toward that direction. The plan is to plant an independent church there in three years. Rev. Liu will then return, leaving the rest of the team there and supporting them as missionary-pastors. Beyond this church planting project, the church also plans to step into international mission. Potential mission fields include Egypt, Africa, and Vietnam. The church council scheduled special discussion sessions regarding the project and was anticipating some decisions by the end of 2016.

ANALYSIS, CRITIQUE, AND CONCLUSION

The urban church movement in China is definitely playing an important role: evangelizing the Chinese people. Urban church movements in various forms from all over China have been contributing to the rapid growth of Christian population in contemporary China. The current article gathered a lot of first-hand data from the church members. We used Chinese Pastors Fellowship to gain access for a general picture of this urban church movement and focused our attention on the detailed studies of these three urban churches. The Hangzhou church represents urban churches in metropolitan settings such as Beijing, Shanghai, Guangzhou, and Chongqing. These are first-tier cities with unique social, political, and kinship patterns. The Zhuhai church stands as a new chapter of mission efforts made by the Five Large Families network in rural areas. Rev. Dai and his church system embodied the type of church made up of migrant workers who usually struggle on the outskirt of major cities. The Xinyang church presents to us a case of an inland urban church located in a third tier city. The pace of these inland cities may not be as fast as those metropolitan ones, yet the passion of urban churches in those cities is no less fervent than the ones in the large coastal cities.

After a careful examination of the data collected in the study, I discovered that the various evangelistic efforts made by different urban churches were a key factor to the rapid growth of the Christian population in China. This remarkable growth came after the expulsion of all Western missionaries in the early 1950s and the devastating persecution during the Cultural Revolution between 1966 and 1976. As the Western missionaries were forced to leave the country, God raised up a generation of local urban church leaders who, driven by burning passions, devoted themselves to evangelism and church planting efforts that yielded remarkable results.

Given the history and the context of these churches, I offer the following concluding remarks:

1. Political environment
    External hostilities did not become major obstacles that hindered the development of these three church movements. Surprisingly, some of these church leaders even hinted at possible hidden benefits of moderate oppression from the government. The external pressure helped the churches to consolidate themselves, to adapt their ministerial strategies, to keep alert about their unique identities, and to keep them away from assimilation by the secular world. However, in at least one case,

political persecution did alter the natural course of development of the church. The Hangzhou church, were it not disrupted by police intervention, would have grown into a mega church today.

2. Local evangelism

    These three church movements did not develop sophisticated theories of missions and evangelistic outreach. Neither were they equipped with modern resources such as TV or radio broadcast. All they relied on were traditional methods such as tracts distribution, evangelistic meetings, or one-on-one gospel sharing. Yet these movements were all characterized by the earnest passion of evangelism among the members. The percentages of members who were involved in evangelistic activities were relatively high. Furthermore, all these churches were seeking ways to break through traditional methods of evangelism, and they have all considered social services as an effective means for outreach. It seems that for evangelism, passion and motivation are much more essential than methods and resources. Massive mobilization of members for evangelism is usually far more effective than training a few elitist evangelistic professionals.

3. Training program

    Based on the data collected from these three church movements, the urban churches in China do not have well-structured training systems and programs. There seems to be no intentionally designed curriculum. The training materials they used were quite simple and old fashioned. Formal theological education could be helpful in developing the urban churches into long-term movement in the future.

4. Global mission

In terms of global mission, it is amazing that during the interview sessions with these church leaders, all of them expressed keen interest in global mission. Furthermore, all three of these urban church movements are very committed to the "Back to Jerusalem" vision. China once was a mission field and is now turning into a mission force. Generations of missionaries didn't labor in vain. The church has now reached the stage of self-evangelizing, with an accelerating pace of growth. It is my belief that the church in China, especially its urban churches, will carry the baton for global mission. As I once said, China's church has unique potential strengths for evangelism, especially in the Middle East (Zylstra 2016). To begin with, China does not raise the same antagonism that Western countries do. In addition, the Chinese, like Middle Easterners, are emerging from a postcolonial era and into a developing-world economy. With these similar backgrounds, they are in a better position to communicate with each other. Chinese people living in Tibet or near countries along the western borders, such as Tajikistan may share some commonality in areas of ethnicity, language, or religion with those in the Central Asian mission field. Their social and cultural context may serve as an ideal environment for training future missionaries who intend to serve in Central Asia or the Middle East. The geopolitical condition is also ripe. China's expansion westward through the "One Belt, One Road" campaign aims to build infrastructure and trade routes—including a high-speed railway—to connect China with the rest of Asia and Europe. This expansion provides a natural avenue for Christian missionaries, much as the early church took advantage of the transportation facilities during the Pax Romana. At this moment, the Chinese church is like a teenager—awkward but energetic. It may not have all the details planned, but at least it has the vitality to tell the world, "We want to do something" (Zylstra 2016).

APPENDIX

SURVEY OF URBAN CHURCHES IN CHINA (CONDUCTED BY THE INTERNATIONAL FELLOWSHIP OF CHINESE PASTORS, 2014)

148 valid questionnaires were collected, representing 148 urban churches across China. Here are some statistics and analyses of this survey

1. **Denominational and/or doctrinal backgrounds of the participating churches**
   Congregational, Charismatic, Evangelical, Pentecostal, Fundamentalist, Reformed, Presbyterian, Lutheran, Jesus Family, Christian and Missionary Alliance Church, Three-Self, Non-denominational and other churches associated with China Inland Mission, Chinese Coordination Centre of World Evangelism, etc.

2. **The year that the church was founded**
   5% before 1980; 11% between 1980 and 1990; 8% between 1990 and 2000; 39% between 2000 and 2010; 22% after 2010; 15% unsure. As the statistics indicates, the majority of the urban churches (61%) were founded after 2000.

3. **Property ownership of the church**
   63% of the churches own no property; 30% own property; 7% unknown.

4. **Theological training of the church leader/ workers**

   6% of the churches indicate that all coworkers were properly trained theologically; 32%, none of the church coworkers was properly trained theologically; 56% only part of the church coworkers were properly trained theologically; and 6% unknown. This results indicates theological training is still an urgent need for these newly founded urban churches.

5. **Gender ratio among the congregational members**

   85% of the churches have more female members than male members; 10% about equal; 5% unknown.

6. **Age groups of church members**

   26% have majority aged members; 37% have majority middle-aged members; 11% have majority young members; 20% have members balanced from various age groups; 6% unknown. The statistics indicates that a large percentage of these urban churches (63%) are made up of members mainly of old and middle-aged members.

7. **Does the church have by-laws?**

   56% yes; 28% no; 16% unknown. The conclusion is that most of these urban churches have by-laws.

8. **Does the church have elders?**

   24% yes; 65% no; 11% unknown. The result indicates that most of these urban churches (65%) have no elders.

9. **Does the church have deacons?**

   47% yes; 39% no; 14% unknown.

10. **Does the church have Bible study groups?**

    73% yes; 17% no; 10% unknown

11. **Does the church have fellowship group for college students?**

    27% yes; 56% no; 17% unknown. The survey reveals most urban churches (56%) do not have fellowship group for college students.

12. **Does the church have cell groups?**

    58% yes; 29% no; 13% unknown. It seems that many urban churches (58%) have adopted the cell-group church model.

13. **Does the church have ministries for married couples, like marriage enrichment retreat?**

    35% yes; 53% no; 12% unknown. It seems that more than half of these urban churches do not have special ministry program dedicated for married couples.

14. **What kind of social services has your church participated/provided?**

    Among all the services include nursing home; orphanage; hospital visitation; intervention to children in poverty; homelessness; drug addiction; donations after natural disasters; etc.

15. **Does your church receive support from overseas?**

    43% yes; 38% no; 19% unknown. The statistics indicates close to half of these urban churches (43%) receive supports from overseas.

16. **Does the church suffer pressure/persecution from government?**

    48% yes; 36% no; 16% unknown. The survey reveals that about half of these urban churches suffer persecution from the government.

REFERENCES CITED

Hattaway, Paul, and Brother Yun. 2002. *The Heavenly Man*. Grand Rapids, Michigan: Monarch Books.

Phillips, Tom. 2014. "China on Course to Become 'World's Most Christian Nation' Within 15 Years." *The Telegraph, UK,* April 19.

Sun, Yanfei. 2015. 千年未有之变局: 近代中国宗教生态格局的变迁 http://wen.org.cn/modules/article/view.article .php/4238/c7 (accessed March 28, 2017).

Watts, J. 2006. "AIDS in China: New Legislation, Old Doubts." *Lancet.* 367: 803–04

Xu, Yiqin. 2012. "Human Capital Accumulation by Low-Skilled Workers with Borrowing Constraints—A Welfare Analysis Based on the Lucas Urban-Rural Migration Model." PhD thesis, National University of Singapore.

Zylstra, Sarah Eekhoff. 2016. "Made in China: The Next Mass Missionary Movement." *Christianity Today.* January/February.

CRISIS AND TRANSFORMATION FROM MONOCULTURAL TO MULTICULTURAL

THE ST. ANDREW'S SCOTS PRESBYTERIAN CHURCH AND THE SIN HENG TAIWANESE PRESBYTERIAN CHURCH

Guillermo Mac Kenzie

INTRODUCTION

Since the second half of the twentieth century we have witnessed an abundance of literature on multicultural ministry. While embracing the important contributions of the homogeneous unit principle in the development and growth of ethnic churches, its applicability is constantly under review because these homogeneous units evolve with the passing of generations and the ministry needs to adapt to new realities which usually include multiple homogenous groups within the same church. While this multigenerational and multicultural reality may be obvious, the right question for Christian leaders should be whether the church is adjusting to these changes or struggling to maintain our undisturbed cultural *status quo*. Due to the growth of the multicultural reality in most global cities, many Christian denominations are seeking to adapt to this new reality by developing multicultural congregations. Some churches have walked through the multicultural transition with great success, while others are struggling or not even attempting to adapt.

Many local churches strive to adapt to the demographic changes in their neighborhoods. These demographic changes, especially in global cities happen faster than ever before. The mission of the local church would suffer if the leaders were not aware of the rapidly changing cultural demographics. This was the case of the St. Andrew's Scots Presbyterian Church in

Argentina during its 157 years of history. It is also the current challenge being faced by the Sin Heng Taiwanese Presbyterian Church in Argentina.

Buenos Aires is a cultural melting pot, just as most global cities today. It is calculated that there were around 300,000 native inhabitants in Argentina from different tribes and cultures before the Spanish colonization in 1492. Between the sixteenth and twentieth centuries, there were large waves of immigration from Europe (mostly Spain and Italy, but also from Great Britain, Germany, Holland, and others), from Africa (mostly slaves), and more recently from Asia and other Latin American countries. Today, Gran Buenos Aires (City of Buenos Aires and its surrounding areas) has a population of more than 13 million inhabitants.

Many of these immigration waves gave birth to churches that were originally intended to serve first-generation immigrants. As immigrant families became assimilated into the new culture, most of these immigrant churches started to experience decline facing the challenge to adapt to their new cultural reality. Some of them are still facing this challenge today.

Through this paper I will outline the history and present challenges of two churches which transitioned from a monocultural to multicultural ministry approach. I will also briefly outline the biblical and theological foundation for such multicultural ministry approach and propose some practical guidelines for enhancing gospel ministry with a multicultural emphasis.

THE ST. ANDREW'S SCOTS PRESBYTERIAN CHURCH IN ARGENTINA

In Argentina, many Protestant denominations coming from Europe in the early nineteenth century experienced some growth during the first one hundred years, especially among immigrants within the first and second generation. During the second half of the twentieth century, however, they all began to decline, while the country in general and the city of Buenos Aires in particular was becoming increasingly multicultural. In his book, *Historia del Protestantismo en América Latina*, Jean-Pierre Bastian proposed three stages to describe this Protestant history in Argentina (Bastian 1990, 24–25): "Colonialist Protestantism" (1492–1808, period of European migration to Latin America), "Protestant Societies and Liberal Modernity" (1808–1959, period of growth and establishment of Protestant groups), and "Transition Crisis?" (1959–?, period in which most Protestant denominations began a process of decline).

The St. Andrew's Presbyterian Church is one of the denominations that went through these stages. The Church of Scotland started its mission in Argentina in 1829 with the main purpose of ministering to the Scottish immigrants. José Míguez Bonino classified those churches coming from Europe into mission churches and immigrant churches. He first wrote, "To speak of these churches as 'residents' or 'immigrant' seems to suggest that what would characterize these churches is their *external* origin" (Míguez Bonino 1997, 80).

Míguez Bonino went on to speak of another way of characterizing these churches by calling them "ethnic churches." He stated, "Here one is not just speaking about origin or mode of entry but rather of the very nature of a church, not of a historical accident but of a constitutive characteristic" (Míguez Bonino 1997, 82).

Míguez Bonino contrasts these "ethnic churches" which focused on the same social group who brought the tradition from Europe with the "mission churches" with a focus on ministering to nationals. The following quote describes very well the reality of the Presbyterian Church in Argentina as an ethnic church with its Scottish origins:

> Frequently there were references that identified them [ethnic churches] as the European Protestantism and Anglicanism, which led to

the decision of the 1910 Edinburgh Missionary Conference to exclude Latin America since it was "a Christian continent" and therefore not a "mission field." Liturgical order, the use of a foreign language, and the unwillingness to engage in "proselytism" were incomprehensible and scandalous to the missionary and evangelizing mentality of the "evangelicals" (Míguez Bonino 1997, 85).

Facing the reality and the complexity of a country that was rapidly becoming multicultural, when Girvan McKay summarized the growth and eclipse of Presbyterian work in Spanish in Argentina, he concluded, "Whenever one of the senior ministers spoke Spanish as his native tongue or felt a personal concern for outreach in Spanish, this work progressed; otherwise it stagnated or was discontinued" (Mckay 1973, 10). His thesis proposal explains very well what was happening in the Presbyterian Church in Argentina in 1973:

We shall endeavor to demonstrate that without drastic restructuring (a process amounting to what we might, in biblical terms, describe as a virtual death and resurrection) a religious body showing the characteristics of St. Andrew's Scots Presbyterian Church in Argentina cannot become an effective instrument of sustained missionary outreach or the basis of an indigenous Reformed Church. A corollary of this is that such an immigrant community church situated in the midst of a "melting pot" society, like that of present-day Argentina, cannot long survive (Mckay 1973, 11–12).

Seventeen congregations were founded during the nineteenth century and the first four decades of the twentieth century. In 1941, however, "it was decided to close down or transfer all the missionary activity [in Spanish] of St. Andrew's Church" (Mckay 1973, 169). After that, the church began declining. In 1973, when Girvan McKay wrote his thesis, there were only five churches left from the seventeen that were originally established in Argentina. Five of those seventeen churches were abandoned and seven were given to other denominations (Mckay 1973, 349–350). In 1986, the Church of Scotland decided not to continue supporting the mission in Argentina. With only five congregations left and one ordained pastor, the St. Andrew's Presbyterian Church started a new stage in its life, deciding to adjust and open its doors to become a more indigenous denomination. Some of the churches were revitalized and church planting efforts were launched. With an inherited Presbyterian structure and a Scottish ministry style, the St. Andrew's Presbyterian Church had to learn to transition from being a dying monocultural denomination to a growing multicultural church.

The following are some of the challenges that the St. Andrew's Presbyterian Church had to face during this period of transition. These challenges were gathered through interviews with many pastors and elders of these local congregations.

LANGUAGE AND COMMUNICATION

The issue of language and communication is one of the most obvious challenges encountered when a local church transitions to become a multicultural congregation. Language is not only the way of relating to one another, but also a way of reinforcing cultural identity. The St. Andrew's Scots Presbyterian Church in Argentina started its ministry in English, because it was the native language of the Scottish immigrants. As decades passed, third and fourth generations began to lose English as their native tongue. Their primary language was Spanish. However, the church insisted on using English as their worship and ministry language. As described in the brief history of this denomination, some outreach works in Spanish were begun at the beginning of the twentieth century but were discontinued in 1941 with a drastic decision to abandon some of these churches, including their church buildings and transfer some other properties and communities to other denominations. Some Spanish Bible study groups kept meeting informally. It was not until 1987 that the church again officially accepted Spanish language work. The first pastor who did not speak English was received in 1988, 159 years after the founding of the church.

With the reinforcement of a unique language, a church can communicate its ethnic emphasis, in this case, giving Scottish descendants the assurance that they would continue to be the main receptors of its ministry, but also sending the message to others that they would always be second class members. Some of the first non-English speaking pastors described how frustrated and despised they felt when others insisted in speaking to them in English, even though all of them knew Spanish perfectly!

Communication in English was understood among the first and second generations of immigrants. But when third and fourth generations found it difficult to communicate, one began to sense the reluctance of adjusting to a new culture together with a defensive attitude and a sense of cultural superiority.

MINISTERIAL TRAINING

In addition to language, the training of ministers is also critical when the church transitions to adjust to a new cultural context. Immigrant churches usually bring their first missionaries and pastors from the country of origin. The Church of Scotland required all pastors serving in Argentina to be educated in Scotland. In fact, all its pastors and missionaries were actually Scottish nationals who have received their theological training in Scotland and went to Argentina to minister without even knowing Spanish. Theological training in Scotland helps assure the church with ministers who would continue its tradition and identity. In fact the St. Andrew's Scots Presbyterian Church brought all its ministers from Scotland for 157 years. It was only in 1986 that the first Presbyterian pastor, born and having studied in Argentina, was ordained with the assistance of the Reformed Churches in Argentina.

In 1912 the Church of Scotland sent a non-Scottish pastor to serve in Argentina. However it is interesting to note that he had also studied in Aberdeen, Scotland. The St. Andrew's magazine states that in 1910 Rev. Dr. James Fleming wrote a series of articles called "On Spanish Evangelization" and started to look for a pastor who could reach out to Spanish-speaking Scottish descendants (*Revista de la Iglesia Presbiteriana San Andrés* 1910). Celebrating the one-hundredth anniversary of Rev. José Felices's work in Argentina, the magazine relates that it was not easy to find a Spanish-speaking pastor that the Church of Scotland could trust (*Revista de la Iglesia Presbiteriana San Andrés* 1910). José Felices, who was born in Spain and ordained by the Andalucía Presbytery in that country, had also studied at Aberdeen so that the Church of Scotland could trust him. His ministry in Spanish had great success and he started many churches and missions.

LITURGY

Liturgy, music, and culture are very closely related to each other. Liturgies often reflect the flavor of the culture it represents. Music can easily become a place of dispute and of preeminence of one culture over the other. Historians remember not only many discussions regarding the language in liturgy but also the use of different instruments and melodies. It is interesting to note that expatriate communities often preserve tradition even stronger than the people in original sending countries. Thus it is not surprising that many leaders in the Scottish churches in Argentina in 1986 were attempting to preserve the same traditional liturgy imported in 1829 even though it had already largely evolved in the Church of Scotland itself.

RACIAL RECONCILIATION

To have a multicultural church is not the same thing as simply accepting that people from other cultures come to our church. Of course, the first step in this transition from monocultural to multicultural ministry is to let different people participate in the church activities. But there are still many more steps to truly becoming a multicultural church. Often times the need for these steps are greatly underestimated. Argentine pastors facing the transition in the St. Andrew's Presbyterian Church have shared the disdain with which they were treated for not understanding or fully committing to the tradition of the church. One of them stated, "One of the biggest conflicts was when we brought homeless people, or even some brothers from a lower social class into the sanctuary. We need to realize that cultural diversity often also means socioeconomic differences. Some cultural groups despise other ones not for their color, but for their social positions" (Roberto Rodriguez 2011, pers. comm.).

One major step in the history of the St. Andrew's Scots Presbyterian Church occurred in 1981 with the only remaining five struggling congregations. At that time the Argentine Kirk Session amended the denominations' official name, removing the word "Scots" to become the "St. Andrew's Presbyterian Church." Although this decision caused heated debate, it ended up creating a new focus and promoted the rebirth of a more indigenous Presbyterian Church in Argentina. This declaration reinforced the idea that the church belongs to the people of God and not to a certain group of founders. Removing the ethnic identity from the name was not the end of the racial discomfort, but it was a necessary step to make Argentineans feel that they were welcomed. It took 152 years since its founding to reach this decision.

FINAL CONSIDERATIONS ON THE ST. ANDREW'S PRESBYTERIAN CHURCH

Seventeen churches or preaching stations were opened from its foundation in 1829 until 1914. Between 1914 and 1989 there were no new churches, except one which was a result of a peaceful split from another church. During that period, the main activity of the denomination was to sell or close churches. This is a good example of a church that had to change before dying. It was unwilling to adjust until there was no other alternative for its survival.

THE SIN HENG TAIWANESE PRESBYTERIAN CHURCH IN ARGENTINA

The first immigration wave of Taiwanese people to Argentina occurred between 1970 and 1980, bringing around three thousand immigrants. Most of them migrated to escape the threat of war and to seek a more prosperous lifestyle. The second wave was between 1980 and 1990 with around fifty thousand immigrants.

The majority of Taiwanese immigrants in Argentina live in Buenos Aires. They founded the first Taiwanese Presbyterian Church in 1978. Only four years later, in 1982, Sin Heng Presbyterian Church was founded. Although there were other churches established over the years, there are four Taiwanese Presbyterian churches still in activity today.

These Presbyterian churches not only have the role of preserving the faith and ministering spiritually to immigrants, but also help them in their arrival and adjustment to the new country. Yet in less than forty years since the first immigration wave, one of these four churches is already transitioning towards becoming a multicultural church. The Sin Heng Presbyterian Church has already launched not only a Spanish worship service but also a Mandarin service with the intention of reaching out to the more recent immigrants from mainland China. These are not separate churches that worship at the same building. In spite of challenges and controversies, it is officially one church that worships in three different languages and is composed by members of different nationalities and cultures.

We will consider the same issues we described previously with the Scots Presbyterian Church, but now applied to the Sin Heng Taiwanese Presbyterian Church, looking for similarities and differences between them. Unlike the Scots case, which was based on more historical data, this Taiwanese church is currently undergoing its cultural transition and some of the information shared in this study will need to be revisited again in the next few years or decades to better assess how the transition is evolved.

LANGUAGE AND COMMUNICATION

Two of these Taiwanese churches in Buenos Aires launched language schools to teach Mandarin Chinese to the future generations in order to preserve their Asian cultural identity and prepare them to go back to Taiwan if needed. Both the Taiwanese Presbyterian Church in Argentina and the Sin Heng Presbyterian Church have maintained their schools until now, admitting also Chinese students to their classes. They have also added Spanish as a Second Language classes for first-generation immigrants. They are mostly immigrants from China, since the Taiwanese immigration to Argentina has practically already ceased for many years.

Because Spanish is such an unknown and distant language for the first-generation immigrants, it creates a barrier for them to adjust their lives upon arrival. But the second generation learned the language very well, studied in Argentinean schools and universities, thus becoming fully integrated to Argentine culture, much more than what their parents may have desired! Most second-generation Taiwanese in Argentina are now in their twenties and thirties. They are well educated, becoming successful professionals, and trilingual (Spanish, Taiwanese, and Mandarin).

Some of the second generation and most of the third generation have already lost the ability to use Taiwanese as a language. Instead, Spanish has become their first language even though some can communicate well in Chinese without the ability to read and write. In this context, the church leaders are confronted with the burden of preserving both their cultural and religious identities among their children. Unfortunately, some second- and third-generation Taiwanese had already left the church or lost interest in their parents' faith. Also, their young sons and daughters had developed relationships with Argentinean friends and could not cross-culturally relate their faith to their daily lives.

As a result, during the first decade of the present century, the Sin Heng Presbyterian Church decided to launch a Spanish worship service. It was mostly focused on its own youth group, but also open to people of other cultural backgrounds. At the beginning, the Spanish ministry was led by volunteers but an Argentinean preacher was later hired to lead this ministry. In 2012, only thirty years after its founding, the Sin Heng Presbyterian Church called its first Argentinean Assistant Pastor to lead the Spanish worship service. It was done in partnership with an Argentinean Presbyterian Church, not only focusing on second and third generations of Taiwanese immigrants, but also intentionally focusing on developing a multicultural community to reach out to people from other nationalities.

This church still has many first-generation Taiwanese members who have little or no language skills in Spanish. Thus, communication is still a major challenge. For this reason, all congregational and leaders' meetings are held in both Taiwanese and Spanish and translated, as well as most written documents.

MINISTRY TRAINING

All current Taiwanese pastors were born in Taiwan, although some of them have received thorough specialized seminary education in Argentina. The program is not directly related to the churches in Taiwan and is locally designed to train Taiwanese and Chinese pastors in Argentina. All these pastors still maintain good relationships with the Presbyterian Church in Taiwan, and consider it their mother church. However, unlike the previous case study, the Church in Taiwan does not influence the nomination of pastors in Argentinean churches.

LITURGY

Liturgy has been a challenge at Sin Heng Presbyterian Church. Each worship service has its own characteristics. Instead of attempting to maintain unity and identity through liturgical traditions, the church has decided to allow each worship service to develop its own liturgy contextualized to its cultural background. So, each worship service is characterized by its own language, music, prayer, and other liturgical expressions. However, what keeps the congregation united with a common identity is the doctrinal standards and ecclesiological form of government of the Presbyterian Church.

RACIAL RECONCILIATION

The Sin Heng Presbyterian Church is currently facing a tremendous challenge in terms of racial reconciliation. Asian people in general are not very well treated and still somewhat discriminated against in Argentina. In general, this discrimination does not include violence but mostly non-welcoming attitudes. In addition, the Taiwanese Christians also sense God's calling to reach out to the more recent immigrants from China. Unfortunately, they still need to face the tension brought by the confrontations in recent history between China and Taiwan.

Most of the Taiwanese churches in Argentina have opened their doors to people of other cultural backgrounds, or opened missionary outreaches to the Chinese immigrants. But the membership is reserved only for the Taiwanese descendants. However, against the practice of all other Taiwanese Presbyterian churches, Sin Heng church has recently taken the step of welcoming both Chinese Christian immigrants and Christians of all other nationalities into formal membership. This was not done without debate and even controversies. Fortunately, Sin Heng decided to move forward with this cultural openness despite fears among some members, especially in regard to the ownership of the church property.

Besides already having a non-Taiwanese pastor, in 2015 the congregation at Sin Heng went even further, voting for and appointing a non-Taiwanese deacon and a non-Taiwanese elder. This was certainly an important step forward demonstrating mutual trust and cultural openness.

FINAL CONSIDERATIONS ON SIN HENG PRESBYTERIAN CHURCH

Only thirty-four years after its founding, the Sin Heng Presbyterian Church is already moving towards becoming a multicultural church. There are still some skeptics, especially among the remaining first-generation immigrants. Fortunately, they do not intentionally obstruct the overall plan either. I am sure some discomfort will continue but the decision and the direction have been firmly secured.

COMPARISON OF CASE STUDIES

Knowing that the Scots and the Taiwanese belong to very different cultures, have different understandings of human nature and social interactions, occupy different statuses in Argentine society, and have immigrated to Argentina under different circumstances, a reflection on their similarities and differences can still help us draw some important lessons to analyze other people groups' experiences. These similarities and differences can be summarized in the following table.

Concept	St. Andrew's (Scots)		Sin Heng (Taiwanese)	
	Year	Years after Founding	Year	Years after Founding
First immigrants	1826	—	~1970	—
Foundation	1829	—	1982	—
First work in Spanish	1910	81	~2006	24
First non-immigrant pastor formally called	1912	83	2014	32
First non-ethnic descendants allowed as members	~1970	141	2014	32
First non-ethnic descendants allowed as deacons or elders	~1980	151	2015	33
Decision to close Spanish work	1942	113	—	—
Change of name	1982	153	—	—
First Pastor who studied in Argentina	1986	157	2014	32
Reopening of Spanish work	1987	158	—	—
Year 2016		187		34

In comparing the two churches, the first thing we need to remember is the difference in time. The St. Andrew's Scots Presbyterian Church was founded in 1829 and the Taiwanese Sin Heng Presbyterian Church was founded in 1982. So, in fact, the Scottish heritage and history of 187 years may serve as a guidebook for the Taiwanese church.

The Scots waited eighty-one years to officially undertake missionary work in Spanish in 1910, while Sin Heng started this same endeavor only twenty-four years after its founding. This is a surprising fact, especially taking into consideration that the

Spanish work of the Scottish church was moved forward by mostly third-generation immigrants, while the Taiwanese started it with some from the first and second generation. Not long after starting ministry in Spanish, both churches called pastors outside of their ethnic ancestry. One main difference is that the Scots called a Spanish pastor who had studied in Scotland because the church did not trust pastors trained in Argentina until 1986, fully 157 years from its founding. On the contrary, the Taiwanese church called its first non-Taiwanese pastor with no link to Taiwan in 2014, only thirty-two years after its founding.

A major difference is that although the Scots Church started ministry in Spanish language in 1910, it was not until the decade of 1970, which is 141 years after its founding that they formally accepted people from non-Scottish ancestry into the membership rolls. Although the church records show the inclusion of some non-Anglo last names a little before 1970, historian Arnold Dodds believes that they were third- and fourth-generation Scottish immigrants who were married to non-Scottish spouses (Arnold Dodds 2012, pers. comm.). Sin Heng, however, received members with no Taiwanese background at all beginning in 2014, only thirty-two years after its founding.

Something similar can be found in regard to the election of elders and deacons. St. Andrews' Presbyterian Church records indicate some Argentinean last names as elders in the sixties and seventies. However, Arnold Dodds asserted that these elders were elected especially to be part of Spanish ministry commissions, but they did not have a vote in the Scottish leadership board (Arnold Dodds 2012, pers. comm.). The actual first elders and deacons with no Scottish ancestry appear in the decade of 1980s, 151 years after its founding, while Sin Heng approved a deacon and an elder with no Taiwanese ancestry as early as 2015, thirty-three years after its founding.

It is not hard to conclude that the Taiwanese are going through the cultural transition much faster than the Scots. It is also true that cultural change in general, in this globalized era, is going much faster than in the previous centuries. In light of the data gathered from both case studies, we can conclude that:

First, the Scots, with a great deal of resistance, took 150 years to accept their loss of identity. The Taiwanese are daily confronted by their loss of identity in society. Generally speaking, the Scots' second and third generation of immigrants felt proud of their identity and ethnic origin, and would openly uphold their traditions. Second- and third-generation Taiwanese cannot avoid being identified with their ancestry due to their genetic features, but would normally attempt to be identified with Argentinean values and lifestyle. This sociological fact helps us understand another reason why the Taiwanese are accepting their loss of identity much faster than the Scots did. In relation to the need of adapting to new realities, Alan Roxburgh asserts that "The loss of identity and coherence . . . suggests that a missional reframing of denominational life today will only come as we live into accepting the loss of our former identity" (Roxburgh 2008, 76).

Second, neither of the cultural traditions in these case studies were flexible cultures. Both the Scots and the Taiwanese have high respect for tradition and the way things have always been done. In this sense, both of them have struggled with the adaptations needed to face the multicultural transition. As quoted above, Harris, Moran, and Moran state, "institutions whose cultures are flexible and adaptive usually outperform their counterparts" (Harris, Moran, and Moran 2004, 100). Adizes also adds that "the organization's emphasis on form affects function. Why? Flexibility suffers when form increases, and in a changing environment, decreasing flexibility implies declining functionality" (Adizes 1999, 124). Following the idea outlined in the previous item, the Taiwanese have developed more flexibility in their daily interactions with society. One would expect that their socially flexible experience would enhance their flexibility at church.

However, that has not been the case yet. This is one aspect that both groups have struggled with.

Third, the defensive mindset is common to almost all ethnic groups. When leaders in organizations start to defend procedures or programs, deny opposing opinions, or demean clear signs shown by reality, a status quo defensive mindset develops. Argyris warns about this situation:

> Reasoning is defensive when its purpose is to protect actors (groups, organizations) from being embarrassed or threatened. They do not test the validity of their diagnosis and actions in the service of discovering some semblance of truth on which they can base their diagnosis, design corrective actions, and evaluate the effectiveness of their implementation. (Argyris 2008, 58)

The Scots and the Taiwanese in Argentina are not exceptions. Both groups of immigrants developed a defensive mindset. The Scots were able to maintain their language and tradition for more than 150 years, and only then the St. Andrew's Presbyterian Church started to decline. The Taiwanese realized their cultural defeat much earlier, but they are still fighting the good fight. They realize that they are losing the battle for language, but most of them will continue to fight for at least some cultural values and traditions. It is interesting to note that the defensive mindset in the Taiwanese is much stronger at church than in society. One reason for this fact can be that, at church, they need to protect what their ancestors did, while in society they are more anonymous and are not identified personally with their parents and grandparents. So generally speaking, second- and third-generation Taiwanese immigrants may not defend their identity in society, but would fight to defend their parents' way of doing church. Nelson Jennings points this out,

What inevitably seems to occur as the generations
go by is a consolidation and protection of systems
(including theological ones), structures (including
organizations), and monuments (buildings,
statutes, and otherwise) that are constructed.
(Jennings 2006, 256)

BIBLICAL AND THEOLOGICAL FOUNDATION FOR MULTICULTURAL MINISTRY

Many books and articles have been written on the biblical foundation of God's mission to unite all peoples to glorify him. While
we cannot include here a full and comprehensive research on this
matter, the following paragraphs will describe a brief summary of
the biblical and theological view of multicultural ministry.

The Bible is clear in stating that God is the Creator of all
human beings and that He desires all nations to come to him.
This can be read at the beginning in Genesis and throughout the
entire Bible until the end in Revelation. In Genesis, we read that
God commands Adam and Eve to fill the earth. The Tower of
Babel, where God causes people to speak different languages, is
an example of his desire to prevent them from going astray. The
use of different languages is not seen in this passage as a curse, but
as a means for God to accomplish his purposes. In fact, reading
carefully, we can see that nations and languages are already
included in the description of the descendants of Noah:

These are the sons of Japheth in their lands,
each with his own language, by their families, in
their nations. . . . These are the sons of Ham, by
their families, their languages, their lands, and
their nations. . . . These are the sons of Shem,
by their families, their languages, their lands,
and their nations. These are the families of the

> sons of Noah, according to their genealogies, in
> their nations; and from these the nations spread
> abroad on the earth after the flood. (Gen 10:5,
> 20, 31–32)

As Romo states, "The story of the Tower of Babel is important
for a theology that considers both our common humanity as crea-
tures of God and the manifold pluralism in the Creator's purpose"
(Romo 1993, 20).

Then in Genesis 12 we read God's call to Abram, asking him
to leave his kindred and his father's house and promising him that
he would become a great nation and a blessing to all families on
the earth.

> Go from your country and your kindred and
> your father's house to the land that I will show
> you. And I will make of you a great nation, and I
> will bless you, and make your name great, so that
> you will be a blessing. I will bless those who bless
> you, and him who curses you I will curse; and by
> you all the families of the earth shall bless them-
> selves. (Gen 12:1–3)

The Psalms is a good place to explore not only the biblical
narratives or theology, but also the experience of God's people in
relation to the other nations. Many times in the history of Israel,
we can read that there may have been a superiority mindset.
However, when it comes to worship in the Psalms, we can read
in many places the importance given to "the nations." We will
quote only two psalms just as a brief example. Psalm 67:1–3 reads,
"May God be gracious to us and bless us and make his face to
shine upon us, that thy way may be known upon earth, thy saving
power among all nations. Let the peoples praise thee, O God; let
all the peoples praise thee!" Then Psalm 117 is a clear invitation
to all peoples to join Israel in worshiping God: "Praise the Lord,
all nations! Extol him, all peoples! For great is his steadfast love

toward us; and the faithfulness of the Lord endures forever. Praise the Lord!" Romo concludes, "The Psalms have a ring of universality: the knowledge of God through Israel's mediation shall bring together the nations—the peoples, *ta ethne*—to worship the only God of both the ethnic and the Israelite" (Romo 1993, 21).

In the New Testament, we can read that Jesus confronted the Jews for considering themselves to be superior to others. Many of his teachings rebuked the Pharisees for this attitude. Analyzing the example of Jesus ministering within a pluralistic society, the passage in Luke 4:16–29 includes a clear example of how important it is to acknowledge cultural differences in order to understand the people's attitude toward Jesus. At the beginning of this passage, Luke tells that Jesus goes to the synagogue. After reading the Scripture from Isaiah, he states, "Today this scripture has been fulfilled in your hearing" (Luke 4:21). It is interesting to note that the first reaction of the synagogue hearers is a positive one: "And all spoke well of him, and wondered at the gracious words which proceeded out of his mouth" (Luke 4:22). What happened that made them change this attitude? The passage ends saying, "When they heard this, all in the synagogue were filled with wrath. And they rose up and put him out of the city, and led him to the brow of the hill on which their city was built, that they might throw him down headlong. But passing through the midst of them he went away" (Luke 4:28–30). What happened is that Jesus quoted two episodes in which the Jews were not the object of the mercy of God, but two foreigners. First, he quotes the episode of the woman from Sidon: "But in truth, I tell you, there were many widows in Israel in the days of Elijah, when the heaven was shut up three years and six months, when there came a great famine over all the land; and Elijah was sent to none of them but only to Zarephath, in the land of Sidon, to a woman who was a widow" (Luke 4:25–26). And then, Jesus dares to quote an episode relating the healing of a Syrian leper instead of the lepers of Israel: "And there were many lepers in Israel in the time of the prophet Elisha; and none of them was cleansed, but only Naaman the Syrian" (Luke 4:27). It is clear that Jesus was challenging the cultural boundaries of the synagogue hearers.

After three years of preaching the kingdom of God and challenging his disciples to share the good news with pagans and sinners from everywhere, it is not surprising that his final commission includes the nations: "All authority in heaven and on earth has been given to me. Go therefore and make disciples of all nations" (Matt 28:18–19).

Finally, the centrality of Pentecost, in Acts 2, cannot be set aside. Reversing the consequences of the Tower of Babel, the Holy Spirit causes God's people to speak different languages so that, in spite of their cultural differences, they could worship God in unison and proclaim the good news. From Pentecost and throughout the whole narrative of the early church, we can draw a line of struggles aiming at uniting the church under Jesus Christ despite race, language, and nationality differences. This trend concludes with John's revelations regarding the new heavens. In Revelation 5, John describes the new song that is sung before the Lamb, "Worthy art thou to take the scroll and to open its seals, for thou wast slain and by thy blood didst ransom men for God from every tribe and tongue and people and nation" (Rev 5:9). Later on, John describes a new vision: "After this I looked, and behold, a great multitude which no man could number, from every nation, from all tribes and peoples and tongues, standing before the throne and before the Lamb, clothed in white robes, with palm branches in their hands, and crying out with a loud voice, 'Salvation belongs to our God who sits upon the throne, and to the Lamb!'" (Rev 7:9–10).

Exploring a biblical theology of culture and analyzing the many passages in Scripture that refer to cultural diversity, it is not difficult to conclude that God himself shared with humanity His own creativity in order to enjoy the diversity in His creation. As Miriam Adeney clearly states it, "What is God's view of ethnicity? God created us in his image, endowed us with creativity, and set us in a world of possibilities and challenges. Applying our God-given creativity, we have developed the cultures of the world" (Adeney 2010).

FINAL CONCLUSION: MULTICULTURAL CHANGE AS A PEBBLE IN ONE'S SHOE

Although the two case studies were drawn from contexts in Argentina, some conclusions may cause challenging reflections in other contexts. The church in the United States is currently being challenged with an amazingly increasing diversity that needs to be evaluated on a regular basis.

Analyzing America's complex society, Oscar Romo states that "[e]thnic groups in America are not only diverse, but they live in changing cultural and linguistic patterns. Each group continually influences others" (Romo 1993, 123). Later, he also adds that "[c]hanging ethnic patterns in the nation, the increasing migration, and the concern to evangelize rather than to "Americanize" have resulted in a response of ethnic persons unparalleled in Christian history" (Romo 1993, 137).

It is interesting to note that the multicultural challenge cannot be solved applying the same type of solution to every context—that is the main point about cultural diversity. So, in light of the specific context of each particular church, the leaders need to find their own unique approach to multiculturalism. For example, Miriam Adeney lays out some of the ministry areas where multicultural thinking can be applied:

> [In ethnic churches] culture remains important in worship. They pray in their heart language, with meaningful gestures, ululations, and prostrations. Their culture affects the way they do evangelism, discipling, teaching, administration, counseling, finances, youth work, leader training,

discipline, curriculum development, relief, development, and advocacy" (Adeney 2010).

We know the challenge is there. We just don't know when is the best time to stop our walk and face the challenge. As long as we keep walking, the pebble of multicultural change will continue hurting us. But if we are courageous enough, taking that pebble out of the shoe will enable the church of God to enjoy and celebrate the rest of the journey towards that ending where God himself will bring all nations together to worship him.

The Bible teaches us that from the beginning of the world, God is uniting his people from every tribe, language, people, and nation (Rev 9:5) and we believe that at the end he will fulfill his will. However, we often struggle as a church to take on that part of God's plan and ignore the multicultural changes that are occurring in society.

Crabtree states that "one of the most important principles for individuals and organizations to flourish in the world is simply to change before you have to" (Crabtree 2008, 6). May God allow us to continue exploring the best ways of adjusting and enjoying the multicultural change that He is bringing about, as well as to stay effective in lovingly reaching out to our neighbors!

REFERENCES CITED

Adeney, Miriam. 2010. "Is God Colorblind or Colorful?" *Mission Frontiers,* 32(3) (May–June), http://www.missionfrontiers .org/issue/article/is-god-colorblind-or-colorful (accessed 28 December, 2016).

Adizes, Ichak. 1999. *Managing Corporate Lifecycles.* Paramus, NJ: Prentice Hall.

Argyris, Chris. 2008. "Learning in Organizations." In *Handbook of Organization Development,* edited by Thomas G. Cummings, 53–68. Los Angeles: SAGE.

Bastian, Jean-Pierre. 1990. *Historia del Protestantismo en América Latina.* Mexico: CUPSA.

Crabtree, J. Russell. 2008. *The Fly in the Ointment*. New York, NY: Church Publishing.

Davis, Stanley M. 1986. "Transforming Organizations: The Key to Strategy is Context." In *The Leader-manager*, edited by John N. Williamson, 105–125. New York, NY: Wiley.

Gornik, Mike and Maria Liu Wong. 2013. "Christ in the Capital of the World." *Christianity Today*, August 30.

Harris, Philip R., Robert T. Moran, and Sarah V. Moran. 2004. *Managing Cultural Differences: Global Leadership Strategies for the 21st Century*. 6th ed. Amsterdam: Elsevier.

Jennings, Nelson. 2006. "Christ-Centered Missions." In *All for Jesus: A Celebration of the 50th Anniversary of Covenant Theological Seminary*, 255–270. Fearn, Ross-shire: Mentor.

Mckay, Girvan Christie. 1973. *Growth and Eclipse of Presbyterian Missionary Outreach in Argentina*. Buenos Aires: Instituto Superior de Estudios Teológicos.

Míguez Bonino, José. 1997. *Faces of Latin American Protestantism*, translated by Eugene L. Stockwell. Grand Rapids, MI: Eerdmans.

Moore, Ralph. 2002. *Starting a New Church*. Ventura, CA: Regal.

Romo, Oscar. 1993. *American Mosaic. Church Planting in Ethnic America*. Nashville: Broadman Press.

Roxburgh, Alan J. 2008. "Reframing Denominations from a Missional Perspective." In *The Missional Church and Denominations: Helping Congregations Develop a Missional Identity*, edited by Craig Van Gelder, 75–103. Grand Rapids, MI: Eerdmans.

Schaller, Lyle. 1976. *Understanding Tomorrow*. Nashville, TN: Abingdon Press.

Part Three

CHURCH ON MISSION IN NORTH AMERICAN PERSPECTIVE

BACK TO MISSION
THE MISSIONAL CHURCH AND THE BLACK CHURCH
Michelle Raven

The black church needs to get back to mission. That declaration causes offense for some and confusion for others. The church's lack of clarity, rather than disobedience, leads to the church's failure to participate in global missions. If the mission of God, the *Missio Dei*, is to reveal himself to the world as the One worthy of worship and to show humanity how to worship (Stetzer and Putman 2006, 44), his church must have the same mission (Busch, Guder, and Guder 2010, 87). God's missional plan to build humanity's capacity to worship him involves choosing and sending Israel, Jesus, and the church to participate in his mission. The missional nature of a church, its missional DNA, is what distinguishes it from any other man-made institution (Hirsch 2006, 18, 143). A church is both chosen and sent. However, a segment of his church, the black church, is not participating in sending in numbers proportionate to the number of African Americans in his church. In this paper, we explore the capacity-building mission of God and the black churches' move away from the sending portion of its mission. Once aware of the church's mission and its lack of fulfillment, the black church and others who have strayed will, hopefully, get back to mission.

THE MISSIONAL CHURCH: TO WHAT MISSION DOES THE CHURCH NEED TO RETURN?

Today every church proclaims, whether in a name, mission statement, or otherwise, that it is missional, though the mission being carried out often reflects only a portion of the *Missio Dei*. In the 1990s, people began to use the term "missional church," claiming that "the church is to be understood not as an organization with a mission; rather the church's very identity is mission" (Ott, Strauss, and Tennent 2010, 197). The focus was on what was being done rather than what the church was being. To counter this, there was a "move from church with mission to missional church" which requires a "reorientation of our theology under the mission of God" (Guder 1998, 6–8). Despite the hope that "missional church" would help realign what the church does with the role of the church stated in Scripture, the term "missional church" has become overused to the point of almost being meaningless (Van Engen 2010, 9–10). The broad, all-inclusive use of the term "missional church" and the focus on what a church does rather than what the church is leads to well-intentioned churches failing to fulfill their part of the *Missio Dei*.

A definition and description of the mission of the church provides a standard by which a church can determine if it is indeed a missional church. The starting point is Scripture, God's mission brief through which he states his mission and his plan of execution. God's capacity-building plan is evident throughout the Bible and is explained beginning with the creation in Genesis. Patrick Cate writes, "Mission begins with God Himself. God has a passion that He be glorified and honored by all people groups on earth" (2013, 3). All of creation, including our very existence, reveals God's glory and manifests a reason to worship the Creator (Wright 2006, 28). God communed with Adam and Eve in the Garden, going out to man to reveal himself. He talked with them, told them what to eat and what to do (dress the garden and keep it), and commanded them to worship him and reflect his glory (Gen 2:15–17). However, when sin entered, man's heart was tarnished. Humanity's capacity to worship God was hindered (Gen 6:5–7). God uses Israel, Jesus, and his church to execute his plan to remove the hindrances (Wright 2006, 61–68).

In the interim between the hindrances to worship appearing and the manifestation of choosing and sending Israel to build capacity, God continued to execute his capacity-building plan, making himself known via nature and communication with his creation. For example, God spoke to Cain asking him where was his brother Abel, walked with Enoch, and talked with Noah (Gen 5:18–24,6–9; Ezek 14:4,20; Heb 11:5,7). The dispersal from the tower of Babel to fulfill the cultural mandate described in the tenth chapter of Genesis is God sending out man to reveal his name. Abram, who was chosen and renamed Abraham, was sent from his home in Ur to Haran to become a great nation and reveal their God to the world (Gen 12:25). Moses was sent to Egypt and God was revealed as greater than the great Egyptian pharaohs (Ex 3:11–15). David went to Goliath and defeated him to show the world that there was a God in Israel (1 Sam 17). Jonah was sent to Nineveh to tell the people what God said so that they might repent and believe (Jonah 1:2). Daniel was sent by God (taken captive by man) to Babylon, which led to a decree that all people would reverence the God of Daniel (Dan 1–6). The dual components of capacity building—God choosing and sending—are evident in pre-Israel.

With Israel, we see "a people with a mission" (Wright 2006, 57). God chose Israel to reflect his glory. He revealed himself to the people of Israel so that they might know him and worship him, and through others seeing God's relationship with Israel, Gentiles might know him and worship him. Blessing Israel to be a blessing, God revealed his glory and his worthiness as an object of worship (Kaiser 2009, 11–16). The *Missio Dei* was carried out by the nations being drawn to the kingdom people, Israel. This drawing is viewed as an attractive force or centripetal movement through which people are drawn to the chosen of God. The *Missio Dei* was also carried out by Israel being sent out to the nations. This sending is viewed as an expansive force or centrifugal movement. Though the main missional strategy was people coming up to Jerusalem, there are instances of Israel going out to the nations to reveal God to the world. Though some argue that Israel's engagement in cross-cultural mission is "beyond the evidence" (Ott, Strauss, and Tennent 2010, 21–22), God did send his people out during the Old Testament and through their going God was revealed as One worthy of worship (Wright 2006, 57). God used Israel as capacity builders though they often failed in their duty.

The New Testament tells of God, the capacity builder, sending his Son as a capacity builder. Removing all hindrances to man's capacity to worship via his offer of salvation and the power of the Holy Spirit, Jesus declared he is "the way, the truth, and the life." If mankind knows Jesus, then they know God. With Jesus's life, death, and resurrection, he glorified God by manifesting God as worthy of worship (John 14:6; 17:4,6) and reminding man how to worship. Jesus was chosen and sent. He participated in up-reach by communing with the Father, in-reach by communing with his followers and showing them how to worship, and outreach by performing miracles and sharing the gospel with those who were not of the household of faith. (Wright 2006, 65, 121–125).

Having been set free to worship and told how to worship, the church is called to participate in capacity building (Moreau, Corwin, and McGee 2004, 84–85; Matt 28:18–20; John 8:31–37). The church is "to worship the Lord and spread the worship of Him among all peoples" (Cate 2013, 4). The church is called out of the world to be reconciled unto God via salvation through Jesus Christ (Marshall 2000, 256). Further, the church is called out to be witnesses of the gospel. This "royal priesthood," both chosen and sent, is called out of the darkness of the world, transformed so that they can reflect God, and then sent to declare and share the Light to the world (Ott, Strauss, and Tennent 2010, 194; Guder 1998, 2, 591; 1 Pet 2:9–12).

Being the church involves centripetal movement—the church, chosen to reflect God in the world, draws people to the Christ they see in the church. The church remains "a city on a hill," beckoning people to join the church universal (Clowney 2002, 46–47; Ott, Strauss, and Tennent 2010, 25–6; Wright 2006, 521). Fulfilling the role of "city on a hill" requires the church to build its own capacity to worship, which is an upward and inward focus. The upward focus, up-reach, is necessary so that the church will continue to be worshipers. The inward focus, in-reach, is the process of growing to be more like Christ so that the church will be an accurate reflection of God in the world.

Though the church is chosen to build its own capacity to worship via up-reach and in-reach, it is also sent to build others' capacity to worship via outreach—a centrifugal movement that sends the church out to the ends of the earth (Clowney 2002, 46–47; Ott, Strauss, and Tennent 2010, 25–6; Wright 2006, 521). God sends the church as the vehicle whereby he and his mission are revealed to the world (Carson 2002, 215; Clowney 2002, 15). There are missional calls or "commissions" in the Gospels which direct Christians to be disciple-makers wherever they are located and tell Christians to go out into the world to share Christ and teach others how to worship (Marshall 2000, 256). Quoting J. G. Davies who described God as "a centrifugal being," Theodore Eastman declares that the church's missional aspect is more than a command or commission with questionable authentic authority. Sending is God's nature, and God chose the church and sends the church as part of his overall plan (Eastman 1971, 15–16).

The capacity-building nature of the church can be gleaned from a survey of descriptions of the early churches found in Scripture. "The church in Acts is not presented as a community of believers with an immediate and urgent sense of commitment to carry out, in an organized and methodical way, the great commission" (Carson 2002, 229). However, each local church was engaged in capacity building and carried out various tasks or responsibilities in fulfillment of their mission to reveal God as One worthy of worship and to show the world how to worship him. After being chosen or called, the church focused inwardly on transformation. People were beckoned to the universal church because of the difference they saw in the members of the body. The results of the inward focus were the catalyst for the centripetal movement.

The church was visible to the outside world (1 Thess 1:8) because of their faith and zeal. Like the other outreach among the early churches, Mark's ministry was based in the urban focal points of Jerusalem, Antioch, Rome, Cyrene, and Alexandria (Oden 2011, 194). Far from the great edifices of later history, the church houses did not draw people and were not visible to the world. The visibility of the "city on the hill" was created by the church going out into the world. The church was active in the community and was therefore visible (Wright 2006, 522). They exhibited the capacity-building process of the church—up-reach and in-reach, then outreach. After being transformed by the Holy Spirit and creating some order in the body, the small local bodies immediately began to share their faith (Carson 2002, 229).

The first sending out, initiated by the Spirit, was primarily to the Jews who were of the same culture and language, but that does not diminish the reality that the centrifugal movement began almost immediately (Carson 2002, 229). They went out from among believers to non-believers to share the gospel. As they went out, largely because of persecution, they spread the gospel as they went to those with whom they came in contact. The Abrahamic covenant by which all peoples on earth would be blessed was being fulfilled (Carson 2002, 229–30).

It is noteworthy that the Holy Spirit takes the initiative in the centrifugal movement of the church and "uses believers as his instruments" (Clowney 2002, 81). Acts 10:9–16 and 11:18 illustrate that the Holy Spirit initiated the actions of Peter. Though the Jerusalem church was shocked, they accepted the missional work of Peter in discipling an uncircumcised Gentile centurion because they knew it was done at the initiation of the Holy Spirit.

The Holy Spirit selected the "target community," first Jews then Gentiles, and the church obeyed the direction it received.

The expansion of the church out from Jerusalem speaks to centrifugal mission being a part of the church's mDNA, capacity building. Rather than a planned strategy on the part of the church (though easily seen as part of God's plan), the gospel spread through Christ followers making disciples as they went. Some traveled because of persecution and others because of other reasons, but all were prompted by the Holy Spirit to act as the sent one called to share the good news with the world (Ott, Strauss, and Tennent 2010, 208). Citing Acts 26:22 and Luke 24:46–47, Wright explains that "the new centrifugal phenomenon of *mission to the nations,* to the ends of the earth" was foretold in the Old Testament and part of God's plan (Wright 2006, 521).

Neither the centripetal nor the centrifugal phenomenon was new. As we discovered earlier, both are parts of the capacity-building plan of God. From the beginning the church participated in both components. The importance of the church being engaged in both is seen in the duties prescribed for the first office of the church. The duties of the office of apostle, the first office in the church, demonstrate the dual requirement that the church have both an inward and outward focus. The office of apostle was deemed a missionary office. The apostle was called not only to proclaim to the members of the church body the teachings of Christ, but was also to go out into the world and spread the gospel (Clowney 2002, 86). This inward focus that helped to transform the church into a "city on a hill" that would beckon the non-believer to come and the outward focus of taking the gospel out to the world were critical to the function or purpose of the church.

This joint focus can also be seen in Paul's practice of continuing evangelism while instructing the local congregation. Paul evidenced the importance of continued evangelism in Rome even though a church was already established. The church was not only there to instruct believers, but was seen to have a role in evangelism in the immediate vicinity as well as spreading the gospel to other parts of the world (Marshall 2000, 258). The up-reach to God and in-reach to the brethren along with the outreach to the world were part of what made the church the church.

The early church's global outreach focused on cities or centers of influence where the gospel message would be shared, a church developed, and from that church the "gospel would be carried into the surrounding areas" (Marshall 2000, 259). Not all churches sent out missionaries "to the ends of the earth," but all had both an inward and outward focus, even if the outward focus was active participation among those in their own community with prayer and/or financial support to those missionaries working beyond the local community. The outreach from the churches at Thessalonica and Philippi illustrate the different ways the early church participated in global outreach.

The church in Thessalonica quickly established itself via up-reach and in-reach and then began sending (outreach). Acts 17:1–15 describes the founding of the church in Thessalonica, a major port city. Paul only ministered there a short time, but in 1 Thessalonians 1:8 we are told of the sending out of the church of Thessalonica. The church spread the word in Macedonia, Achaia, and everywhere else their faith in God had gone forth (Marshall 2000, 259). A member of the Thessalonian church, Aristarchus, traveled on missionary journeys (Acts 27:2). Their outreach was so effective that they "turned the world upside down" (Acts 17:5). The church at Philippi was also effective in outreach. The Philippian church, rather than sending a missionary from its local body immediately, financially supported missionaries of the universal church and prayed for the spread of the gospel to the world through the missionaries they supported (Ott, Strauss, and Tennent 2010, 202; Phil 14:15–16).

The church at Antioch had "genuine worship, mutual edification, and fellowship to share with the lost world" (Acts 13:1–3). Once the church reflected Christ and could, therefore, be a legitimate catalyst for a centripetal movement, they were sent out to replicate themselves in the world. This same process is seen among the churches in Crete described in Titus (Bush 1986, 89–90). These churches modeled up-reach and in-reach followed by outreach.

The early church experienced a maturing process where up-reach and in-reach led to outreach. Self-identity, the realization in doctrine and practice of the community of believers that they are people of faith in Jesus Christ whose very existence is "rooted in the way of Jesus Christ," is the first task towards a missional mindset (Nessan 2010, 6–7). The first task includes the up-reach and in-reach that flows from the church being chosen. This is the part of capacity building when the church is placed in position to worship through salvation and works out its salvation or, in other words, builds its own capacity to worship. The second task is to begin "sending out" locally and abroad (Nessan 2010, 6–7). The outreach or outward focus flows from the church being sent which is the church's engagement in building the capacity of others to worship. The biblical outward focus that is necessary cannot be achieved until the upward and inward self-identity is established. Luis Bush concludes, "The outreach to the world comes after the up-reach to God and the in-reach to the brethren" (1986, 89).

This progression seen in early churches is important to the discussion of the black church's failure to participate in global outreach. It is reasonable to conclude, as the author did, that a church that is not engaged in global outreach is not a biblical church. However, a close analysis of the progression of the early churches sufficiently counters that conclusion. Arguably, the black church will continue in the maturing process and eventually begin to substantially participate in global sending. However, as the title of this paper suggests, there was a time when the black church participated in global sending. The black church's regressive history provides insight into the impact of a church that has gotten away from one of the essential components of its mission: sending.

THE BLACK CHURCH

From its beginnings, the black church participated in all aspects of capacity building. Up-reach and in-reach were high priorities but outreach, locally and globally, was also considered a part of the mission of the church. The black church is a unique phenomenon in the universal church because it evolved among African slaves in search of a collective identity. Slaves responded favorably to evangelism efforts, as they concluded that the Christian God was the same "universal guide" of their religions. The chiefs or spiritual guides of their tribal ethnic origins were eventually replaced with the role of preachers. Slaves migrating through the plantations transcended language and cultural barriers to form societies centered on evangelical Christianity. The church became the focal point of black Christian life and the great connector of African American society (Frey and Wood 1988, 117–19). From these distinctively black churches, "citadels of African evangelism," flowed the "first generation of black missionaries" (Frey and Wood 1988, 117). Congregationalist, Baptist, Methodist, Episcopalian, and Presbyterians sent missionaries in the nineteenth century. Most raised funds by portraying Africans as uncivilized, immoral, ignorant, unclothed, and diseased (Jacobs 1982, 6–7). Nonetheless, some of the earliest American missionaries were African Americans, including the first Baptist missionary from America, George Liele (Morrison 2015, 18; Jacobs 1982, 8–9; Sutherland 2004, 501; Johnson 2002, 12).

African Americans began to plant churches as they transitioned to religious leadership, and they made sending a key part of their ministry. Churches became the only place of belonging, cultural expression, and exercise of community leadership (Frey and Wood 1988, 118). Many black churches were started by African Americans who had been members of biracial churches that were engaged in evangelical outreach. These black churches, some including "Missionary Baptist" in their name to emphasize the point, knew the importance of evangelical outreach to their mission. One association's mission stated, "The church is to evangelize the world, she is told to preach the gospel to every creature. The church is told to teach all nations, when the church fails to do this, she fails to discharge her most sacred duty for which she was organized'" (Zou and Hope 2015, 27–30). The black church began as capacity builders.

There was a decline in black church sending in the late nineteenth and early twentieth century from which participation never recovered (Walston and Stevens 2002, 3–5). When white mission leaders refused to use African Americans as missionaries after reconstruction because they feared negative responses by colonial governments to freed African Americans and mixing races among missionaries, African Americans started their own sending societies (Johnson 2002, 12). African Americans who felt called to serve in the mission field were sent by African American denominations or went independently when they did not meet denominational requirements (Jeter 1999, 164–65; Jacobs 1982, 9). African Americans also focused sending efforts in areas where there was not a lot of activity. Prior to the end of the nineteenth century, some mission boards sent African Americans to Liberia and other places in Africa because they looked like those being evangelized. Many thought African Americans could withstand diseases and the hot climate better than Caucasian missionaries (Seraile 2002, 29). African American missionaries served in the West Indies, Canada, Haiti, and other locations (Sernett 1975, 148).

After 1900, participation continued to decline. White-led mission boards changed from desiring African Americans to go to Africa to refusing to send them as missionaries. This was because Jim Crow laws were the law of the land and Marcus Garvey's popularity ("Africa for Africans") influencing African Americans to teach Africans about freedom caused them concern (Johnson 2002, 27–29). In addition to the changes in white-led sending agencies' attitude towards African American missionaries,

African colonial governments began refusing or discouraging the use of African American missionaries. The only two countries where African Americans were permitted to continue organized missionary efforts were Liberia and Sierra Leone (Johnson 2002, 27–29; Sutherland 2004, 501–2). African Americans had fewer fields from which to choose and few churches and agencies to support them. Moreover, African Americans interested in global sending had very few options for training and education. As late as the mid-twentieth century, several prominent Bible colleges and seminaries refused to admit qualified African Americans, and evangelical mission boards, including the Southern Baptists, refused to accept qualified African American candidates for missions (Sutherland 2004, 502). Sending from the 1960s to 2000 remained essentially the same. African Americans continued to go to Kenya, Uganda, the Caribbean, Central and South America, Liberia, Nova Scotia, southwest India, and other countries (Jeter 1999, 158–65), but the overall number of African Americans participating in global sending remained small.

Determining the participation level of African American missionaries is difficult because of a lack of information; however, an estimated level can be garnered using available statistics.

Though the numbers of African Americans that have gone on short-term mission trips continues to grow and there were about 125 African American mobilizers in 2012, the number of African American career missionaries has never been estimated over three hundred (Sutherland 2004, 502–3; Raven 2012, 82–83), a very low number considering there were approximately 17 million African American churchgoers in the United States in 2012 (Williams 2014, 18–20). With approximately 127,000 of the world's estimated 400,000 missionaries being sent from the United States (Gordon-Conwell 2013, 76), African American missionaries are about 0.24 percent of the missionary force sent from the United States.

The pervasive lack of participation in African American sending is due to many obstacles that have generally been described in terms of past and present hindrances. In the past, the main hindrances were slavery and subsequent Jim Crowism (Sutherland 2004, 502–3). Racism and limited resources were the catalyst for many churches turning their focus inward. With Jim Crowism, the local church was the only place where many African Americans felt true freedom. Terror from the Ku Klux Klan and others caused the black church's mission to become survival rather than helping others around the world. There were very few black churches that were "open to missionaries being involved in evangelism and discipleship." Most churches that are engaged in capacity building have "home missions" to evangelize and do outreach in their local area (Jeter 1999, 157–59; Sutherland 1998, 75). Feelings of not having enough are rampant in the African American community. Many African Americans want to see that their churches are "doing well," meaning outward signs of prosperity rather than focus on how many souls they have helped lead to Christ (Johnson 2002, 17). With the perceived need for the outward show and the local needs, many pastors do not feel there is enough money or resources to give to overseas missions. Moreover, with all the race issues and problems that exist in the United States, churches do not want to turn their focus outside their own community (Walston and Stevens 2002, 4). In the present, residue from the realities of the past, along with economic and worldview hindrances, cause many African Americans and the black churches they attend to decide not to participate or to limit participation in global sending. These hindrances result in an overemphasized centripetal component and little to no focus on the centrifugal component (Raven 2012, 83). Despite the hindrances, the current impediments are based on perceptions that can be changed.

The change of perceptions needed in order to get back to mission requires a clear understanding of the scriptural basis for capacity building, awareness programs, collaboration with others, and the support of the pastor. A change of perceptions and a move toward become a capacity builder engaged in up-reach, in-reach, and outreach is underway at a historically black church, Diamond Hill Baptist Church (DHBC).

REVITALIZATION OF DHBC

DHBC is one example of a black church that started with a focus on up-reach, in-reach, and outreach. DHBC was established in 1872 in Lynchburg, Virginia and provided spiritual edification as well as social interaction. Dealing with the after-effects of slavery and subsequent Jim Crow laws, the church worked diligently to improve the lives of its members and members of the community at large. From 1958 to 1963, the church became a destination for civil rights activists, and church members coordinated the participation of Virginia during the historic march on Washington. DHBC was "where leaders strategized and activists planned campaigns to register and turn out voters, desegregate lunch counters and protest discriminatory hiring practices" (Diamond Hill 2011). Reverend Haywood Robinson, the pastor of DHBC for many years, was an advocate for what was called interchurch cooperation and founded the Lynchburg Community Action Group, Lyn-CAG (Laurant 2011). Lyn-CAG is a community outreach organization in which community partners work toward "the prevention, reduction or elimination of poverty and adverse situations" in people's lives. This outward focus of the church, through interchurch cooperation and Lyn-CAG, was a continuation of the church's commitment to "go out" sharing the gifts they had to point people to Christ. Their efforts were geared towards improvement of the capacity of all in the community. DHBC also focused on those outside the community—others in the United States and abroad. Keys to the success of their outreach efforts were the input and involvement of diverse community partners, a focus on the entire community, and representation and participation by the citizens of the communities to make policy and manage efforts. Because of the guiding principles, comprehensive services were provided which increased the citizen's ability to live better lives.

Though members of DHBC remained active in community outreach, the focus of the church turned inward. Difficult financial times, moves by many in the congregation out of the downtown community, and contentment with past achievements without focus on the future have been cited as reasons for this change from an outward focus to an inward focus. About 90 percent of the congregation is over the age of fifty-five. The congregation that once had over eight hundred members now has approximately 250 members with even less as active participants. The inward focus resulted in a diminished visible presence in the community and a lack of perceived relevance to the community. DHBC became a church focused on the centripetal component at the expense of the centrifugal component.

The pastor recognized the need to get back to mission and started revitalization efforts that reflect both components of the mission of the local church. Reverend Warren Anderson and the author began efforts in 2011 to return the church to an outward focused missional mindset. With renewed intentional activity towards reaching lost souls, a monthly community outreach was started. It was geared mostly toward youth but included activities for all ages. This community effort, initially called Diamonds in the Rock, blossomed from a program led by a church member and college student volunteers to a program adopted by the church at large. Community partners and other local churches and organizations participated in this endeavor. The goal was to share the love of Christ and help transform the lives of people in the downtown community. The monthly outreach was the beginning of the plan which includes a discipleship program, an educational improvement/after school tutoring initiative, boys to men/girls to women training, financial education/stewardship training, and health awareness initiatives to remove hindrances to global outreach.

To prepare for and revitalize a desire for outreach, Pastor Anderson renewed and expanded efforts towards church maturity—up-reach and in-reach. He started a weekly midday prayer gathering which concentrated on praying for the lost. He reinvigorated the Wednesday night Bible study and began a study on the biblical family—the importance of and the roles of Christ followers in their immediate families, their local church families, and the universal church. The subsequent study focused on the importance of and the roles of Christ followers in evangelism. Emphasizing church unity and spiritual growth, DHBC saw fruit in increased attendance at prayer gatherings, Bible study, and Sunday school. There was increased attendance at worship service and activities by members of the community under the age of fifty-five. Moreover, more church members participated in the monthly outreach efforts. DHBC became a practical laboratory for putting into practice the principles of comprehensive capacity building in partnership. With focus on building the church member's capacity to worship—up-reach and in-reach via training, Bible study, and worship focused on living as Christ followers—and exploring ways to build other's capacity to worship via local outreach programs and focus on salvation of lost souls, DHBC is beginning to positively impact African American global sending.

The outward focus emerging at DHBC—with emphasis on pointing souls towards Christ through efforts that involve sharing of the gifts and skills of the local body, unity with other churches, participation of other organizations in the community, as well as participation throughout the process by those being reached— has resulted in revitalization of sending by DHBC. DHBC hosts Perspectives courses, helps support members who are going on short-term mission trips, and partners with a ministry in Haiti through prayer support and providing resources. Their most recent Perspectives class included approximately forty students from various churches in the area, and African Americans represented 80 percent of the participants. The church sent out its first missionary in 2012 and is now providing the missionary monthly support. DHBC is getting back to full participation in the mission of God.

CONCLUSION

God's restorative plan to build man's capacity to worship him is seen throughout the Old and New Testament. As part of his plan, the church is chosen and sent to build its own capacity to worship and help others to build their capacity to worship. Scripture explains that God desires that the church participate in capacity building.

It is imperative that the black church get back to God's mission. The church, when on its mission, is "the most potent force for transformational change the world has ever seen" (Hirsch 2006, 17). The black church is uniquely suited to serve as "centers for mission, both ministering to the needs of members and carrying forth the gospel to their communities and the world" (Nessan 2010, xii). The entire church is chosen and sent to the entire world to make disciples with a message of repentance and forgiveness of sin. Where there is a lack of knowledge of the outreach requirement, we must provide insight. Where there is a lack of maturity, other churches should participate in in-reach, walking alongside the church as they evolve into a sending church. The black church must participate in sending. The black church must get back to mission.

REFERENCES CITED

Busch, Eberhard, Darrell L. Guder, and Judith J. Guder. 2010. *The Barmen Thesis Then and Now: The 2004 Warfield Lectures at Princeton.* Grand Rapids, MI: Eerdmans.

Bush, Luis. 1986. "The Identity of the Local Church: Biblical Principles." In *The Church: God's Agent for Change,* edited by Bruce J. Nicholls, 85–90. South Africa: Oxford University.

Carson, D. A. 2002. "Church and Mission: Reflections on Contextualization and the Third Horizon." In *The Church in the Bible and the World: An International Study,* edited by D. A. Carson, 213–257. Eugene, OR: Wipf and Stock.

Cate, Patrick O. 2013. *Through God Eyes: A Bible Study of God's Motivations for Missions.* Pasadena, CA: William Carey Library.

Clowney, Edmund P. 2002. "The Biblical Theology of the Church." In *The Church in the Bible and the World: An International Study,* edited by D. A. Carson, 13–87. Eugene, OR: Wipf and Stock.

Diamond Hill Historical Society. 2011. "Two Local Places Nominated to VA Landmark Register." 2011. *Diamond Hill News 33(2).* http://www.diamondhill.org/dhhs/

Eastman, Theodore. 1971. *Chosen and Sent: Calling the Church to Mission.* Grand Rapids, MI: Eerdmans.

Frey, Sylvia R., and Betty Wood. 1988. *Come Shouting to Zion: African American Protestantism in the American South and British Caribbean to 1830.* Chapel Hill, NC: University of North Carolina. Retrieved from Questia.

Gordon-Conwell. 2013. *Christianity in its Global Context 1970–2020: Society, Religion, and Mission.* http://www .gordonconwell.edu/ockenga/research/documents /2ChristianityinitsGlobalContext.pdf

Guder, Darrell L., ed. 1998. *Missional Church: A Vision for the Sending of the Church in North America*. Grand Rapids, MI: Eerdmans.

Hirsch, Alan. 2006. *The Forgotten Ways: Reactivating the Missional Church*. Grand Rapids, MI: Baker.

Jacobs, Sylvia M. 1982. "The Historical Role of Afro-Americans in American Missionary Efforts." In *Black Americans and the Missionary Movement in Africa*, edited by Sylvia M. Jacobs, 5–29. West Port, CN: Greenwood Press.

Jeter, Sr., Joseph C. 1999. "Help Wanted: Missionaries for the Harvest." In *Evangelism and Discipleship in African-American Churches*, edited by Lee N. June, 157–68. Grand Rapids, MI: Zondervan Publishing.

Johnson, Michael. 2002. "Am I My Brother's Keeper? The Search for African-American Presence in Missions." In *African-American Experience in World Mission: A Call Beyond Community*, edited by Robert J. Walston and Robert J. Stevens. 11–18. Pasadena, CA: William Carey Library.

Kaiser, Walter C. 2009. "Israel's Missionary Call." In *Perspectives on the World Christian Movement: A Reader*, edited by Ralph D. Winter and Steven C. Hawthorne, 11–16. Pasadena, CA: William Carey Library.

Laurant, Darrell. 2011. "Diamond Hill Baptist Joins National Historic Register." *The News and Advance*, Local News, March 9.

Marshall, I. Howard. 2000. "Who Were the Evangelists?" In *The Mission of the Early Church to Jews and Gentiles*, edited by Jostein Adna and Hans Kvalbein, 251–64. Tubingen: Mohr Siebeck.

Moreau, Scott A., Gary R. Corwin, and Gary B. McGee. 2004. *Introducing World Missions: A Biblical, Historical and Practical Survey*. Grand Rapids, MI: Baker.

Morrison, Doreen. 2015. *Slavery's Heroes: George Liele and the Ethiopian Baptists of Jamaica* 1783–1865. Birmingham, AL: Liele Books.

Nessan, Craig L. 2010. *Beyond Maintenance to Mission: A Theology of the Congregation* Minneapolis, MN: Fortress Press.

Oden, Thomas C. 2011. *The African Memory of Mark: Reassessing Early Church Tradition.* Downers Grove, IL: InterVarsity Press.

Ott, Craig, Stephen J. Strauss and Timothy Tennent. 2010. *Encountering Theology of Mission: Biblical Foundations, Historical Developments, and Contemporary Issues.* Grand Rapids, MI: Baker.

Raven, Michelle L. K. 2012. "Back to Mission: A Possibility Center Approach to Revitalizing African American Sending." MA thesis, Liberty University.

Seraile, William. 2002. "Black American Missionaries in Africa: 1821–25." In *African-American Experience in World Mission: A Call Beyond Community,* edited by Robert J. Walston and Robert J. Stevens, 25–29. Pasadena, CA: William Carey Library.

Sernett, Milton C. 1975. *Black Religion and American Evangelism: White Protestants, Plantation Missions, and the Flowering of Negro Christianity.* Metuchen, NJ: Scarecrow Press.

Stetzer, Ed, and David Putman. 2006. *Breaking the Missional Code: Your Church Can Become a Missionary in Your Community.* Nashville, TN: Broadman and Holman.

Sutherland, James. 1998. African American Underrepresentation in Intercultural Missions: Perceptions of Black Missionaries and the Theory of Survival/Security. PhD diss., Trinity Evangelical Divinity School.

———. 2004. "Time for African American Missionaries." *EMQ* 40(4): 500–510.

Van Engen, Charles. 2010. "'Mission' Defined and Described." In *MissionShift: Global Mission Issues in the Third Millennium*, edited by David J. Hesselgrave and Ed Stetzer, 7–29. Nashville, TN: Broadman & Holman Publishing.

Walston, Rebecca and Robert Stevens. 2002. "Moving Beyond the Community." In *African-American Experience in World Mission: A Call Beyond Community*, edited by Robert J. Walston and Robert J. Stevens. Pasadena, CA: William Carey Library.

Williams, Chester. 2014. *Last Call for the African-American Church: The Death of Global Missions.* Blue Ridge Summit, PA: University Press of America.

Wright, Christopher J. 2006. *The Mission of God: Unlocking the Bible's Grand Narrative.* Downers Grove, IL: InterVarsity Press.

Zou, Hang, and Warren Hope. 2015. "Black Missionary Baptist Ministers and the Burden of the Great Commission." *Baptist History and Heritage* 50(3): 27–42.

ENGAGING THE AFRICAN AMERICAN CHURCH IN GLOBAL MISSIONS BY RECRUITING AFRICAN AMERICAN YOUNG ADULTS FOR MISSIONS EDUCATION AND TRAINING

Linda P. Saunders

INTRODUCTION

MOTIVE

The twenty-first century finds the North American Christian with more means financially, technologically, and theologically for *doing* global missions than at any other point in history. Yet, many Christians sit on the sidelines of global missions endeavors; and, the African American church community is less engaged in global missions than ever before. This paper will articulate methods for engaging the African American church community in global missions. David Cornelius believes, "the African American church is a sleeping giant in the area of international missions" (2009, 303). To awaken this "giant" African American young adults should be recruited, educated, and trained as missionaries, cross-cultural workers, and leaders for twenty-first century global missions.

I am a missionary serving the people of Venezuela since 2003. Prior to moving to Valencia, Venezuela, I engaged in missions, predominately with underprivileged inner city youth in North America. I am called to work with youth and young adults in Venezuela as well. Additionally, to help facilitate the ministry endeavors in Venezuela, I created a missions training program specifically geared towards missions teams who volunteer to assist the ministry in Venezuela. Over the last two decades of serving as a missionary, I recognized the lack of global missions engagement by African American Christians. That realization inspired my thesis research project; this paper is an excerpt from my thesis.

PURPOSE

The percentage of African Americans engaged in missions is barely quantifiable. If African American young adults are trained and educated in missions, will this cultivate their interest in missions culture? Furthermore, college-aged young adults are still impressionable enough to be discipled as global missionaries who will in turn influence their community, specifically, the African American church community. Tina Rosenberg, author of *Join the Club: How Peer Pressure Can Transform the World*, contends, "along with genetics, peer pressure is probably the most important influence on who we are" (2011, xx). Therefore, recruiting African American young adults for their participation in global missions may play a significant factor in increasing the African American church community's participation in global missions.

Moreover, peer pressure positively affects as well as fosters participation in worthy causes. Therefore, perhaps the influence of African American young adults who have joined the global missions endeavor will provoke their friends to engage in like activities. The author of Hebrews admonishes Christians to encourage or provoke one's fellow Christian to good works (Heb 10:24). From this viewpoint, peer pressure could play a prominent role in influencing other African American young adults to pursue global missions.

AFRICAN AMERICANS' LACK OF PARTICIPATION IN GLOBAL MISSIONS

Every summer, thousands of young adults participate in global missions to evangelize the world for the sake of the gospel. There are several missions agencies and organizations that recruit young adults to engage in global missions for the cause of Christ. These young adults have been trained, educated in missions, and sent out on adventures to rescue the lost. The great news: Christian young adults have answered the call that Jesus sounded over two thousand years ago. Nonetheless, a closer look reveals a somber commentary among the demographics of the young adults who engage in global missions. Youth with a Mission (YWAM) has over eighteen thousand young adults engaged in global missions (YWAM.org), and African Americans are a tiny representation of these young people. According to statistics, African Americans are not engaged in global missions endeavors. American young adults have engaged in missions to proclaim the good news worldwide; yet, this picture is incomplete.

Based upon recent statistics, the percentage of African Americans who participate in global missions is barely quantifiable (Rivers 2013a). The numbers paint a sad portrait concerning the African American church community with regard to their global missions participation. According to the International Mission Board's (a related organization of the Southern Baptist Convention) Keith Jefferson, African Americans comprise less than one percent of all American global missionaries actively engaged in international missions (Rivers 2013a). Furthermore, Fred Luter, former Southern Baptist Convention (SBC) president, said African Americans are a minute percentage of global missionaries even among an organization that boasts a membership of one million African Americans (Rivers 2013b). SBC has about 4,900 global missionaries, twenty-seven of whom are African Americans.

The total number of African American global missionaries does not improve the sad portrait of the African American church's global missions participation. According to The Traveling Team, the total number of global missionaries in 2015 is 400,000 (thetravelingteam.org); but the estimated total number of African American missionaries is three hundred (Sutherland 2002, 136). While there are a few scholars and missionaries who have written about African Americans' lack of engagement in missions, the issue has not been thoroughly explored; likewise, the grim realities of African Americans' lack of involvement in missions seems to go unnoticed by the body of Christ as a whole. Not only is there little discourse with respect to African Americans' lack of presence in global missions, there is even less discussion focused on a viable resolution to engage African Americans in global missions.

A resolution cannot be actualized without clear and focused discourse concerning the dilemma, and while a focused discourse will illuminate the problem, the discourse should be driven by a commitment to solve the problem. A dialogue for the sake of discussion will not produce a lasting solution, if it produces a solution at all. This paper will suggest a solution that is worthy of implementation. The development of a missions training center that will focus on recruiting African American young adults who will be trained and educated as global missionaries is one such solution. Actively recruiting African American young adults may compel them to engage not just intellectually, but practically as well. A brief inquiry into the history of African Americans and missions will highlight these complexities.

A HISTORICAL PERSPECTIVE

BACKGROUND

Historically, the African American church community has rich roots in missions. African Americans began engaging in global missions during the late eighteenth century. Even though the vast majority of them were enslaved, their desire to spread the gospel pushed them out from the home front to distant lands. "From the time slaves began accepting Christianity, it was in their hearts to carry the Gospel of Christ not only back to their father-lands, but also to other parts of the world" (Cornelius 2002, 48). Many African Americans left America's shores for Africa, believing God had called them to rescue their ancestors. Many others served in the Caribbean islands and in Canada, taught among Native Americans, or traveled to the Pacific islands (Cornelius 2002, 48). One of the first missionaries to leave America for foreign lands to proclaim the gospel was a former slave named George Liele (or Lisle). Liele ministered in Jamaica (Cornelius 2009, 300). "Many historians regard Liele as the first American-born missionary" (Fariss 2013, 66). George Liele left South Carolina in 1783. In 1790, another freed slave, Reverend Prince Williams, also left US soil to preach the gospel in the Bahamas (Stevens and Johnson 2012, 296). Lott Carey, born 1780, was another forerunner of African American missionaries, and it is noteworthy that Carey "led in the organization of the African Baptist Foreign Missionary Society. It was the first organization for world missions founded by African Americans in the United States" (Cornelius 2009, 300).

Space will not allow for a full review of the African American missionary heroes of faith. Although there are many whose names do not appear in the anthology of missions history, from the late eighteenth century until the early twentieth century African American missions history is replete with free men and women, as well as former slaves, who left the shores of the United States to spread the Good News of Jesus. Methodists, Baptists, Presbyterians, Lutherans, and other denominations, contributed to sending African American missionaries around the globe. African Americans were not afraid, ashamed, or reluctant to leave America and travel to lands unknown to carry the gospel to those who did not know Jesus. However, the disconnect that has occurred in their global missions participation is dismal. Statistics bear proof that African Americans too soon became introspective and their outlook turned inward. They no longer felt compelled to leave America's shores, but instead began to fight the injustices suffered in their homeland. Many scholars, as well as African American pastors, believe that the beginning of the twentieth century marked the decline of the African American church involvement in global missions (Stevens 2012, 59–61). Cornelius believes that the onset of Jim Crow laws precipitated the African American church's inward look. He asserts, the black church was "the only institution that African Americans had under their control, [and therefore] had to lead in the struggle of her people for full citizenship and human rights in the country of their birth. Somewhere in the struggle, the vision for world evangelization . . . blurred" (2002, 53). "The Protestant Episcopal Church, which had boasted more than four times as many blacks as whites on its Liberia staff in 1876, was all white by 1943" (Gordon 2002, 57). Baptists, as well as Presbyterians, noticed the decline in African American missions participation. However, "there were exceptions. . . . Blacks on the Congregationalist staff numbered 10 percent in 1943, and their contribution was so valuable that they were being sent to non-African fields" (Gordon 2002, 57). Sadly, the exceptions were few. Whether the lack of global missions engagement commenced immediately following the Civil War or several decades later, the truth remains that the African American church fell away from her passion to evangelize the lost in foreign lands. Notwithstanding, Cornelius insists that the African American church never lost her passion for global missions. He contends that various circumstances have prohibited the African American church community from full involvement in global missions throughout the decades following the Civil War (2002, 51). Nevertheless, much can be learned about the African American church community if one takes an in-depth look at her historical background and her involvement or lack of involvement in global missions.

STATISTICS FOR AFRICAN AMERICANS AND GLOBAL MISSIONS

African Americans led the way in the global missions endeavors when Americans began to traverse the world to take the gospel to foreign lands. For many decades beginning in the late eighteenth century, African Americans' hearts burned with a passion to fulfill the Great Commission. George Liele, John Marrant, John Day, Amanda Berry Smith, Lott Carey, and Reverend Prince Williams to mention a few, left their families and friends to teach and preach the Good News of Jesus to those as far away as Africa, and as nearby as the American Indian. Now, the landscape for African Americans' engagement in global missions is nearly a blank canvas. There are less than three hundred documented African American career missionaries (the most optimistic estimate) serving in foreign fields (Rivers 2013a).

The total number of global missionaries serving worldwide is 400,000. The percentage of African Americans serving in global missions is less than one-tenth of one percent of the total number of global missionaries worldwide (Saunders 2015, 12). With African Americans representing less than one percent of all missionaries serving globally, the gap is too great to ignore. A clarion call should be made to enlist the participation of the African American church community in the Great Commission that Jesus gave to all His followers. This paper explores and investigates the *how* and *whys* for enlisting African Americans in global missions. The statistics paint a grim portrait of the African American church regarding global missions; however, this does not mean that the story will end on the same somber note. While engaging the African American church community in global missions is a complex task, it is not impossible. Motivating and mobilizing African American young adults through education and training them in global missions may be one way to jump-start this monumental undertaking.

EDUCATION AND TRAINING TO INCREASE PARTICIPATION IN GLOBAL MISSIONS

Education and training are prominent factors with regard to mobilizing African American young adults for global missions participation. These young adults may propel the African American church community to global missions engagement, especially since many *revolutionary* movements have commenced with college age young adults. For example, the civil rights movement in the United States had its beginning in the late 1950s when students from North Carolina A&T and other historically black colleges, sat at a Woolworth Five and Dime lunch counter and waited peacefully to be served. Students at Berkley led a protest against the United States government in the late 1960s protesting the Vietnam War and other issues. The Tiananmen Square protest of 1989 was also student-led. In March 1991, Yugoslavian students in Belgrade began a movement (*Otpor*—"resistance" in Serbian) that eventually overthrew Slobodan Milosevic in 2000 (Rosenberg 2011, xvii; 216–248). Student led movements have inspired revolutionary changes that have captivated the world as young adults sought to actualize change in their respective societies. African American young adults who have been educated and trained concerning global missions may possibly be the catalyst for engaging the African American church in the global missions endeavor. More importantly, training and education are not just idealistic concepts, they are biblically based precepts as well. Missions education will give the African American church the knowledge to engage effectively in global missions, while training will equip them with the skills and strategies necessary for global missions participation.

The research conducted for the thesis was not exhaustive; however, it did identify a few key areas within the African American church community as it relates to global missions participation. First, there is a somber and disheartening realization that the African American church community places little, if any, emphasis on missions and missions education and training. Secondly, the lack of global missions teaching and preparation within the African American church community is staggering. The pastors interviewed for the research project were in unanimous agreement regarding the lack of teaching, discipleship, training, and education regarding global missions within the African American church. With few exceptions, global missions is a missing component of ministry, a non-entity, within the African American church. How does one rectify this issue? Will training and educating about global missions directly correlate to increased involvement in global missions?

The void, found within the African American church community, is the lack of missions education, training, and teaching. This is a delicate situation. Perhaps, if training and education began first with African American pastors, they could then teach and disciple their congregations. Maybe the key for increased involvement of the African American church in global missions would be to train and educate the pastors first, then educate, train, and recruit African American young adults. This could prove effective since, "African-Americans do not join white or black evangelical missions in significant numbers" (Sutherland 2002, 136). Therefore, the purpose for educating and training African American pastors is to create a global missions training environment within the local African American church. As meaningful as this may be, recruiting African American pastors for global missions education and training would be an arduous task. African American pastors do not make global missions a priority, as discovered through the interviews conducted for the research. Of the thirteen pastors interviewed, six had never been on a missions trip and five had been on three or four missions trips. However, the problem is actually more profound than what the research uncovered. "Most African-American pastors have never been exposed to missions. The African-American church experience with missions has been primarily within and around the four walls of the church" (Robinson 2002, 67). The chief objective remains the recruitment of African American young adults. Since the pastor of the African American church directly influences the culture within his or her local assembly (Saunders 2015, 58-59), it is crucial to garner the pastor's support and endorsement. The African American church is one of the avenues through which to recruit African American millennials. So, the role of the pastor in the African American church is linked to the recruitment of African American young adults for global missions participation.

THE ROLE OF RECRUITMENT

RECRUITMENT AND INCREASED PARTICIPATION IN GLOBAL MISSIONS

If missions training and education are vital components for increasing the African American global missionary population, then the recruitment of African American young adults to participate in the training is also a critical component. It is noteworthy that 76 percent of the African Americans who participated in an online survey admitted that they would participate in a global missions training and education program if given the opportunity (Saunders 2015, 83); therefore, there appears to be a trend that points toward an interest in global missions training and education among African American young adults. Based solely on the responses received from the survey, recruiting African American young adults to a global missions training program for the express purpose of educating, training, and mobilizing them for global missions engagement is still the best solution for engaging the African American church community in global missions. Once trained, African American young adults could be mobilized for global missions participation and begin a movement that would involve the African American church community at large.

A more strategic approach may be to equip African American pastors with the tools and skill sets to conduct global missions training in their local churches. Also, this would mean providing African American pastors with experienced missions trainers as mentors. If these pastors realized the great need for their church's involvement in missions, the African American young adults would be mobilized under the scope of their influence. According to the survey of forty-two participants, 73.7 percent agreed that if their local pastor supported global missions they would engage in global missions (Saunders 2015, 78). Likewise, as stated earlier, if given the opportunity, 76.2 percent of the participants agreed that they would participate in a global missions training program.

One concern, though, for endorsing a missions training center, deals with African American men. One of the pastors interviewed mused, "If the local church has no strategy to reach them [African American men], how can we send them?" (Saunders 2015, 99). This is a critical dilemma within the African American church community. Men are underrepresented in the African American church. Lincoln and Mamiya estimate 66 to 80 percent of African American church membership is female (1990, 304). "All of the seven mainline black denominations are characterized by a predominately female membership and a largely male leadership, despite the fact that the major programs of the Black Church . . . depend heavily upon women for their promotion and success" (1990, 275). Lincoln and Mamiya further claim, "both historical and contemporary evidence underscore the fact that black churches could scarcely have survived without the active support of black women" (1990, 275). This is true on the missions front as well. As mentioned earlier, the African American church community is most familiar with the term *missionary* as it relates to women wearing white on designated Sundays. In *Last Call*,

Chester Williams also laments the somber situation of the African American church's predominantly female membership. Williams attests, "what modest representation there is of African Americans on mission fields consists of, mostly, black women . . . because the church has directly and indirectly gender-assigned missions—as especially a woman's avocation—black men have not been attracted to the profession [of global missions]" (2015, 65).

Thus, the question is not whether African American men will volunteer for global missions training; the quandary at hand is, how will the African American church reach African American men? As one pastor lamented, how can African American men be recruited to global missions, if the African American church cannot reach them? Moreover, according to Lincoln and Mamiya, imprisonment among African American males is a common problem within the African American community (1990, 323). Therefore, if African American men are not prevalent in the African American church and there is a problem of high incarceration rates among African American males, the African American pastor is left to contemplate another crucial issue for endorsing a missions training program. Furthermore, this is possibly a contributing factor to African Americans' lack of participation in global missions. This only reinforces the concept that African Americans must reach their own, in their own backyard, before they can engage in global missions. During the focus group discussion in the research stage of the thesis, this concern was mentioned among the young adults as well. One participant lamented, "you look at the African American community and a lot of us are just trying to help *Pooky* [sic] get out of jail . . . that's our mission, and so, to go all the way to Africa or somewhere else . . . a lot of us can't see that far yet, because we're doing . . . our own personal missionary things" (Saunders 2015, 101). Vaughn Walston offers a similar commentary in his article, "Mobilizing the African-American Church for Global Missions." Walston makes this observation concerning the African American church community, "they cannot see the needs of the world because they are focused on the needs right next door" (Walston 2002, 189). Therefore, in light of these difficulties, the role of recruitment is one that can ill afford to be downplayed or misdirected. The recruitment of African American young adults for global missions participation must be investigated and solutions should be sought in order to remedy the myriad of problems and obstacles that still exist. Another prevalent perception for lack of participation concerns the African American church and resources.

FINANCIAL RESOURCES

One of the greatest fears causing African Americans' lack of participation in global missions is the perceived lack of resources or severely limited resources. This topic was discussed in the focus group as well as among the pastors who were interviewed. For African Americans, the lack of funding with regard to missions is a major concern. Many of the pastors acknowledged that if they had more resources, they would participate in global missions. One pastor even cited lack of funding as the major reason that his congregation does not participate in global missions (Saunders 2015, 63). Of the thirteen pastors interviewed, eight cited lack of finances, lack of funding, or lack of resources as the number one fear factor among African Americans concerning global missions. Of the remaining five who did not cite lack of finances as the number one fear, minimal financial resources was mentioned at some point during the interview. Whether in regard to training, sending, or supporting missionaries, financial concerns weighed heavily on the minds of the African American pastors who were interviewed. Scarcity of resources was listed as a major fear or as the primary reason that global missions is all but ignored in the African American church; however, the lack of priori- tizing global missions may be a more appropriate response to the lack of African Americans' participation in global missions.

When examining the financial resources of the African American church at large, another picture begins to emerge.

THE AFRICAN AMERICAN CHURCH AND RESOURCES

There are few sources that offer legitimate accounting for African American church income; therefore, to research African American church income or try to report specifically on the income of the African American church becomes a monumental, if not impossible, task.

> Black churches . . . are themselves significant economic and financial institutions. As a community-based institution, the finances of the local black church often reflect the economic conditions of its members. Much of the class character of the churches, from elite ones to storefronts, is determined by this important index. Nevertheless, as important as black churches are in the profiles of their respective communities, not much hard information is known about their financial activity. Any research on the economic character of black churches is severely limited by the inadequate records kept by many of these churches, or by the extreme difficulty in gaining access to these records if they exist. (Lincoln and Mamiya 1990, 253)

Furthermore, based on the interviews conducted during the research phase of the thesis, financially supporting global missions is not a top priority in the African American church. Programs directly related to the church are the beneficiaries of the money raised. The African American church is preoccupied with community outreach or missions work within their own backyard to the neglect of global missions. Chester Williams surmises, "as there exists no annual budget for children and youth in the average black church, there is none for home-and-away-from-home missions" (2015, 107). This is certainly a dismal explication. The African American church has to accept global missions as a ministry priority before she will prioritize her resources to be utilized for such an endeavor. The appropriately allocated resources for the use of global missions would fund a missions training program within the African American church to train future global missionaries for service. The illustration below (drawn from Bureau of Labor Statistics data) presents the possible giving potential within the African American church community. According to the Bureau of Labor, financial statistics of the African American Christian community paint a different picture than what many African American pastors purport. Statistically, one-third of one percent of all denominational giving is allocated for benevolence (Ronsvalle and Ronsvalle 2013). While the African American church community may be fearful of engaging in global missions based upon their perceived idea of the lack of financial resources, if even this same one-third of one percent was utilized for missions, there would be significant support for global missions. This could eliminate the fear factor associated with the lack of finances available for global missions. As the chart below demonstrates, the African American church is financially able to participate in global missions. *Is she willing to participate financially? Is she willing to allocate funds to global missions?* These are the questions that should be contemplated. There is a perception that the African American church does not have the financial resources to participate in global missions. However, if the African American church decided to allocate one-third of one percent of the church's income to global missions, which would be an extremely low commitment and would still fall tremendously shy of even tithing to missions, it would nonetheless be a start. While statistics point to the idea that the African American church community has the resources to engage in global missions, the fact remains that education and training are necessary if the African American church is to become an effective participant in global missions in the twenty-first century.

The following chart illustrates the giving potential of the African American church community. The funds that *could potentially* be given towards missions is $765,422,755. This is less than one percent of the total income of the African American church (Saunders 2015, 101).

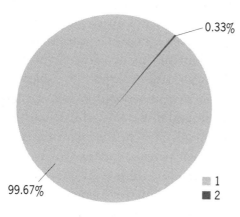

0.33% — 1) Total annual income of AA households affiliated with Christianity 2012.
$231,643,259,118

2) Amount of AA annual income that *could potentially* go towards benevolence and missions *IF* the AA church supported missions at the same level as all other Christian churches of USA.
$764,422,755

99.67%

■ 1
■ 2

Total income from 8,763,279 households

Finding AA composite annual income	Amount
Median income of AA household	$33,460
# Households X median income	$239,219,315,340

Total annual income of AA households affiliated with Christianity

AA Christian households
Total funds pertaining to AA churchgoers
79% of AA claim affiliation with Christianity and the church

79% of total AA income	$231,643,259,118

Total amount that *COULD* be given towards benevolence from AA church

% of income that goes toward benevolence	.33% (all denominations)
.33% national figure which includes all Christian churches	
.33% of total AA income affiliated with Christian churches	$764,422,755

AA Church Giving Potential

THE CONCEPT OF "BACKYARD" MISSIONS: HOME MISSIONS AND THE AFRICAN AMERICAN CHURCH

Historically, missions held a prominent position in the African American church. Incidentally, many African American churches received their names because of the African American church's strong concept of missions both locally as well as globally (Williams 2015, 16). At the dawn of the twentieth century, African Americans found themselves under a different kind of bondage. While slavery was no longer legal, segregation, discrimination, and other forms of civil rights oppression were legal. African Americans began to fight causes at home, and looked less and less at the opportunities to travel overseas to spread the gospel. The "mission field" for the African American church soon became what African Americans call their "own backyard." This phrase refers to the African American church doing missions in their own community. One of the challenges for creating a missions training center to recruit African Americans for global missions involves moving the African American church community beyond the four walls of the church and her own community. While home missions and community outreach is a necessary part of missions, as two of the pastors contended, why not do both (Saunders 2015, 111)? The results of the research showed that this concept may potentially turn into a major roadblock within the African American church community and their participation in global missions. The need to provide for home first has actually overshadowed the need to go globally. So, the question is how to do both? This query was actually posed by two pastors during the interview, as mentioned above (Saunders 2015, 111). The training would have to incorporate the need to act locally, while still evangelizing globally. The perceived value of missions is accepted and generally received when the African American church engages in home missions; however, as one pastor pondered, the lack of perceived value of missions may prohibit many African Americans from participating in global missions (Saunders 2015, 111). Therefore, there is a multiplicity of challenges that must be addressed.

CHALLENGING QUESTIONS

Will the recruitment of African American young adults increase African American participation in global missions?

The information that has been collected and analyzed is inconclusive as to whether specifically recruiting African American young adults would increase African American participation in global missions. The primary contention for this finding is based on numerous challenges that emerged while conducting the research. The primary challenges: lack of resources, lack of teaching and training about global missions, lack of African American men in the African American church, and home missions and the African American church. While these are not the only challenges for implementing a program of this kind, they are a few of the major quandaries.

Based upon the data analyzed from the focus group and survey, African American young adults seem open and willing to participate in a missions education and training program. Moreover, if the research expanded the scope of its investigation to include a prototype training center that recruited, educated, and trained participants, the researcher would be able to provide conclusive evidence to the hypothesis of this thesis research. Though the research did not determine definitively whether recruiting African American young adults for global missions education and training would increase the participation of the African American church for global missions participation, it points to a specific trend. According to the survey, due to the high incidence of African American young adults willing to participate in a global missions training program if given the opportunity and those willing to participate in a global missions trip if a group of people were going, there appears to be a positive correlation between these two characteristics. Therefore, if African American young adults are recruited, the possibility exists that they would participate in a global missions trip if a group of their peers was going. This leads to another crucial question.

WHAT ABOUT HOME MISSIONS AND THE AFRICAN AMERICAN CHURCH COMMUNITY?

Home missions or the concept of taking care of home and doing missions in their own backyard are challenges that must be addressed. Home missions consumes the struggles of the African American church community. While there are multiple struggles, the scarcity of African American males in the African American church was one of the issues brought to the foreground of this discussion. Other challenges involve funding and resources to make global missions plausible. Therefore, the lack of global missions engagement for the African American church community is more than a perceived idea in the mind of the African American church. The African-American church is on a collision course regarding reconciling home missions with global missions; there is a conflict between giving to the needs of the African-American community that they see daily and giving to the needs of others whom they do not see or know. Global missions, then, is a concept that the African American church community at large has a difficult time visualizing. Making the transition from home missions to global missions appears to be an insurmountable chasm.

A few of the pastors interviewed offered this suggestion: engage in both "backyard missions" and global missions. This may be a difficult obstacle to hurdle because as Walston claims, "some African American pastors will discourage, even rebuke, anyone who endorses sending resources outside the black community" (Walston 2002, 189). He further admits, "the church is correct in its concern for the needs of the community, but with almost

2 billion people outside of the reach of the Gospel, we are not released from our responsibility to reach the world" (2002, 189). If the African American church community is ever to embrace global missions wholeheartedly, it will probably be because they have reconciled the concept of doing both home missions and global missions. From the information gathered, it is unimaginable that the African American church community will relinquish their contributions in the community, nor should they. A well-developed missions training program will train the African American church community to engage in both home missions and global missions, and not at the expense of either. Also, engaging in both will satisfy many of the pastors' perceived needs, not only that missions begins at home, but also the idea that one must first prove themselves in home missions before becoming a viable candidate for global missions. This is accomplished through a strong global missions education and training program.

Educating the African American church about global missions is a task that will require time, patience, cooperation, and collaboration within the Christian community. The curriculum has to include methodologies that intertwine the basics of global missions while meeting the needs of the African American church community to prepare them for cross-cultural evangelization. Roland Allen's *Missionary Methods: St. Paul's or Ours* tackles the basics of teaching and training using the strategies of the Apostle Paul. Allen's recommendations for implementing strategic plans for missions training are applicable for educating and training the African American church community in global missions. Utilizing these methods for the training curriculum for the African American church will lay a solid foundation upon which to build a stable global missions training program that focuses on recruiting African American young adults for global missions. Allen speaks of the Apostle Paul's "fully equipped and well established church[es]" (1962, 84), churches that were established and equipped during Paul's brief tenure at each location.

The question that Allen poses is, how did the Apostle Paul accomplish such a task? How did Paul leave well-trained, educated, and fully-functioning church bodies without the people having a prior knowledge of Christianity and the way of Jesus? Allen's response: "St. Paul left a tradition . . . hence we may conclude that the doctrine involved in the preaching was reinforced, in the tradition delivered to converts, by . . . detailed teaching of the facts in the life of Christ upon which the doctrine rested" (1962, 84). Applying this principle to the education and training curriculum for global missions, the African American church could be fully educated and trained for successful global missions engagement in a relatively short time. Focused and in-depth teaching of global missions, based upon biblical precepts of global missions, would help propel the African American church into global missions. Therefore, if the African American church is well-equipped, they could confidently participate in global missions endeavors. This is not an indication that one should ignore the issues that have been previously discussed. However, it is a reminder that properly executing a global missions training program is feasible, especially if African American young adults are willing to participate, if given the opportunity, in such a program. Such a program would equip the African American church with the essential skills for productive global missions engagement. If the African American church community embraces the concept of global missions, "backyard" missions will continue to flourish. Global missions will enhance home missions, making it possible for the African American church to thrive in both endeavors. When the African American church community begins to engage in global missions, the objective of this research will be resolved.

CONCLUSION

KEY COMPONENTS: EDUCATION AND TRAINING

Recruit, educate, train, and mobilize: this is the recommended formula for successfully engaging the African American church into global missions. The structure of the training program is an integral component to the success of the program. Also, the administrators, teachers, and curriculum developers must be voices of those who understand the African American church community. The voice of an experienced global missionary is a necessary element in the formation of the curriculum; additionally, it is imperative to listen to the voice of African American pastors. Most importantly, the voice of the African American young adult will shape this program. The education and training program is the link that will unite the past of the African American church with her future. If such a program is accomplished, it will be achieved through education and training. Education and training are the greatest resources for engaging the African American church community in global missions.

Another critical component to the training program is the necessity to be linked to one or more established mission agencies such as YWAM or AIM. A partnership with an established missions sending organization to send out missionary apprentices once they have been adequately educated and trained would be a powerful connection in bridging the great divide of African Americans and global missions.

ENGAGING AFRICAN AMERICANS IN GLOBAL MISSIONS

Cornelius speaks of the African American church as a sleeping giant (2009, 303). It seems evident that the African American church is indeed a sleeping giant with regard to global missions. The African American church community has over 20 million members, based on statistics gathered by the Pew Research

Center.[1] If there are more than 20 million African American churchgoers, there are enough African Americans to send one million and leave millions home to continue involvement in "backyard" missions. Even if the numbers are off by 50 percent, there would still be enough in the African American church community to send one million, and leave the remainder behind to take care of the needs of home missions. The African American church community has the manpower to go. The more urgent question is: will they answer the call?

Global missions is a mandate; Jesus said go. Global missions is also a need to reach the world with the gospel before it is too late. The need is present; the call has sounded. Perhaps the call is drowned out by the fears of *what if*. Even so, the call has gone forth, and the African American church is strong enough and large enough to answer that call. If a program existed that would recruit, educate, train, and mobilize African American young adults for global missions, the African American church would have a plausible means by which to answer the call to engage in global missions.

FINAL WORDS

To engage the African American church community in global missions, there are critical issues that must be resolved. The African American church is a missing link in the world of global missions and among global missionaries. Without doubt, an enormous task looms over the African American church community as well as the Christian community at large to engage the African American church in global missions. There are no short cuts and there are no easy solutions; however, it is imperative to discover a workable solution and implement it.

Such an endeavor would involve creating a global missions training center in Atlanta, Georgia. Why Atlanta? First, Atlanta

---

1. The Pew Research Center's statistics are extrapolated from the 2015 United States Census Bureau.

is home to the Hartsfield-Jackson Atlanta Airport, the world's busiest airport. This means that from Atlanta one can travel to nearly anywhere in the world. Second, it means that Atlanta is easily accessible as well. Additionally, Atlanta's African American population is one of the largest in the United States (United States Census Bureau 2015). The goal is to catapult the African American church community into global missions participation. Yes, it is time to awaken the *sleeping giant*.

REFERENCES CITED

Allen, Roland. 1962. *Missionary Methods: St. Paul's or Ours?* Grand Rapids, MI: Eerdmans.

Bureau of Labor Statistics. https://www.bls.gov/cps/cpsaat37.htm (accessed September, 2015).

Cornelius, David. 2002. "A Brief Historical Survey of African-American Involvement in International Missions." In *African-American Experience in World Mission: A Call Beyond Community*, edited by Vaughn J. Walston and Robert J. Stevens, 48–54. Pasadena, CA: William Carey Library.

———. 2009. "A Historical Survey of African Americans in World Missions." In *Perspectives on the World Christian Movement: A Reader*, edited by Ralph D. Winter and Stephen C. Hawthorne, 299–304. 4th ed. Pasadena, CA: William Carey Library.

Fariss, Michael V. 2013. *Vanguards of a Missionary Uprising: Challenging Christian African-American Students to Lead Missions Mobilization*. Norfolk, VA: Urban Discovery Ministries, Inc.

Gordon, Robert. 2002. "Black Man's Burden." In *African-American Experience in World Mission: A Call Beyond Community*, edited by Vaughn J. Walston and Robert J. Stevens, 55–60. Pasadena, CA: William Carey Library.

Lincoln, C. Eric, and Lawrence H. Mamiya. 1990. *The Black Church in the African American Experience.* Durham, NC: Duke University Press.

Pew Research Center. http://www.pewresearch.org (accessed September 5, 2015).

Rivers, Tess. 2013a. "SBC President Recruiting More Black Missionaries." *The Triangle Tribune,* Feb 24: 1. http:// ezproxy.liberty.edu:2048/login?url=http://search .proquest.com/docview/1316626123?accountid=12085.

————. 2013b. "SBC President: We Need African Americans Out on the Foreign Mission Field." *IMB Commission Stories,* February 13, 2013. http://stories.imb.org/stories/view /sbc-president-we-need-african-americans-out-on-the -foreign-mission-field (accessed April 8, 2015).

Robinson, Wendell. 2002. "An Interview with Elder Donald Cantey." In *African-American Experience in World Mission: A Call Beyond Community,* edited by Vaughn J. Walston and Robert J. Stevens, 65–68. Pasadena, CA: William Carey Library.

Ronsvalle, John, and Sylvia Ronsvalle. 2013. "The State of Church Giving through 2011: What Are Christian Seminaries and Intellectuals Thinking—or Are They?" 23rd ed. Champaign, Illinois: Empty Tomb, Inc. http:// www.emptytomb.org/scg11chap8.pdf.

Rosenberg, Tina. 2011. *Join the Club: How Peer Pressure Can Transform the World.* New York: W.W. Norton & Company, Inc.

Saunders, Linda P. 2015. "A Feasibility Study to Develop a Missions Training Center to Recruit African-American Young Adults for Global Missions through Education and Training." Master's thesis, Liberty University Baptist Theological Seminary.

————. August 14, 2015. Focus Group Panel. Lansing, MI: EOW, MP4: 9:30–10:05.

————. September, 2015. Personal interviews via telephone, MP3 Reference #12: 27:05–27:15.

Stevens, Robert J., and Brian Johnson, eds. 2012. *Profiles of African-American Missionaries*. Pasadena, CA: William Carey Library.

Stevens, Robert J. 2012. "The Second Great Awakening and Missionary Rise: African-American Missionary Movement." In *Profiles of African-American Missionaries*, edited by Robert J. Stevens and Brian Johnson, 59–61. Pasadena, CA: William Carey Library.

Sutherland, Jim. 2002. "How Black is the Harvester? A Profile of the African-American Intercultural Missionary Force, the Extent of the Problem." In *African-American Experience in World Mission: A Call Beyond Community*, edited by Vaughn J. Walston and Robert J. Stevens, 135–140. Pasadena, CA: William Carey Library.

The Traveling Team. "Missions Stats." http://thetravelingteam.org/stats (accessed April 5, 2015).

United States Census Bureau. http://www.census.gov (accessed September 22, 2015).

Walston, Vaughn J., and Robert J. Stevens. 2002. *African-American Experience in World Mission: A Call Beyond Community*. Pasadena, CA: William Carey Library.

Williams, Chester. 2015. *Last Call for the African-American Church: The Death of Global Missions*. Blue Ridge Summit, PA: University Press of America.

YWAM. "About Us." http://www.ywam.org (accessed October 15, 2015).

FROM THE PROMISED LAND TO EGYPT

IMMIGRATION, TRANSNATIONALISM, AND MISSION AMONG HISPANIC EVANGELICAL CHURCHES IN NORTH AMERICA

Daniel A. Rodriguez

INTRODUCTION

For the past two decades, colleagues in the Evangelical Missiological Society have been contributing to a growing body of literature in the relatively new field of "diaspora missiology," understood as "a missiological framework for understanding and participating in God's redemptive mission among people living outside their place of origin" (Tira 2011, 1). My goal today is to advance the diaspora discourse among evangelicals, especially in North America, by drawing attention to the evangelistic opportunities and theological challenges presented by the Hispanic[1] evangelical church, particularly by those dominated by foreign-born Latinos.

Concerning the field of "diaspora missiology," our colleague Enoch Wan observed that

> the tasks of missiologist and missions leaders are to realize the scale, frequency and intensity of people moving both internally and internationally. They are, not only demographically to

---

1. Latino or Hispanic. These terms are used interchangeably to refer to all individuals of Latin American ancestry or with ties to the Spanish-speaking world who reside either legally or illegally within the borders of the United States of America. Generally, Latino will be used as a noun (e.g., native-born Latinos/as) and Hispanic will be used as an adjective (e.g., Hispanic churches). Any prolonged debate over which term should be used is self-defeating because both terms ultimately fail to deal with the complexity of Hispanic existence in the United States.

describe and analyze such phenomenon, but to also responsibly conduct missiological research and wisely formulate mission strategy accordingly. (Wan 2007, 6)

Accordingly, I will first describe and analyze the relevant demographic phenomenon among Latinos in the US, then proceed to formulate mission strategy based upon sound missiological research.

In 2015, worldwide, the number of people residing in a country other than their country of birth reached a historic high of more than 244 million. However, over the past decades the share of the world population that consists of international immigrants has remained stable at 3 percent (Global Migration Data Analysis Center 2015). Closer to home, in 2014 a record 42.2 million immigrants were living in the US representing 13.2 percent of the nation's total population. This means that the foreign-born[2] population has quadrupled since 1960 when only 9.7 million immigrants lived in the US. While growth in the number of immigrants living in the United States has begun to slow in recent years the US Census Bureau projects that number will double by 2065 (Brown and Stepler, 2016).

NOT ALL UNDOCUMENTED IMMIGRANTS ARE FROM MEXICO

During his campaign, United States President Donald Trump, promised to immediately "Begin working on an impenetrable physical wall on the southern border" to keep illegal immigrants out of the US (Donald Trump 2016). Unfortunately, Mr. Trump's provocative proposal reinforces two common misconceptions:

---

2. Foreign-born, first-generation and immigrant-generation. These terms will be used interchangeably to refer to all individuals of Latin American ancestry who have legally or illegally immigrated to the United States.

first, that the majority of immigrants in the US are from Mexico; and second, that most Latinos in the US are undocumented immigrants from Mexico. While it is true that the largest share of immigrants in the US are from Mexico, in 2014 that share was just 27.7 percent, followed by those from Asia (26.4%) and immigrants from Latin American countries other than Mexico (23.9%). Furthermore, of the 42.2 million immigrants living in the US in 2014 only 11.3 million (26%) were undocumented. Finally, only 5.8 million (52%) of all undocumented immigrants were from Mexico (Brown and Stepler, 2016). However, it would be a mistake to assume that the majority of Latinos in the US are undocumented immigrants, or immigrants at all.[3]

Recent political rhetoric aside, we are witnessing a momentous change in the makeup of the Hispanic population in the United States. The Hispanic population has more than doubled since 1990, growing from 22 million to more than 50 million in 2010 (US Census Bureau, Decennial Census 1970–2010). By 2014 the number of Latinos in the US grew to more than 55.3 million, comprising 17.3 percent of the total population (Brown and Stepler, 2016). More significantly, unlike the 1980s and 1990s when immigration accounted for most of the growth in the Hispanic population, in the early twenty-first century native births are now outpacing immigration as "the key source of growth" (Fry 2008, i). Today 65 percent of all Hispanics are native born,[4] that is, they are the children and grandchildren of immigrants to the US (Fry and Passel 2008, i, 3). Reflecting on these momentous changes, Juan Martínez remarks, "The Latino community in the

---

3. Illegal immigrant, unauthorized immigrant, and undocumented immigrant are used synonymously in this paper.

4. Following the precedent established by the US Census Bureau and the Pew Research Center, Native-born Latino and US-born Latino will be used synonymously to refer to those Latinos born in the US, Puerto Rico or other US territories and those born abroad to at least one parent who was a US citizen.

United States is dynamic and changing. Every ministry within this community ought to be as well" (Martinez 2009, 111). These demographic changes are forcing many Hispanic church leaders to reexamine ministry paradigms designed with foreign-born Spanish-speaking Latinos in mind. As Martinez insists, "Effective leaders in the Latino community will reorient their ministries to respond to these changes" (ibid.,10). Two significant changes to traditional ministry paradigms among Latinos are worth noting.

A PARADIGM SHIFT IN US HISPANIC MINISTRY

Demographic changes in the Hispanic population of the United States are forcing church leaders to reconsider historic ministry paradigms in Hispanic ministry. My scholarship in the past several years has focused on Hispanic evangelical churches that are responding in creative and contextually-appropriate ways to the demographic and linguistic changes taking place in some of the oldest and largest Hispanic communities in the United States including Los Angeles, New York, Houston, Chicago, Dallas/Fort Worth, Miami, Phoenix, and San Antonio. I have observed that when considering Hispanic ministry in the United States, many denominational and local church leaders continue to equate Hispanic ministry with ministry conducted almost exclusively in Spanish. While this approach continues to be very effective for reaching and nurturing the faith of first-generation Latinos, it is generally not successful when targeting the growing number of native-born English-dominant Latinos in the United States.[5] The problem I discovered is that conventional Spanish-speaking ministry models are unintentionally designed to

---

5. See Daniel A. Rodriguez, A Future for the Latino Church: Models for Multilingual, Multigenerational Hispanic Congregations (Downers Grove, IL: IVP Academic, 2011), for several examples of Hispanic churches that are now successfully targeting second- and third-generation Latinos in the United States through programs and ministries conducted in English.

preserve the language and cultural preferences of foreign-born Latinos. Sadly, this is usually done at the expense of their native-born English-dominant children and grandchildren. Though they represent more than 65 percent of all Latinos in this country, native-born Latinos, especially those who are English-dominant, have been largely ignored by denominational and local church leaders who uncritically equate "Hispanic ministry" with "Spanish-language ministry." Like the Greek-speaking Jews described in Acts 6:1–4, "Hellenistic Latinos" (i.e., English-dominant Latinos) are going overlooked, at least in so far as most Hispanic Protestant, evangelical, and Pentecostal churches are concerned.

My research has led me to a rapidly growing number of Hispanic evangelical congregations that strategically moved beyond "Spanish-speaking ministry models," toward different "multigenerational and multilingual models." The new models seek to address the needs of two or three different generations of Latinos under the same roof where the linguistic and cultural preferences of each generation are accommodated in an effort to become "all things to all Latinos," where language is not a barrier. Nevertheless, despite the unprecedented spiritual as well as numerical growth experienced at virtually all the churches responding to the shift from foreign-born to native-born majorities, many Hispanic evangelical churches remain committed to traditional models of ministry that reflect the preferences of the immigrant generation.

RESISTANCE AGAINST ACCOMMODATING US-BORN LATINOS

Why do many Hispanic church leaders continue to resist the changes that have helped other churches grow significantly without compromising what they understand to be the essential nature of the gospel? Recent studies suggest important social as well as theological reasons for opposing the expanded use of

English and more accommodating stances toward native-born Latinos who do not share the linguistic, cultural, and religious idiosyncrasies of foreign-born Spanish-dominant members.

Hispanic church leaders observe that continued immigration from Latin America and the Caribbean reinforces the cultural values, traditions, and language of immigrants living as "foreigners and aliens" in the United States. This is particularly evident in communities throughout California and the Southwest with large immigrant populations from Mexico. The same is true in South Florida where many immigrants from Cuba reside. Similar observations are made by pastors in Orlando, the Southside of Chicago, and the Bronx in New York, where continued migration from Puerto Rico reinforces the values, language, and practices of the immigrant generation.

The cultural values, traditions, and language of immigrants from Latin America and the Caribbean are also reinforced by improvements in international transportation and by advances in telecommunications, especially the smartphone. Thanks to smarter phones and inexpensive data and cell-phone plans, immigrants can instantly communicate via text and voice calls as well as emails with the simple touch of a button. Video chat applications including Skype, Facebook Messenger, Facetime, and Google Hangouts allow Hispanic immigrants and many of their second-generation children to maintain very close relationships with family and friends in their countries of origin, thereby creating and nurturing transnational identities. In other words, smartphone applications and social media help immigrants to cross the border into the United States and still preserve the values, traditions, and language of their countries of origin while simultaneously creating new hyphenated identities *en el extranjero* (abroad in a foreign land).

For many in the dominant group, these observations reinforce the fears of new nativists, including Samuel P. Huntington. In *Who Are We? Challenges to America's National Identity*, Huntington has argued that unlike earlier immigrant groups, the Latin American diaspora's refusal to learn English and assimilate into American society is now threatening to split the United States into two nations, one English-speaking and the other Spanish-speaking (2004, 316–324). It is important to note that Huntington is correct when he observes that—thanks to continued immigration, improvements in international transportation, and advances in telecommunications and social media—Latinos are holding on to their ancestral language longer than did earlier immigrant populations.[6] However, those who have carefully examined the available US Census figures and subsequent Pew Research Center surveys conclude that the data "reveal both a high degree of assimilation among American Hispanics, and no real difference between Hispanics and other [immigrant] groups in their ability to use English" (Brown 2009, 5)." The most obvious difference in language use between earlier immigrant groups and Latinos is bilingualism, which persists among a greater percentage of second- and later-generation Latinos than it did among earlier immigrant groups (Pew Hispanic Center and Kaiser Family Foundation 2004, 5).

MISSION TO AND THROUGH THE LATIN AMERICAN DIASPORA

Unlike nativists, including Samuel Huntington, many Hispanic church leaders recognize the transnational nature of the Latin American diaspora as a blessing in disguise. They are now considering creative ways to leverage the transnational character of many first-generation Latinos. In other words, they are beginning to recognize what Enoch Wan refers to as "the immense

---

6. Among earlier immigrant groups, foreign-language use usually becomes extinct by the third generation, when English proficiency becomes universal. See Alejandro Portes and Lingxin Hao, "E Pluribus Unum: Bilingualism and the Loss of Language in the Second Generation," Sociology of Education 71 (1998): 269–94.

potential of 'diaspora missions' in ministering to diaspora and ministering through diaspora" (Wan 2010, 95, 99). Not only is it true that "people on the move are receptive to the Gospel," but now, thanks to the proliferation of smartphones and the world-wide popularity of social media, the Latin American diaspora in the US is spreading the gospel throughout Latin America and the rest of the world, particularly among millennials.

For instance, thanks to video chat applications and social media sites including Facebook and Twitter, Sixto Rivera encourages members of his church in Dallas to share their new-found faith under the Lordship of Jesus Christ with family and friends back in El Salvador. Ongoing relationships between expatriates living in Dallas and their homelands have led to fruitful mission trips to Central America that have resulted in many conversions and the planting of missional communities where holistic spiritual formation is promoted, modeled, and nurtured with strong and mutually beneficial ties to the Salvadoran diaspora in Dallas (interview with author, September 30, 2016).[7] The availability of ever-improving videoconferencing applications like Zoom and GoToMeeting help Sixto Rivera to facilitate discovery Bible studies and even recruit, train, and coach church planters in Central America from his desk in Dallas. Similarly, leaders at the Sunset Church of Christ and Latin American Mission Project in Miami encourage members of the Latin American diaspora to use social media, including Facebook, to stay connected to friends and family back home.[8] They make annual mission trips to Latin America planned and led by Christians who are members of the Central and South American

---

7. Learn more about Sixto Rivera at Genesis Alliance at http://www .genalliance.org/.

8. See Trevor Castor, "Mapping the Diaspora with Facebook©," in Diaspora Missiology: Reflections on Reaching the Scattered Peoples of the World, edited by Michael Pocock and Enoch Wan, Evangelical Missiological Society series, 23 (Pasadena, CA: William Carey Library, 2015), 21ff.

diaspora communities in South Florida. Another Hispanic church near Fort Lauderdale, Florida encourages members of the Latin American diaspora to strategically use smartphone video chat apps as well as Twitter and Facebook to introduce people back home to their new church in South Florida, directing those interested to websites where they find links with many helpful resources including contact information for missional churches in the countries of origin (pers. comm.).[9]

Enoch Wan reminds us that diaspora mission challenges "the traditional missiological distinction between 'foreign mission' and local missions" replacing it with "a 'multi-directional' conceptualization of 'world missions'" (Wan 2012, 9). This is also evident in mission efforts initiated in Latin America by Christians putting family and friends living in the United States in contact with Christians who are members of churches dominated by the Latin American diaspora. Once again, it is impossible to overstate how invaluable smartphone app usage has been in efforts to reach immigrants with the gospel, especially those who have recently arrived in the United States.

CULTURAL RESISTANCE AMONG THE LATIN AMERICAN DIASPORA

As alluded to earlier, one unwelcomed consequence of missions *to* and *through* the Latin American diaspora has been the reluctance on the part of Hispanic churches dominated by foreign-born Latinos to accommodate the needs of the growing number of native-born English-dominant Latinos. In his study of Hispanic Protestant churches, Edwin Hernández noted that sociologically, traditional Spanish-speaking churches help foreign-born Latinos adapt to life in the United States while at the same time serving as

---

9. Learn more about the Latin American Mission Project at https://lampmiami.com/.

"an important mechanism for sustaining cultural values, language, and practices" (Hernández 1999, 223). Consequently, for some churches dominated by foreign-born Latinos, incorporating English-language programs and ministries to accommodate the preferences of native-born Latino teens and young adults undermines their efforts to sustain and reinforce the values, language, and practices of the Latin American diaspora. Similarly, Daniel Sánchez has observed that many immigrant parents pressure their pastors to help them "preserve the Hispanic language and culture" (2006, 85). In response, visionary and missional pastors try to help reluctant foreign-born parents and members to recognize that they are often more concerned with conserving their ancestral culture and language than with the spiritual welfare of their children and grandchildren.

Reverend Samuel Rodríguez, president of the National Hispanic Christian Leadership Conference (NHCLC), is one of the most well-known and respected Hispanic evangelicals in the United States.[10] As president of the NHCLC, Samuel Rodríguez has had a front-row seat and has been extended invitations to preach in hundreds of Hispanic churches in the United States. Given his extensive knowledge of the Hispanic evangelical church in the United States, I asked him what he perceived to be at the heart of the ongoing debate in Hispanic evangelical churches to accommodate native-born Latinos, especially teens and young adults. He reiterated what several Hispanic pastors have shared with me: "Some first-generation pastors and Christians are driven by a desire to preserve their culture. Consequently, they are isolationists" (telephone interview with author, December 10, 2009). Instead, Hispanic evangelical church leaders would do well to consider the wisdom expressed by Pastor Juan Carlos Ortiz. "If our effort to maintain our culture in

---

10. Learn more about the National Hispanic Christian Leadership Conference at www.nhclc.org/.

a foreign country makes our children leave the church, we have gained nothing" (quoted in Martinez 2008 110).

THEOLOGICAL RESISTANCE AMONG THE LATIN AMERICAN DIASPORA

In addition to the commitment to preserve the culture and traditions of the Latin American diaspora communities, there are also significant theological presuppositions that strengthen the resolve to resist the call to accommodate the linguistic and cultural preferences of native-born English-dominant Latinos. For instance, Christians are called to be holy in all their conduct (1 Pet 1:14–16) which above all else is characterized by "nonconformity" to the pattern of this world (Rom 12:2). To the first generation, their cherished traditions and prohibitions are not viewed as "cultural preferences," but rather as reflecting the value of personal and communal holiness *(la santidad)*, "without which no one will see the Lord" (Heb 12:14). Therefore, for many first-generation Latino Christians it is untenable to consider accommodating the younger generation's needs and preferences, many of which have been influenced by secular society. Samuel Solivan-Román sheds additional light on this theological source of resistance. He argues that many Hispanic evangelicals

> understand themselves to be the bulwark against death and the forces of evil that are overwhelming the world. They are a fortress against the cultural forces that seek to destroy them and their value system—a system that they understand as reflecting the values of the kingdom of God and their Lord Jesus Christ. (1996, 45)

FROM THE PROMISED LAND TO EGYPT

In all fairness to the immigrant generation, frustrated native-born Hispanic Christians are often unable or unwilling to see their own "subculture" and the broader American society through the eyes of foreign-born Hispanic Christians. For example, many Spanish-dominant Latinos do not equate the United States with the Promised Land or the "Chosen Nation" as do many American Christians, including many US-born Latinos. Instead, many foreign-born Latinos draw analogies between their experience in the United States and that of the Hebrews in Egypt. Like the sons of Jacob (Gen 46–50), many Hispanic immigrants leave their beloved homelands and come to the United States (i.e., Egypt) for one primary reason: to survive. They come to the United States because here they can carry on until they are in a position to return to their *patria* (homeland) to live out their dreams. In the meantime, they resolve, like the descendants of Jacob, to maintain a necessary distance from the "Egyptians" (i.e., Anglo Americans) and their materialistic and decadent culture, pejoratively referred to as *el mundo* (the world).

Consequently, Latino evangelicals, especially the foreign-born, feel compelled to create spiritual as well as cultural ghettos like the land of Goshen (Gen 46:28) where they can sustain and reinforce the culture, values, language, and practices of their *patria* while they "live in exile" surrounded by a foreign, hostile, and worldly society. Seen sympathetically from this standpoint, incorporating English and accommodating the cultural preferences of highly assimilated Latinos is tantamount to opening the doors of the church to "the forces of evil that are overwhelming the world." (Solivan-Román, 45). Dr. Isaac Canales, pastor of Mission Ebenezer Family Church in Carson, California, reminds us that many well-meaning and pious first-generation Latino Christians sincerely believe they must resist assimilation and acculturation, including encouraging the use of English in the church, because *el diablo habla inglés,* that is, "the devil speaks English!" (Canales, pers. comm.).

Canales and other pastors insist that statements like *el diablo habla inglés* and regular references to the decadent culture of *los anglos* (i.e., the dominant group) reveal a sense of cultural superiority prevalent among many first-generation Hispanic evangelicals. Wilfredo De Jesús, pastor of New Life Covenant Church in Chicago, has heard many well-meaning Hispanic church leaders repeatedly remark that *el español es el idioma del cielo* (Spanish is the language spoken in heaven). Pastor De Jesús insists that statements like these betray "a racist and ethnocentric attitude" that unnecessarily alienates and offends English-dominant native-born Latinos (Jesús, pers. comm.). Manuel Ortiz also noted that the ethnocentrism described by these Latino pastors brings with it an anti-American bias that inadvertently reinforces "the paradox of living in two hostile worlds." As a result, young US-born Latinos are unintentionally excluded from the church in favor of the foreign-born and second-generation Latinos who embrace "the value system of their native country—rural, monolingual, embodying conservative Hispanic values" (1993, 63). In response to the unconscious cultural superiority revealed in such statements as *el diablo habla inglés* and *el español es el idioma del cielo,* Pastor Isaac Canales reminds members who long for the good old days when the church was entirely Spanish-speaking that *el diablo es bilingüe* (the devil is bilingual)! Of course, when it comes to ethnocentrism and nativism, first-generation Latinos don't have a corner on the market. Members of the dominant group in the United States have very similar self-understandings.

THE MYTH OF THE CHOSEN NATION

In his book *Myths America Lives By,* Richard Hughes examines the sources of such American myths as the Nature's Nation, the Christian Nation, the Millennial Nation, and the Innocent Nation. He then offers a critique of each myth from the perspective of those marginalized by the dominant group (e.g., African Americans and Native Americans). Hughes argues that among the most powerful and persistent of all myths that Americans suggest about themselves is the myth that America is a Chosen Nation (i.e., the Promised Land) and that its citizens constitute a Chosen People, that is a New Israel (2004, 19). He traces the stages of the myth of the Chosen Nation from the arrival of the Puritans in the sixteenth century until the late twentieth century.

> Since the days of Tyndale, English Protestants had drawn a parallel between England and ancient Israel. Now, in their migration to New England, Puritans found the parallel even more compelling. Centuries earlier, for example, God had led the Jews out of Egypt, through the Red Sea, and into the Promised Land. Now God led the Puritans out of England, across the Atlantic Ocean, and into another promise land. The Puritans made the most of this comparison. In the Puritan imagination, England became Egypt, the Atlantic Ocean became the Red Sea, the American wilderness became their own land of Canaan, and the Puritans themselves became the new Israel. (Hughes 2004, 32).

The myth of the chosen nation has always had its critics including the likes of Roger Williams. But by the early nineteenth century the myth was becoming deeply rooted in the American psyche and found one of its greatest proponents in none other than Thomas Jefferson. For example, in his second inaugural address in 1805, Jefferson once again appealed to the image of ancient Israel as an appropriate model for the United States.

"I shall need the favor of that Being in whose hands we are, who led our fathers, as Israel of old, from their native land and planted them in a country flowing with all the necessities and comforts of life" (quoted in Hughes 2004, 35). In 1937, H. Richard Niebuhr observed that "As the nineteenth century went on, the note of divine favoritism was increasingly sounded." The belief that Americans, more precisely White Anglo-Saxon Protestants, constituted a chosen people gradually turned into the belief of America as a chosen nation (quoted in Hughes 2004, 37). According to Hughes, it was not difficult for the myth of the chosen nation to become a badge of privilege and power, justifying oppression and exploitation of those not included among the chosen (e.g., Native Americans, black slaves, and later the Spanish-speaking Catholic inhabitants of the southwest) as our country's Manifest Destiny (2004, 41).

Today a growing number of evangelicals are speaking out against the worst consequences of cultural superiority and ethnocentrism endemic in most societies. For instance, missiologists speak of *cultural validity* or *cultural relativity* to refer to an anthropological perspective that assumes that all cultures are essentially equal to one another and therefore should not be quickly judged by outsiders. The terms imply that every culture must be evaluated according to its own standards, not according to those of another society. Thus, an Anglo-American missionary in Honduras or a foreign-born Cuban evangelist in Tampa, Florida, should never imply that his or her culture is superior to that of others. Instead, they assume that all cultures are created by humans. Therefore, all cultures have inherent strengths and weaknesses. Our colleague Gailyn Van Rheenen reminds us that "All cultures simultaneously demonstrate the original goodness of the creation and the satanic brokenness resulting from the Fall. Cultures exhibit both a proclivity to sin, which alienates them from God, and attributes of goodness, reflecting divine presence" (2014, 240).

EVERY SOCIETY IS EGYPT

All cultures including Anglo-American and Hispanic cultures (plural) are what Sherwood Lingenfelter calls "palaces" and "prisons of disobedience." They are "palaces" because they provide human beings with "comfort, security, meaning and relationships." But they are also "prisons of disobedience" because they restrict our freedom to live the abundant life we were created for, the life provided for by Jesus Christ (John 10:10). Instead, every culture sets barriers between people, God, and others. As such, every culture is judged by God (2004, 20). This rejection and rebellion against God is often manifest in what we call "religion" (cf. Rom 1:18–23). Consequently, in word and deed Jesus challenged the traditional ideas, behavior, products, and institutions of his society and culture. This is obvious not only in the Sermon on the Mount (Matt 5–7) but also in his critique of the teaching, behavior, and institutions of the religious leaders of his day (Matt 15:1–20; 21:33–46; 23:1–36). Ultimately, it cost him his life. The same is true of many believers who took the gospel from Jerusalem to the ends of the earth (Acts 1:8). Implied in the message that Jesus is Lord and Savior and the only mediator between God and humanity (John 14:1–7; Acts 4:8–12; 1 Tim 2:3–7) is a critique of every culture, including Anglo-American and Hispanic cultures, as "prisons of disobedience."

THE CHURCH AS A COLONY OF RESIDENT ALIENS

In their ground-breaking countercultural ecclesiology, Hauerwas and Willimon offer a biblical corrective to the cultural superiority and ethnocentrism prevalent among many first-generation Hispanic evangelicals and dominant-group Christians in the United States. Concerned with the nature and purpose of the church in a post-Christendom context, the authors ask, "What does it mean for us to live in a culture of unbelief" (1989, 115).

They insist that to be a Christian, is to accept "the invitation to be part of an alien people who make a difference because they see something that cannot otherwise be seen without Christ" (1989, 24). To be a disciple of Jesus Christ implies joining "a countercultural phenomenon, a new *polis* called church." (1989, 30).

Hauerwas and Willimon insist that the political and ethical response of the church as a colony of "resident aliens" (Phil 3:20–21; Heb 11:13; 1 Pet 1:17; 2:11–12) is informed by the *telos*, the end. "It makes all the difference in the world how one regards the end of the world, 'end' not so much in the sense of its final breath, but 'end' in the sense of the purpose, the goal, the result" (1989, 61). The end, the goal towards which the Christian colony moves is nothing less than the "unity to all things in heaven and on earth under Christ" (Eph 1:9–10 NIV). The mechanism by which this reconciliation of all things and all peoples take place is the death, burial, and resurrection of Jesus Christ resulting in a new household, which brings an end to all particularisms, including the hostility between Jew and Gentile. The result is a new *polis*, a new society, the church.

> Consequently, you are no longer foreigners and strangers, but fellow citizens with God's people and also members of his household, built on the foundation of the apostles and prophets, with Christ Jesus himself as the chief cornerstone. In him the whole building is joined together and rises to become a holy temple in the Lord. And in him you too are being built together to become a dwelling in which God lives by his Spirit. (Eph 2:19–22 NIV).

Juan Francisco Martinez would add that the church as colony embraces the opportunity "to teach kingdom values that transcend culture and society" to their children and teens, especially to those coping with life at the margins of US society (i.e., Egypt) in at-risk underserved neighborhoods. They do so by demonstrating in word and deed that the kingdom of God is superior to any human culture or society. In this way, they are forming "young people to be Christians with a worldwide vision, not just with a Latino or a US mindset" (2009, 14). Furthermore, as they challenge the socially constructed barriers that keep us apart they rehearse before a divided world the multinational, multiethnic and multilingual celebration envisioned in Revelation 7:9–10:

> After this I looked, and there was a great multitude that no one could count, from every nation, from all tribes and peoples and languages, standing before the throne and before the Lamb, robed in white, with palm branches in their hands. They cried out in a loud voice, saying, "Salvation belongs to our God who is seated on the throne, and to the Lamb!"

CONCLUSION

It seems clear to me that one important step for missiologist and leaders in the worldwide mission of God is to embrace and actively promote our true identity as resident aliens whose true citizenship is in heaven (Phil 3:20–21). When we do, we will recognize that we have infinitely more in common with an undocumented immigrant Christian from Mexico than we do with our non-Christian native-born American neighbors who stand with us at baseball games singing the national anthem.

REFERENCES CITED

Brown, Anna, and Renee Stepler. 2014. "Statistical Portrait of the Foreign-Born Population of the United States." Washington, DC: Pew Research Center. http://www

.pewhispanic.org/2016/04/19/statistical-portrait-of-the -foreign-born-population-in-the-united-states-2014/

Brown, Dennis. 2009. "English Spoken Here? What the 2000 Census Tells Us About Language in the USA." Department of English, University of Illinois. http://www.english .illinois.edu/-people-/faculty/debaron/403/403readings /english%20spoken.pdf (accessed October 15, 2016).

Castor, Trevor. 2015. "Mapping the Diaspora with Facebook©." In *Diaspora Missiology: Reflections on Reaching the Scattered Peoples of the World*, edited by Michael Pocock and Enoch Wan, Evangelical Missiological Society series, 23. Pasadena, CA: William Carey Library.

Fry, Richard. 2008. "Latino Settlement in the New Century." Washington, DC: Pew Hispanic Center.

Fry, Richard, and Jeffrey S. Passel. 2009. "Latino Children: A Majority Are U.S.-Born Offspring of Immigrants." Washington, DC: Pew Hispanic Center. http://www .pewhispanic.org/2009/05/28/latino-children-a -majority-are-us-born-offspring-of-immigrants/

Global Migration Data Analysis Center. 2015. "Global Migration Trends Factsheet." http://iomgmdac.org/global-trends -factsheet/ (accessed October 15, 2016).

Hauerwas, Stanley, and William H. Willimon. 1989. *Resident Aliens: Life in the Christian Colony*. Nashville, TN: Abingdon Press.

Hernández, Edwin, I. 1999. "Moving from the Cathedral to Storefront Churches: Understanding Religious Growth and Decline among Latino Protestants." In *Protestantes/ Protestants: Hispanic Christianity within Mainline Traditions*, edited by David Maldonado Jr., 216–235. Nashville, TN: Abingdon.

Hughes, Richard T. 2004. *Myths America Lives By*. Chicago, IL: University of Illinois Press.

Huntington, Samuel P. 2004. *Who Are We? The Challenges to America's National Identity.* New York, NY: Simon and Schuster.

Jefferson, Thomas. 1907. "Second Inaugural Address." In *The Writings of Thomas Jefferson*, Vol.10, edited by A.E. Bergh. Washington, DC: Thomas Jefferson Memorial Association.

Lingenfelter, Sherwood. 2004. *Transforming Culture: A Challenge for Christian Mission*, 2nd Edition. Grand Rapids, IL: Baker Academic.

Martínez, Juan Francisco. 2009. "Acculturation and the Latino Protestant Church in the United States." In *Los Evangélicos: Portraits of Latino Protestantism in the United States.* Ed. Juan F. Martínez and Lindy Scott, 105–118. Eugene, OR: Wipf and Stock.

———. 2008. *Walk with the People: Latino Ministry in the United States.* Nashville, TN: Abingdon Press.

Niebuhr, H. Richard. 1959. *The Kingdom of God in America*, Reprint. New York, NY: Harper and Row.

Ortiz, Manuel. 1993. *The Hispanic Challenge.* Downers Grove, IL: InterVarsity Press.

Portes, Alejandro and Lingxin Hao. 1998. "E Pluribus Unum: Bilingualism and the Loss of Language in the Second Generation." *Sociology of Education* 71: 269–94.

Pew Hispanic Center and Kaiser Family Foundation. 2004. Bilingualism. Washington, DC: Pew Hispanic Center (March 2004).

Rodriguez, Daniel A. 2011. *A Future for the Latino Church: Models for Multilingual, Multigenerational Hispanic Congregations.* Downers Grove, IL: InterVarsity Press Academic.

Sánchez, Daniel R. 2006. *Hispanic Realities Impacting America: Implications for Evangelism & Missions.* Fort Worth, TX: Church Starting Network.

Solivan-Román, Samuel. 1996. "Hispanic Pentecostal Worship." In *¡Alabadle! Hispanic Christian Worship*, edited by Justo L. González, 43–55. Nashville, TN: Abingdon Press.

Tira, Sadiri Joy. 2011. "Diaspora Missiology." *Global Missiology* 2 (8), January. http://ojs.globalmissiology.org/index.php /english/article/viewFile/478/1178 (accessed on October 1, 2016).

Trump, Donald J. 2016. "Immigration." https://www .donaldjtrump.com/policies/immigration/ (accessed October 15, 2016).

U.S. Census Bureau. 1970, 1980, 1990, 2000 and 2010 Decennial Censuses.

Van Rheenen, Gailyn. 2014. *Missions: Biblical Foundations and Contemporary Strategies*, 2nd ed. Grand Rapids, MI: Zondervan.

Wan, Enoch. 2007. "Diaspora Missiology." *Global Missiology*, 4 (4), July. http://ojs.globalmissiology.org/index.php/english /article/viewFile/303/848 (accessed on November 10, 2016).

———. 2010. "Global People and Diaspora Missiology." In *Tokyo 2010 Global Mission Consultation Handbook*. Ed. Yong J. Cho and David Taylor, 92–100. Pasadena, CA: Tokyo 2010 Global Mission Consultation Planning Committee.

———. 2012. "The Phenomenon of Diaspora: Missiological Implications for Christian Missions." *Global Missiology*, 4 (9), July. http://ojs.globalmissiology.org/index.php/english /article/view/1036/2416 (accessed October 15, 2016).

11 THE CASE FOR MISSIONS IN ETHIOPIAN DIASPORA CHURCHES OF AMERICA

Mehari Korcho

American Christians are discussing the need for local churches and mission agencies to evangelize immigrants. This is a good focus, but there is a segment of the immigrant population that has the potential to effectively contribute to global missions. Not all immigrants are non-believers; rather, there are many believing immigrants who can be one of the major forces in global missions. For instance, there are thousands of immigrant churches in the United States, of which over 140 of them are Ethiopian diaspora churches. In order to see the impact of these churches on a global scale, they need to revise their definition and practice of missions. This study attempts to develop an understanding of how missions is defined and practiced among the Ethiopian immigrant churches in America and how this affects their missionary endeavors on a global scale. As such, it investigates their understanding and practical ways of doing missions including their mobilization, recruitment, passing down the responsibility of missions to future generations, and transnationalism.

It is hoped from this study that Ethiopian diaspora churches in America will come to realize the missional aspect of their displacement by revising their definitions and practices of missions. This will help them to actively engage in missions as diaspora witnesses in the hosting nation and beyond. Non-Ethiopian immigrant churches and local American churches may also take some lessons from this study.

HISTORY OF ETHIOPIAN IMMIGRANTS IN AMERICA

There are approximately 251,000 Ethiopians living in the United States. Today, Ethiopian-born immigrants constitute the United States' second largest African immigrant group after Nigeria (Migration Policy Institute 2014, 1). Ethiopian migration to America can be understood in three waves. The first wave was prior to the 1970s. The presence of Ethiopians in America in this period of time began with the sending of a handful of Ethiopians for further education in the 1920s (Getahun 2007, 3). In addition to students, tourists, businessmen, and government officials also migrated to America. However, permanent migration was virtually unknown among Ethiopians prior to the revolution in 1974. The second wave of migration began during the revolution of 1974 and completely changed this scenario. At this time, Ethiopia came under the rule of the communist government while American immigration policy was being highly influenced by cold war politics in which anyone who was against communism was welcomed. This allowed many Ethiopian immigrants who were victims of the "Red Terror" to be accepted in America as refugees. This wave of migration also included those people who were brought to the US in the 1980s from refugee camps, mainly from Sudan (Getahun 2007, 3). The third wave of Ethiopian immigrants to America encompassed those who came through diversity, lottery programs, and family reunification. For instance, from 1997 to 2000, Ethiopians ranked among the top five sending countries under the lottery program, and in 2004 and 2009, Ethiopia ranked first (Scott and Getahun 2013, xxi).

As far as Ethiopian settlement in America is concerned, most Ethiopian immigrants are widely distributed across a number of metropolitan areas of the United States. They are concentrated in California, Washington, Virginia, Maryland, Minnesota, Colorado, and Texas, each having about fifteen thousand Ethiopians, with Washington DC area having a population of thirty-five thousand, making it the largest population center for Ethiopians in the United States (Migration Policy Institute 2014, 5). The majority of Ethiopian immigrants to the United States (87%) arrived during or after 2000, thereby making the community as a whole quite young (ibid.).

ETHIOPIAN DIASPORA CHURCHES IN AMERICA

It is difficult to tell the exact number of Ethiopian diaspora believers in America. However, the North American Ethiopian Evangelical Churches Association director, Pastor Gizaw D. Derseh, says that there are over 140 Ethiopian diaspora churches in America. Most of these churches are planted in metropolitan areas following the pattern of the Ethiopian immigrant distribution in the US. According to Pastor Derseh, Ethiopian diaspora churches in America began in the early 1970s by Ethiopian Christian students living in the United States. Their purpose at the beginning was to preserve their faith and culture through fellowship and social support. Even today most Ethiopian churches are influenced by the agenda of culture and faith preservation. For instance, social responsibility is the main priority that keeps pastors busy. Because the majority of Ethiopian immigrants arrived during or after 2000, Ethiopian diaspora churches in America have a very young second generation. The Ethiopian diaspora church youth ministries in Washington DC, Atlanta, Dallas, and Denver are some examples of strong second-generation efforts that can set the tone for the work among the majority of upcoming Ethiopian youth.

METHODOLOGY

In this study, twenty-two Ethiopian diaspora church pastors and ministers in America were contacted. These participants have been chosen from various states including Colorado, Washington, Kansas, Illinois, Washington DC, Florida, Texas,

North Carolina, California, and Georgia. These locations were chosen because most Ethiopian immigrants are living in the metropolitan areas of these states. Data was collected between January and March 2016 through phone interviews. An unstructured interview method was followed in which all questions in the questionnaire were open-ended questions (see Appendix at the end of this chapter). This method was used because it would allow for further explorations that could bring a broader understanding of the subject. Data collection is also utilized through the author's personal experience and observations, as well as literature and research that have been done on the subject.

DEFINITION AND PRACTICE OF MISSIONS AMONG ETHIOPIAN DIASPORA CHURCHES IN AMERICA

"Missions" is not a biblical term. "Missions" comes from the Latin *mittere*, "to send," and *missio*, "sending." Prior to the sixteenth century the words "apostolate" or "apostolic office" were used (Little 2016, 2). Using the concept of sending, William Larkin noted that "mission is the divine activity of sending intermediaries whether supernatural or human to speak or do God's will so that God's purposes for judgment or redemption are furthered" (Larkin and Williams 1998, 3). The Bible shows us that Jesus is the Sender of his church. In Matthew, he said "Go and make disciples of all nations" (28:19 NASB); in Mark, he said "go and preach the gospel to all creation" (16:15 NASB); in Luke, he said that "repentance for forgiveness of sins would be proclaimed in His name to all the nations, beginning from Jerusalem" (24:47 NASB); in John, he said "as the Father has sent me I also send you" (20:21 NASB); and in Acts, he said "you will be my witness . . . to the ends of the earth" (1:8 NASB). This implies that all followers of Jesus Christ, everywhere, are called to engage in this mission. Historically, however, the terms "missions" and "missionary" have been understood in association with Western Christians and their service of helping the poor in the Global South.

In relation to this, Jonathan Bonk points out that the sense of entitlement with which Western missionaries regard their personal material and economic advantage can be traced to the beginning of the modern missionary era. This perspective remains deeply embedded, for good and ill, at the very core of Western missionary thinking, strategy, and policy (1991, xx). In other words, the historical understanding of missions as an activity from the "haves" (Westerners) to the "have-nots" (poor non-Westerners) is the norm even today. For instance, when I ask about their understanding of missions, most of my Ethiopian friends reflect an idea that missions is the burden of the white man to help poor people in the Global South. One participant of this study said: "When I think about missions, what first comes to mind is a white man with money and projects." Furthermore, my American friends laugh at me when I tell them that I am called to be a missionary in America. My Ugandan friend even told me about the experience of a non-Western missionary who was not accepted as a missionary by the kids in a Ugandan orphanage. All of these examples show that there is a misconception about missions and missionaries that pose a serious challenge for those that God desires to raise up as missionaries from the poor nations of the Global South. Breaking the norm of missions as an activity from the "haves" to the "have-nots" is the assignment of Christians in diaspora and others who are coming up as missionaries from the Global South. Christian missions is not all about poverty alleviation. For that matter, poverty is not the main problem of humanity—sin is. Sin made salvation necessary and sin makes Christian missions necessary (Peters 1972, 15). Hence, the definition and practice of missions in the church today needs to be revised according to its universal demand and God's primary agenda of redeeming people from their sins.

DEFINITION OF MISSIONS IN THE ETHIOPIAN DIASPORA CHURCHES

The definition of missions in the Ethiopian diaspora churches tends to reflect one of the following four ideas.

EVANGELISM IS ONE PART OF MISSIONS

This definition implies that evangelism is a subset of missions. For Ethiopian churches the dichotomy between missions and evangelism is understood as missions being social/humanitarian work and evangelism as verbal proclamation of the gospel. When one of the participants explained this dichotomy he said, "Mission is holistic ministry and evangelism is just one part in mission. . . . Mission is not only focused on winning souls but serving the whole person; it should involve compassion ministry or social work." He added that the church needs to address the physical, emotional, economic, social, and spiritual needs of a person. Another participant explained holistic ministry this way: "Holistic ministry is everything we do to glorify God and serve others." This shows that by definition Ethiopian diaspora churches understand missions in a broad sense. This perspective is supported by Andrew Walls and Cathy Ross who define mission with five marks: (1) To proclaim the good news of the kingdom; (2) to teach, baptize, and nurture new believers; (3) to respond to human need by loving service; (4) to seek to transform unjust structures of society; and (5) to strive to safeguard the integrity of creation and sustain and renew the life of the earth (2008, xiv). The problem with such a broad definition is that proclaiming the message of the gospel might be sidelined as we put a great deal of emphasis on social or humanitarian work. Stephen Neill is well known for saying, "If mission is everything, mission is nothing. If everything that the Church does is to be classed as mission, we shall have to find another term for the Church's particular responsibility for the heathen, those who have never yet heard the name of Christ" (1959, 81). Timothy Tennent also argued that in recent years the word mission has broadened even further to mean "everything the church should be doing," and this makes the term slowly migrate from a theocentric connotation to a more anthropocentric one (2010, 54).

In contrast to the holistic view, another participant said that missions should result in church planting. In other words, a mission that does not result in church planting is not Christian mission. This view emphasizes the need for communicating the gospel, converting people, and planting a church. This is the difference between the church and other humanitarian organizations. If the church considers humanitarian work as missions, then the church is not a church any more but a humanitarian organization.

For instance, this is what the biggest Ethiopian diaspora church in Washington DC is reflecting on its website. Their ministry focus includes family ministry; orphanage ministry in Ethiopia; educational ministry for full-time ministers; and holistic ministry that offers a wide range of free services to refugees, other immigrants, and low income residents to help them become self-sufficient members of their communities ("International Ethiopian Evangelical Church, Ministries"). One can see from the website that their ministry is more about serving the well-being of a person from an economic point of view. In fact, what they describe as mission work below reflects how evangelism is sidelined in this church.

> The church is involved in holistic activities, where Ethiopians and Eritrean [sic] are facing hardship due to various conditions.
>
> In recent years, the church has been working on a project involving Ethiopian and Eritrean migrant workers in Lebanon. According to IOM (International organization of Migration) there are approximately 70,000 women who are working as domestic help in Lebanon. Many of

these migrant women have been subjected to undue exploitation and abuse.

This is a serious problem! Since 2008, in order to address the plight of the migrant workers, The International Ethiopian Evangelical church is mobilizing support to those victims in dire need. The Church has managed to help a number of Migrant workers to be rehabilitated and or re-integrated into society. ("International Ethiopian Evangelical Church, Outreach Ministry")

Notice that there is no mention of evangelism or proclamation of the gospel, yet they believe that they are accomplishing mission among Ethiopians in Lebanon.

MISSION IS PERSONAL

This definition comes from an individual who is leading the church or anyone who claims to have a "vision." When most Ethiopian diaspora church pastors plant a church, they claim to have a "vision" which they want to accomplish through the church. Anyone who believes in that vision will come under the leadership of that pastor. One participant stated, "Mission is a personal vision as Paul had been sent to the Gentiles and Peter to the Jews." He added, "For us, our pastor is a visionary and all members of the church are operating under his specific vision." Another participant who is a senior pastor affirmed this point when he said, "At this point we are not sending missionaries from our church; I am the only one traveling back to Ethiopia and in different parts of the world to accomplish the vision God has given me, so in this case you can consider me as a missionary sent by our church." Some of the visions of the church leaders include "Ethiopians for Christ," "Compass Ethiopia Ministry," "Destination Ministry," "From Dallas to Addis Ministry" and "Vision Leadership Institute."

Their definition of missions as a personal task indicates two things. First, this definition makes believers in the church leave the task of missions to those who have the pastoral title. John Piper said this about professionalism in the church:

> We pastors are being killed by the professional-izing of the pastoral ministry. . . . Professionalism has nothing to do with the essence and heart of the Christian ministry. The more professional we long to be, the more spiritual death we will leave in our wake. For there is no professional childlikeness (Matt. 18:3); there is no professional tenderheartedness (Eph. 4:32); there is no profes-sional panting after God (Ps. 42:1). (2002, 1)

For pastors this notion of professionalism gives a sense of "I am good enough to teach, lead, counsel people, or do anything in the church" but leaves church members as passive consumers of the professional. Jessica Udall notes that the professionalization of ministry is insidiously at work in the Ethiopian community (2015, 188–89). That is, the idea that the person with the title "evangelist" or "pastor" is the only one who can legitimately do real ministry is a major hindrance to the daily life witness of the majority of title-less (but nevertheless gifted) Ethiopian Christians. I strongly agree with Udall when she states, "The impact of a diaspora church—even a large church—is greatly diminished if the majority of its members are passively waiting for their leaders to do the ministry of the harvest" (2015, 188–89). Secondly, this understanding may result in creating conflict in the church. This has been a reality for the Ethiopian diaspora churches for the last decade. The source of the conflict derives from the shift of their leadership style, from the "elders/team leadership model" they used to have in Ethiopia to the "pastoral/one-man leadership model" they have adopted from American churches. Professionalism is one of the reasons for the emergence of pastoral leadership in Ethiopia. Before full-time ministers and evangelists were introduced to the Western model of pastoral leadership in theology schools, there was elders/team leadership in most Ethiopian churches. I know some evangelists who had to go to school to earn their professional credibility and get the position they want in the church or plant their own church.

Here is my experience with this. I remember as a youth in Ethiopia when some evangelists and pastors went to theology schools for further education. It was good that they decided to get more education, but the sad thing was that right after they graduated, they started to claim their position over the elders/team leadership. That was what happened at my church in Ethiopia, which resulted in the church being divided. Those who believed in the elders/team leadership moved from that place, and those who believed in pastoral leadership stayed.

MISSION DOESN'T NECESSARILY INVOLVE GOING OVERSEAS

By referring to Acts 1:8, most participants have explained the meaning of "mission to all nations" as an act of crossing geographical, cultural, and ethnic boundaries. However, they noted that this does not necessarily involve doing missions by going overseas. For instance, one participant said, "We need to change our mindset; what we have seen from the Western churches is the expensive way of doing mission; mission doesn't necessarily involve going overseas." Another participant said, "We don't have to go overseas in order for us to say we are doing missions; reaching out and serving our community here in the United States is missions for us." He added, "We don't have any regrets for we are not even reaching non-Ethiopians in America; the clear assignment for us is to reach out to our community since no one else would do it as effectively as we do it." It is correct to say that the church would be effective in reaching and discipling people from the same background. But this cannot be an excuse for the church to overlook the Great Commission given in Acts 1:8. According to this verse, it is necessary that churches should start their mission in their Jerusalem, but they should also consider going to the ends of the earth even as they are accomplishing their local mission wherever they may be. This means that Acts 1:8 is a call to witness for Christ both locally and globally. We can't say that the church has to finish here and then go there; both need to happen simultaneously.

Another participant explained the reason why Ethiopian churches do not necessarily need to go overseas. The reason is because as immigrants, they already have crossed geographical, cultural, and ethnic boundaries. He said, "We are encouraging our church members to realize that they are missionaries here in America." He used the 3D's to describe the role of diaspora churches: divinely designed diaspora. This means that Christian immigrants are sent by the sovereign God to be his witnesses wherever they are. In line with this perspective, another participant added that he is trying to encourage his congregation by putting emphasis on cross-cultural discipleship in his teachings. I agree with this point that God is sovereignly working through the movements of people. Diaspora believers can be used as a harvest force in hosting countries. However, it is wrong to limit the ministry of diaspora churches to the hosting nation alone. Their agenda for missions should not end at the country of destination but it should continue to impact other nations. It is important for diaspora churches to have the attitude of serving all nations, even nations beyond the hosting country. Particularly, this helps them pass down their missional heart to the younger second generation.

MISSION IS PARTNERING WITH GOD

Mission is partnering with God in finding the lost and restoring relationship with God. This definition reflects the view of those who believe that mission should be understood based on the truth from the beginning of Scripture. One participant said, "Mission is the primary reason for the existence of the Church. . . . All believers are called to take part in God's mission of finding and redeeming the lost, and this mission has begun in Genesis 3 right after the fall of humanity." Participants traced the Great Commission in Scripture from Genesis 12 in the Old Testament to Matthew 28:18–19 and Acts 1:8 in the New Testament where Jesus sent out his disciples. This definition shows us the importance of basing our understanding of missions on Scripture.

PRACTICE OF MISSIONS IN THE ETHIOPIAN DIASPORA CHURCHES

This part of the study attempts to answer two questions: "What are the mission practices of Ethiopian diaspora churches?" and "How are they practicing them?"

WHAT ARE THEIR MISSION PRACTICES?

The scope of the mission work in the Ethiopian diaspora churches is limited to serving Ethiopians here in America and back in Ethiopia. In America, they carry out a compassion ministry with the intention of helping Ethiopians settle in America. Yared Haliche rightly said,

> The socio-cultural changes leave immigrants in the state of bewilderment as they struggle to cope with the rapid and intense change they undergo. While the churches provide cultural and religious maintenance, it loses sight of the bigger picture, and continues propagating mono-cultural ministries. As a result, the churches loose [sic] the broader aspect of mission and focus on serving existing members' interest and protect the status quo. In this sense mission is seen as a maintenance and protection mechanism. (2008, 237)

Ethiopian diaspora churches also have a heart for proclaiming the gospel in America fervently. Almost all Ethiopian diaspora churches have a monthly evangelism outreach campaign which includes giving food and clothes to homeless people. They organize evangelistic conferences and they try to do evangelism through their daily Christian living. One participant said, "What is lacking in this regard is that the Ethiopian diaspora churches have no readiness to serve people from other nations if they come to their church as a result of the evangelism outreach." I agree with his point. For instance, the church I am attending has a monthly outreach, yet we don't have anything set up in our church for those who may come from another nation as a result of our outreaches.

When it comes to missions back in Ethiopia, almost all Ethiopian diaspora churches assist local churches in Ethiopia through training and material and financial support. Participants noted that a huge amount of support goes to church planting, evangelism outreach campaigns, salaries and training for church planters, and material and financial support for Bible schools. For example, one participant mentioned that seven hundred church planters are trained in Ethiopia through their support. Most participants also noted that they are helping the effort of church planting in the most challenging and unreached areas of Ethiopia, namely, Arsi, Bale, Harar, Welo, Kefa, and Afar. Doing humanitarian work in Ethiopia was not given much emphasis by the Ethiopian diaspora churches except for a few churches that work in collaboration with American churches to help orphanages and to open schools and clinics.

HOW ARE THEY PRACTICING MISSION?

Organization and structure: Technically many Ethiopian churches in the US have an evangelism and mission department, but most of them are not strong. A participant noted that the church is full of activities with less attention given to the purpose for why they are doing things. Another participant said that there is a lack of unity among Ethiopian diaspora churches when it comes to bringing their efforts together for kingdom work.

He added that their efforts are fragmented and instead of complementing one another, they are competing with each other.

The tension between pastoral leadership (Western model) and elders/team leadership (the model they are used to in Ethiopia) is another aspect of church organization that is negatively affecting the church's missionary endeavor. There is no intentional task structure in most Ethiopian diaspora churches (Haliche 2008, 177). In most churches the pastor is in charge of everything. I agree with Haliche when he says that overwhelming social demands coupled with impoverished task structures tend to overshadow members and leaders' commitments in the church's ministry (2008, 235). This means that the social aspect is one of the most important founding purposes of the Ethiopian diaspora churches.

The other issue which needs to be discussed concerning organization and structure is the pastoral leadership style. In his study, Haliche discovered that participants made a clear distinction between home country and host country churches' perspectives on positions of power (2008, 181). Home country churches mainly promote an elder-oriented leadership style, whereas the host country churches principally focus on pastoral leadership. These two leadership styles result in personal and organizational clashes in Ethiopian diaspora churches (Haliche 2008, 181). With regard to the pastoral leadership style, pastoral ministry is the only active ministry in the church. For instance, most churches have a senior pastor, junior pastor, youth pastor, mission pastor, family pastor, and children's pastor. However evangelist, prophet, apostle, teacher, and other ministry gifts are not well-recognized in the church. This has been a source of conflict in Ethiopian diaspora churches since the pastoral leadership style doesn't give room for other ministry gifts to operate in the church.

Mobilization and recruitment: There is a need for mobilization among the Ethiopian diaspora churches in America. One participant indicated that there is an individual desire and spiritual commitment for missions, but mobilization is not done effectively. He added that there is no intentional training or follow-up. Most pastors in the Ethiopian diaspora churches view mobilizing potential leaders as a threat to their church because potential leaders may split the church. One of the participants pointed out that the pastoral leadership system doesn't embrace upcoming ministers in the church because the pastor feels insecure when potential leaders are mobilized.

Transnationalism: By this term I mean the missionary sending and cross-cultural ministry activity of Ethiopian diaspora churches in America. From my observation, Ethiopian diaspora churches are inwardly focused. That is, their mission task is restricted only to Ethiopians. But the question here is why are they inwardly focused? First, it is because they believe mission is too expensive—a luxury. Most participants indicate that they have a lack of financial resources. A participant said that one can do mission only if he/she has the resources. To explain this he used the Amharic quote: *Yemitlebsew yelat yemitikenanebew amarat.* This means for the Ethiopian diaspora churches to have the task of missions outside of their own community is like someone who is looking to wear luxurious clothing on top of his normal clothing when he doesn't even have normal clothing on. This implies that mission is wrongly associated with the "haves" or "have-nots" mentality. Another participant noted that mission has nothing to do with having resources but rather having a burden for the nations and obedience to the Lord Jesus Christ, the Sender. He added that whenever money is powerful, the gospel loses its power.

Second, a dependency mentality pervades Ethiopian diaspora churches resulting in them being even more inwardly focused. One participant explained this situation with the analogy of human blood types. Blood type "AB" refers to non-Westerners who are considered to be receivers all the time whereas "O" refers to Westerners who are considered to be donors all the time. He stated, "Who said that our blood type is AB; we need to be liberated from this dependency mentality."

Lack of burden for the nations is the third reason why Ethiopian diaspora churches are inwardly focused. Participants noted that ethnocentrism and being preoccupied with their own mission of winning their bread are the main reasons that hold them in their own comfort zone. Abeneazer Urga asks the question, "Can they also win souls, not just bread?" (2015, 14). He pointed out that there are Ethiopians who have lived in America for decades but just speak their own language and have been swallowed up by their own people group (2015, 14).

Participants also noted that the language barrier and the lack of experience and resources are the main challenges of Ethiopian diaspora churches. In response, a participant noted that even though these challenges are real, they cannot be an excuse for Ethiopian churches not to be missional. If they had a burden for the nations, they would take the necessary steps to explore the need of global missions and obey the Great Commission based upon the resources of the sovereign God who empowers and sends his people to the harvest.

Second generation: To truly fathom what is happening within Ethiopian diaspora churches, it is necessary to understand the unique nature of the second generation. There is no way the next generation is going to look like the first. A participant noted that the first generation will die out eventually, and the second generation will either continue keeping its unique identity or be scattered among the host country churches. Another participant stated that in churches where there is a gap between the first and the second generation, the latter thinks that they have graduated from the first-generation churches when they graduate from high school. There are some churches who have second-generation individuals who are ready to lead in the church in hopes of keeping their unique nature. Second-generation English services in Washington DC, Dallas, Denver, and Atlanta are good examples. Participants emphasize that the second generation hold great promise for global missions because of their unique identity.

Most of them are bilingual and almost all of them have multi-cultural experience. One participant noted they can be effective tools for global missions since they already have overcome various cultural and language barriers.

The fact that most Ethiopian immigrants have arrived to America during and after 2000 indicates that Ethiopians have a very young second generation. This implies that much is expected from the Ethiopian diaspora churches in terms of equipping the second generation for global missions. However, some participants indicate that there are certain challenges in the area of handling the second generation. For instance, the first generation is not effective in equipping the second generation since there is a language limitation, and it is a challenge to get pastors and teachers for them. Another challenge is that, like the first generation, the second generation is also pursuing the American dream. A participant said, "We are not preparing them for future ministry; parents are only encouraging them to be doctors or engineers. . . . Only few of them are interested in joining seminary for further ministry in the church." The fact that the first generation is not letting the second generation have their own independent church based on their unique identity can also be seen as another challenge. One participant said, "They need to have a church, not just an English service." The advantage of letting the second generation have their independent church is that this would create an opportunity for attracting all nations to their church, unlike the first-generation churches.

CONCLUSION

There is great potential among the Ethiopian diaspora churches for global missions. However, in order to have an impact on a global scale, they need to revise their definition and practice of mission, which is inwardly focused, negatively affected by leadership struggles, and wrongly associated with having or not having resources. Moreover, there is great potential for the second generation in global missions. The first generation needs to intentionally concentrate on equipping and helping them plant their own independent churches based on their unique identity.

Ethiopian diaspora churches should continue to give priority to evangelism without confusing it with holistic ministry. Holistic ministry associates missions with having resources. This implies that it is only those with resources who can be missionaries. Ethiopian diaspora churches need to change this mindset of understanding missions as an expensive task. One of the participants noted that we do missions not because we have the resources but because we have the passion and the burden for the nations to come back to the worship of the one true God. Rather than deriving our authority for missions from our economic power, it is important for the believer to recognize that we need to base our source of authority on the Holy Spirit. Mission is all about preaching the gospel through the power of the Holy Spirit (Acts 1:8; 1 Cor 1:18; 4:19–20; 1 Thess 1:5). Preaching the gospel is not merely communicating human words or simply talking about three steps to heaven. But as we preach, the gospel has the power to transform lives for eternity. The mission practice of Ethiopian diaspora churches shows that they have an amazing commitment and zeal to preach the gospel in this way and they need to maintain that spirit.

Pastoral leadership should be examined biblically. The question to consider is, "Is it healthy for the church when only pastoral ministry is active?" Most churches have a senior pastor, junior pastor, youth pastor, mission pastor, family pastor, and children's pastor. The issue is, where are the other gifts in the church (Eph 4:11; 1 Cor 12:28)? A church where all gifts and all believers in the church are not actively engaged in the mission task, is a dying church. There is a strong desire among Ethiopian diaspora believers to be missional, but they are not equipped and mobilized properly. Pastors need to change their attitude of securing their own positions in the church and welcome others to work with them in the mission harvest. Moreover, the North American Ethiopian Churches Association needs to organize consultations to seek solutions for their leadership problems. This Association must play the role of unifying churches and promoting missions among them.

Ethiopian diaspora churches need to change their inwardly focused mission by repenting and opening their hearts to serve all nations. One of the participants suggested that Ethiopian diaspora churches need to activate the spirit of fervent prayer which is diluted because of the materialistic lifestyle in America. Prayer is very important in missions. Jesus said, "The harvest is plentiful but the workers are few. Ask the Lord of the harvest, therefore, to send out workers into his harvest field" (Matt 9:36–38 NIV 1984). The other way that Ethiopian diaspora churches can take corrective measures is through working and learning together with Western churches in global missions as one body (1 Cor 12:27). Local American churches should share their global missions experience with Ethiopian diaspora churches for the benefit of all involved.

Ethiopian diaspora churches need to be intentional in equipping and helping the second generation to operate independently based on their new identity. Pioneering second-generation English worship services in Washington DC, Dallas, Denver, and Atlanta can set a standard for the second-generation church movement and its impact for global missions. This can result in a huge impact on the majority of upcoming second and third generations all over America. The good thing about these pioneering second-generation English services is that they are welcoming anyone from any background because there is no mention of "Ethiopia" in their new name. For instance, the one in Denver is named Avenue. Those churches who have challenges reaching their second generation due to language barriers could collaborate with local American churches to find teachers for their second generation.

All of these suggestions are meant to encourage and motivate Ethiopian diaspora churches to intentionally engage in missions among all nations on a global scale.

APPENDIX

INTERVIEW QUESTIONNAIRE

Definition of missions:

1. What is mission? Or how do you define mission?
2. What are the elements that shape your understanding of mission?

Practices of missions:

1. Share the mission practices you have in your church.
2. How do you mobilize and recruit believers in your church for missions? What resources do you have in your church for missions? Are you mobilizing them well?
3. How does your church structure look like in relation to missions?
4. Do you have cross-cultural/global mission programs?
5. In what ways do you think the second generation is an instrumental force for global missions? What does your church do to equip the second generation for missions work?

Problems and recommendations:

1. What are some of the challenges and problems that hinders your church's growth in missions work?
2. Give some recommendations and suggestions for the Ethiopian diaspora churches to grow and flourish in their effort for global missions.

REFERENCES CITED

Bonk, Jonathan. 1991. *Missions and Money: Affluence as a Western Missionary Problem*. Maryknoll, NY: Orbis.

Getahun, Solomon A. 2007. *The History of Ethiopian Immigrants and Refugees in America 1900-2000: Patterns of Migration, Survival and Adjustment*. New York, NY: LFB Scholarly Publishing.

Halche, Yared. 2008. "A Socio-Cultural Analysis of Leadership Approaches in Ethiopian Immigrant Churches in the United States: Leadership Styles and Implications for Missions." PhD diss., Concordia Theological Seminary.

"International Ethiopian Evangelical Church, Ministries." http://www.eecdc.org/ministries.

"International Ethiopian Evangelical Church, Outreach Ministry." http://www.eecdc.org/missions.

Little, Christopher R. 2016. "Biblical Theology of Missions." Class Notes for BIB/ICS 6030. Columbia International University, Columbia, SC.

Migration Policy Institute (MPI). 2014. The Ethiopian Diaspora in the United States. Prepared for the Rockefeller Foundation-Aspen Institute Diaspora program (RAD). http://www.migrationpolicy.org/sites/default/files/publications/RAD-Ethiopia.pdf (accessed on July 8, 2017).

Neill, Stephen. 1959. *Creative Tension*. New York, NY: Doubleday.

Peters, George W. 1972. *A Biblical Theology of Missions*. Chicago, IL: Moody.

Piper, John. 2002. *Brothers, We Are Not Professionals: A Plea to Pastors for Radical Ministry*. Nashville, TN: Broadman & Holman.

Scott, Joseph W., and Solomon A. Getahun. 2013. *Little Ethiopia of the Pacific Northwest*. New Brunswick, NJ: Transaction.

Tennent, Timothy. 2010. *Invitation to World Missions: A Trinitarian Missiology for the Twenty-first Century*. Grand Rapids, MI: Kregel.

Udall, Jessica A. 2015. "The Ethiopian Diaspora: Ethiopian Immigrants as Cross-cultural Missionaries; Activating the Diaspora for Great Commission Impact." In *Diaspora Missiology: Reflections on Reaching the Scattered Peoples of the World*, edited by Michael Pocock and Enoch Wan, 183–95. Pasadena, CA: William Carey Library.

Urga, Abeneazer. 2015. *A Reflection on Diaspora Cross-Cultural Evangelism: An African Perspective*. Clemson, SC: East Park Printing.

Walls, Andrew and Cathy Ross, eds. *Mission in the Twenty-First Century: Exploring the Five Marks of Global Mission*. Maryknoll, NY: Orbis.

Part Four

CHURCH ON MISSION IN PRACTICAL PERSPECTIVE

APATHEISM

ENGAGING THE WESTERN PANTHEON OF SPIRITUAL INDIFFERENCE

K. Robert Beshears

A few years ago, while living in Cambridge, England, I made a habit of meandering through the narrow, winding streets of the revered university town to soak in its rich heritage and architecture. On one such occasion, passing through the Market Square, I took notice of a Muslim missionary passing out some material. Most of his pamphlets made it into the hands of passersby, but quickly ended up in the trash bin. Week after week, I watched the dejected man try in vain to spark any meaningful conversation about spirituality. After a few months, on one particularly soggy afternoon, I felt compelled to buy him a cup of coffee. I offered him the drink, which he happily accepted. He asked me why I had offered him kindness. I replied that Jesus would have done the same thing. "So, you're a Christian?" he asked. I confirmed his suspicion. "Well, then, you know my pain," he replied. Not believing that we had much in common when it came to converting people to Islam, I was a bit confused by his response. I asked him what he meant. "These people," he said with a sigh, "they care nothing of God or spirituality. They are spiritually apathetic, totally indifferent to the biggest questions of life. They simply do not care. How can that be?"

He was right; I had experienced the same thing. Just a month earlier, after a public lecture, I was privy to a conversation in which a respected historian flippantly dismissed another lecturer's talk on soteriology by calling it "whatever magical nonsense the Christians want to call it." At a popular café, I once overheard a conversation between two students discussing the utter uselessness of theology, a mere psychological crutch that helped their grand-parents through the war. At a book release, an author explained his unwillingness to investigate the theological implications of his work because it would "only be interesting to a few Americans," which I assumed was a jab at the number of people in the United States who would find theology interesting.

Back in the Market Square, standing next to the Muslim missionary on that soggy afternoon, I came to the realization that spiritual indifference was not simply an isolated phenomenon in the lives of a few individuals. It was permeating an entire culture. Naturally, this is not to say that all Britons had abandoned their faith and cared nothing for their religious heritage. After all, for three years I participated in a local congregation that exuded all the dedication and passion one would expect from a vibrant Christian community. What I could not deny, however, was the ubiquity of spiritual aloofness. This apathetic attitude is not merely isolated to Great Britain. Upon my return to the United States, I found a similar indifference to spiritual matters, especially among my fellow millennials (ages 18–33). Many people have cast aside theism and exchanged it not with the opposite worldview, atheism, but something far worse: *apatheism.*

WHAT IS APATHEISM?

In his 2003 article "Let it Be" in *The Atlantic Monthly*, journalist Jonathan Rauch, a senior fellow at the Brookings Institution in Washington, offered a brilliant, pithy definition of apatheism: "a disinclination to care all that much about one's own religion, and an even stronger disinclination to care about other people's [reli-gion]" (2003, 34). Rauch described precisely the cold, spiritual apathy I had experienced in Cambridge and among my fellow millennials in the United States. More concisely, apatheism, a portmanteau of apathy and theism, may be defined as the lack of reason, motivation, and/or will to express interest in theism.[1]

Earlier British biologist Thomas Huxley (1825–95) coined the term *agnostic* to distinguish himself from those who believed they had "solved the problem of existence" through attaining a certain knowledge, or *gnosis*, of God (1910, 93). Huxley, however, neither denied nor affirmed the immortality of man and, by extension, the theistic system that immortality implies. His belief that the problem of existence was "insoluble" led to his self-description as an agnostic, but it did not lead him to express apathy toward the question of theism (1910, 93). Thus, agnosticism maintains that it is impossible to know presently whether or not God exists while apatheism is the emotional and psychological response of apathy that results from agnosticism.

The progenitor of apatheism, practical atheism, has long accompanied humanity. The Psalms bemoan people—foolish people—who suppress their belief in God's existence to indulge in moral corruption (Ps 14:1; 53:1). These "fools" never intellectually rejected God's existence, but habitually denied his input for moral decision-making. Paradoxically, they believed in God while craving his nonexistence. Later in the West, the Enlightenment experienced practical atheism as the outcome of a deistic theological system. In deism, where God allows his creation to self-govern and never imposes his will upon it, any ethical code

---

1. Philosopher Trevor Hedberg has rightly called apatheism "uncharted territory in philosophy" (2013). Consequently, there are many definitions for apatheism, especially in contrast to agnosticism. Hedberg and Jordan Huzarevich recently defined apatheism as "a general attitude of apathy or indifference regarding how we answer [existence questions]" (2016, 1). Yet, their definition does not address the why question of apatheism, that is, why does such an attitude of apathy or indifference exist within a person? Others view apatheism as a subset of agnosticism (cf. Mavrode, 2005); however, agnosticism merely claims that belief in God is ultimately unknowable without speaking to the usefulness of postulating God's existence or nonexistence.

must be derived from reason, not sacred revelation. Consequently, in general, Enlightenment-era practical atheism acknowledged God's existence while rejecting his ethic on the grounds of rationalism. Thus, practical atheism, unlike apatheism, has always recognized the importance of God's existence. Practical atheists care about religion, but not enough to allow it the duty of guiding their morality. Instead, they intellectually suppress the truth about God's character to ease their guilt and nullify any moral obligation to him. Nevertheless, the Enlightenment marked a time when practical atheism took a step toward apatheism, the character of which is perhaps best summarized by French philosopher Denis Diderot's famous quip, "It is very important not to mistake hemlock for parsley, but to believe or not believe in God is not important at all" (Buckley 1987, 225).[2]

It would not be until the turn of the millennium that true apatheism fully introduced itself to North America. It is likely that, among other reasons, 9/11 was a catalyst for spiritual apathy as a viable religious choice. If the terrorists cared too much for religion, which resulted in the death of thousands of victims, then apatheism would care too little for religion to prevent such an atrocious attack in the future. Rauch in a bid to convert his readers to apatheism, pointed to 9/11 as evidence that religion is the most "divisive and volatile of social forces" (2003, 34). To protect our culture against religious extremism, it must care for religion in the exact opposite direction. It must adopt apatheism as its worldview—a laudable social construct that will protect our culture against future religious extremism. Rauch writes:

> Apatheism, therefore, should not be assumed to represent a lazy recumbency, like my collapse into a soft chair after a long day. Just the opposite:

---

2. Such disregard for theism would later evolve into ignosticism—a failure to place any value on the question of God's existence—which lies at the philosophical foundation of apatheism.

> it is the product of a determined cultural effort
> to discipline the religious mindset, and often of
> an equally determined personal effort to master
> the spiritual passions. It is not a lapse. It is an
> achievement. (2003, 34)

This social "achievement" manifests itself in the passionless, detached "meh" that a high school youth mumbles after being asked about her spiritual life. It is present in the option "None" that young adults are circling more frequently on surveys about religious identity. Apatheism is the paradoxical nonchalance that accompanies many people on the most important issue of their existence.

Apatheists, like atheists, deny the gospel; however, unlike atheists, apatheists lack the reason, motivation, or will to spark a conversation about spirituality in the first place. At a minimum, atheism (and agnosticism for that matter) share a mutual interest with theism—the philosophical question over God's existence—that acts as a platform for talking about spirituality. In fact, the primary philosophical commonality between a theist, agnostic, and atheist is their shared concern for religion and interest in God. The apatheist, though, finds no value in such concern or interest, thus denying Christians access to common ground upon which they might build a case for the gospel. This is the reason why I have suggested that apatheism is far worse than atheism. Furthermore, apatheism obviously presents a challenge to the mission of the local church.

THE CHALLENGE OF APATHEISM TO THE LOCAL CHURCH

The opening remarks of Paul's gospel presentation at the Areopagus—the speech so often utilized by church leaders to motivate Christians to engage culture—presupposes a minimally common interest in theism. Addressing the "men of Athens," Paul shrewdly leveraged their mutually shared belief in the existence of the divine to present the gospel by pointing to the Athenian statue of the "unknown god" as evidence for their foundational conviction of God's existence (Acts 17:22). Today, this famous Acts 17 sermon is popularly cited as a model for contextualizing the gospel in the modern world.[3] Yet, citing Paul's Areopagus discourse overlooks an obvious difference between first and twenty-first century Western cultures. While (presumably) most ancient Athenians were theists and expressed interest in religious matters, many modern Westerners—especially millennials—are beginning to reject theism for spiritual apathy. Indeed, in certain contexts, many local churches now find themselves in an Athens without a statue to the unknown god.

This is especially true of the American context where, according to a 2015 Pew Research Center poll, the growth of religiously unaffiliated US adults—or "Nones,"[4] under which a

---

3. For example, see Paul Copan and Kenneth D. Litwak, The Gospel in the Marketplace of Ideas: Paul's Mars Hill Experience for Our Pluralistic World (Downers Grove, IL: IVP, 2014). Daniel Strange called the speech "subversive fulfillment par excellence" and an "exemplar of the apostolic preaching to pagans" in his Their Rock is Not Like Our Rock: A Theology of Religions (Grand Rapids, MI: Zondervan, 2014, 286). K. Scott Oliphint described Paul's address as an "instructive" model for evangelism in his Covenantal Apologetics: Principles and Practice in Defense of Our Faith (Wheaton, IL: Crossway, 2013, 229). A popular apologetics based study Bible commented on the Areopagus sermon in favorable terms, opining that Paul spoke "in terms understandable to Athenians" (Ted Cabal, et. al., The Apologetics Study Bible, Nashville, TN: Holman Bible Publishers, 2007, 1653). A notable exception is F. F. Bruce, who observed that while Paul had enjoyed several years as a "successful evangelist in the pagan world," he nevertheless fell into a "mood of dejection" after his Aeropagitica received "outright ridicule and polite dismissal" (cf. Paul: Apostle of the Heart Set Free, Grand Rapids, MI: Eerdmans, 1977, 244–48).

4. The term "Nones," not to be confused with monastic order nuns, describes religiously unaffiliated people who select "None" for their religious preference on polls and data collection. These include, but are not limited to: atheists, agnostics, apatheists, "spiritual" but not religious, and actively religious people who shy away from religious labels.

portion of apatheism falls—increased from 16.1 percent to 22.8 percent between 2007 and 2014 (Pew 2015, 4, 10). The increase of Nones, which includes apatheists, constituted the fastest-growing religious identity during the same period. Millennials represent 70 percent of all Nones (Pew 2015, 11), and, as sociologist Vern Bengtson lamented, their "none-ism" is notoriously difficult to describe coherently (Bengtson, Putney, and Harris 2013, 46).[5] Consequently, it must be noted that the percentage of religiously affiliated US adults (22.8 percent) does not represent the nation's total population of apatheists. In fact, there are many Nones that care very much about religion, e.g., New Atheists, agnostics who study religion, and the "spiritual" but not religious. Speaking of the New Atheist movement, Bengtson rightly observed that "while some nones may simply be passively indifferent to religion, others are actively engaged against it, perhaps intensely so" (Bengtson, Putney, and Harris 2013, 146). These "intensely" active Nones who are opposed to religion are commonly—and very often pejoratively—referred to as militant atheists, and lay at the complete opposite spectrum of secularism from apatheists. This observation alone is enough to explain why Bengston lamented the heterogeneous "None" category as notoriously difficult to define. Sociologist William Bainbridge also recognized this problem when he noted that while some Nones may be atheists

---

5. According to the Longitudal Study of Generations (LSOG), 22 percent of Millennials self-identify as "not at all religious"—more than any other cohort in the seven-generation study—while an additional 33 percent reported they are "not very religious" (Bengtson, et. al., 2013, 45). Only 16 percent thought of themselves as "very religious" (Bengtson, et. al., 2013, 45). These numbers paint a picture of the millennial generation as "far less coherent" than any previous generation while simultaneously "espousing a much wider range of religious perspectives than their predecessors" (Bengtson, et. al., 2013, 46). Perhaps this is due, at least in part, to an undercurrent of apathy: regardless of a religious opinion one way or another, does it ultimately matter what one believes or whether one believes at all?

who hesitate to don the label for fear of reprisal from the religious community, and while other Nones may be agnostics who merely misunderstand what the term means, some Nones "may simply be uninterested in religion, having no opinions about it" (Bainbridge 2009, 320). These "uninterested" Nones are generally apatheistic.

Additionally, people can (and often do) evolve from one type of None to another without ever leaving the category, for example, an agnostic who later self-describes as an atheist and later still may lose interest altogether, becoming an apatheist. All three sub-categories of Nones—atheist, agnostic, and apatheist—are fluid, and Nones may drift in and out of them throughout their life. To further add to this confusion, some people that self-identify as religiously affiliated may, in all actuality, exhibit apatheistic traits. These Nones associate themselves with a religion via non-religious motivations, for example, personal, familial, cultural, or ethnic reasons. Certainly, the latter is the case with Rauch, who self-identified as both an apatheist and an "unrepentantly atheistic Jewish homosexual" (2003, 34). So, while the exact number of apatheists is unknown, the recent jump in the number of Nones, whatever they may be, nevertheless indicates that apatheism is growing.

This presents an emerging and unique challenge to the local church in North America—a challenge that may not be receiving adequate development and implementation of strategic responses at the lay level. Under the umbrella of secularism, we tend only to think in terms of atheism and agnosticism, both of which typically provide an audience that is interested in religion. Apatheism, while closely related to both atheism and agnosticism, does not care to join the conversation. Secularism is a "Triple-A" world-view of atheism, agnosticism, and apatheism. Our missiological strategies toward secularism and the Nones must include all three.

THE PANTHEON OF APATHEISM

Carrying on the theme of Paul's Areopagus sermon amid the Greek deities, we must first recognize that the West has added new gods to its pantheon. Unlike the gods of old, these new gods demand no attention and require no consideration. In fact, they would prefer you not care for them at all. They are the pantheon of Spiritual Indifference, the polytheistic representation of apatheism, and of the numerous deities represented in the apatheistic pantheon, we will explore three in particular: *Inratio* (the apatheistic god of a lack of *reason* to believe), *Incausam* (the apatheistic god of a lack of *motivation* to believe), and *Involuntas* (the apatheistic god of a lack of *will* to believe).

INRATIO: THE LACK OF REASON TO CARE

Inratio (Latin for *no reason*) is the patron god of those who express spiritual apathy due to their lack of *reason* to care. Often, their apathy toward religion is fueled by confidence in secularism, which is the great success that the New Atheist movement has enjoyed in the post-9/11 milieu of skepticism toward religious belief. In the existential vacuum created by Salafi jihadism, New Atheism quickly rallied to offer the alternative to the some-thing people were looking for—nothing at all. Yet, unlike the hot-blooded, pugnacious attitudes that so often accompany New Atheist approaches to interreligious dialogue, worshipers of *Inratio* are completely indifferent and aloof to religion. In stark contrast to their atheistic kin, *Inratio* worshipers happily spend American currency without giving thought or care to the contested phrase "In God We Trust" that greets them each time they open their wallets. They could care less when politicians ask God to bless the nation or when celebrities thank him in their pursuit of acco-lades. It does not matter if someone believes or disbelieves. What matters is that it does not matter.

For these apatheists, Christianity is not something to be rationally considered because, at least externally, *Inratio* worshipers are completely satisfied with the secular worldview that their god represents. Secularism is unassailable, verified by science, and bolstered by all the scientists and philosophers they most respect. Their worldview has been baptized in the waters of what German philosopher Max Weber (1864–1920) called *entzauberung* ("demagification"), which has enabled them to trade superstition and mysticism for science and rationality as tools for understanding the world around them. Perhaps they have never even considered an alternative, rival worldview, but neither do they believe their worldview is susceptible to critique. Secularism simply is the way things are. There is no more reason to justify logically the fundamental truth claims of secularism as there is to justify logically why one plus one equals two. Secularism is the ironclad worldview that every human is born into, only to have the various forms of theism added later through tradition, childrearing, or spiritual exploration and study.

Religion is seen as a crutch, a handy psychological tool that previous generations utilized to make sense of the world around them. However, given scientific advances, religion has exhausted its usefulness and is no longer needed. Indeed, having no reason to desire a religious affiliation communicates confidence in this fact. If religion is a crutch, then only the weak need it. *Inratio* worshipers are strong, having cast aside the crutch, and are stronger than their atheist and agnostic kin who still feel the need to continue talking about the crutch. In a culture that rewards the confident and punishes the humble, there is a sociological incentive to distance oneself from religion. Our culture values Nietzschean individualism—where the self is the sole motivating power—as the peak of human prowess to boldly navigate the intimidating waters of existentialism. Thus, worshipers of *Inratio* are completely satisfied with secularism and have no reason to care about religion. They certainly lack both the motivation and will to care as well.

INCAUSAM: THE LACK OF MOTIVATION TO CARE

Incausam (Latin for *no motivation*) is the patron god of those who express spiritual apathy due to their lack of *motivation* to care. Often, their spiritual apathy is fueled by impatience. This is not necessarily a unique problem to any specific generation; yet, because of advances in technology, millennials are particularly prone to impatience. As digital natives, they were born into a world where many tasks are accomplished instantly, requiring only a little amount of patience and effort. Unlike generations before them, where hours in a library might be required to find the answer to a difficult question, today a simple search engine query for any topic, including religion, will yield the same result in seconds. This trend is only moving toward faster and easier access to information.

Consequently, religion seems like an outdated and tedious medium for answering existential questions. Most religions have sacred texts that, at best, are centuries old and require the reader to have at least some kind of historical framework to understand them. Furthermore, the texts are typically much larger portions of information than millennials are used to consuming. If an idea cannot be communicated in a 250-character microblog post or in a fifteen-second GIF or five-celled comic meme, then it will likely not receive an immediate audience among millennials. This is especially true of Christianity and the way the faith is presented. Regardless of the simplicity of the gospel, the message itself is often shared in a manner that assumes the hearer knows what it means to be "born again" for the "justification" of their "sins." It takes time to understand these terms, the gravity of their reality, and the character of their messenger. If time is a commodity in the modern world, then its cost might be too high for some individuals to invest in spiritual matters. Thus, some worshipers of *Incausam* lack the motivation to care about spirituality due to the perceived sacrifice of time and effort required to understand a worldview other than their own.

INVOLUNTAS: THE LACK OF WILL TO CARE

Involuntas (Latin for *no will*) is the patron god of those who express spiritual apathy due to their lack of *will* to care. Often their spiritual apathy is caused by a fear of what they may uncover if they were ever to step outside the boundaries of secularism. They were perhaps raised in a religious environment only to throw it off later in life for one reason or another, for example, rational, emotional, or moral reasons. Simply because they are now secular does not mean they have no reason or motivation to exhibit interest in religion. Quite the contrary, perhaps they have felt the desire to explore beyond the boundaries of secularism after noticing inconsistencies or shortcomings in their non-theistic worldview. Yet, because adopting a religious worldview—especially Christianity—forces the individual to change at a fundamental level, they are unwilling to yield to their desire of exploring spirituality. They do not want to learn because they are afraid of what they will find. So, they remain indifferent to religion as a self-defense mechanism to protect their autonomy.

Arguably, worship of *Involuntas* is merely an evolved form of practical atheism from generations past. However, whereas practical atheism recognized the importance of religion without wanting to acknowledge that fact, worshipers of *Involuntas* do not recognize the importance of religion and, likewise, do not want to acknowledge that religion may have importance. Previously, in a world without widespread secularism, the practical atheist practiced his autonomy within the confines of Christianity or deism. Today, because secularism has grown in popularity, an *Involuntas* worshiper may practice his autonomy outside the confines of any theistic belief whatsoever. Any intrusion of religion into his worldview constitutes a threat to the moral and ethical autonomy that secularism offers him. Thus, worshipers of *Involuntas* choose to remain in secularism by denying themselves the will to leave non-theism despite any real reason or motivation to explore theism.

ENGAGING THE WESTERN PANTHEON
OF SPIRITUAL INDIFFERENCE

As it has been briefly demonstrated, apatheism manifests itself in various forms, whether it be a lack of reason, motivation, or willingness to care about religion. How should the local church engage apatheists? Let us assume that common, fundamental Christian practices for evangelism are included in any missiological strategy regardless of the worldview being engaged. We must then recognize that the challenge in engaging apatheism is not intellectual or philosophical, but emotional and psychological. For the more apologetically-minded Christian, the desire to engage apatheism may manifest itself in the temptation to create compelling arguments to shock the apatheist out of their detached, blasé daze. This will likely not work for the simple reason that religious, intellectual propositions are meaningless to a person who does not care about religious, intellectual propositions. Regardless of the persuasiveness and clarity of the apologist's argument, it will fall on deaf ears. Apologetics must play an ancillary, albeit important, role when engaging apatheism.

Relatedly, as previously argued, we must recognize that we do not have common ground concerning the apatheist's interest in theism, let alone theism in general. If we do not even have the common ground of interest in theism, then we must find other common ground deep in universal commonalities that all humans share. As beings created in the image of God, certain elements of the human experience are shared across time, culture, and worldviews. It is here in the *Imago Dei* where we may find a platform from which to jolt an apatheist out of their indifference. While this paper does not claim to have the final authoritative answer—since I believe a multi-faceted approach is in order—it will offer one suggestion. A good strategy for engaging apatheists is to leverage the untapped universal resource of human curiosity.

As evangelicals, we seem to have an underdeveloped theology of curiosity even though we are inherently familiar with its power to capture attention and carry us to the conclusion of exploration, discovery, or learning. For example, a preacher relies on human curiosity to hold his audience's attention until the conclusion of his sermon. A theology professor will employ curiosity to spark genuine interest of a topic in her students. The Bible itself is organized in a metanarrative that entices human curiosity to hear the story out from beginning to end. Writing on mythopoeia, of which curiosity plays an important role, C. S. Lewis observed that:

> It arouses in us sensations we have never had before, never anticipated having, as though we had broken out of our normal mode of consciousness and 'possessed joys not promised to our birth.' It gets under our skin, hits us at a level deeper than our thoughts or even our passions, troubles oldest certainties till all questions are reopened, and in general shocks us more fully awake than we are for most of our lives. (1946, xxvii–xxviii)

Narrative stokes our curiosities, it guides and shapes them, all the while bidding us toward the exploration of things about which we never previously considered or cared. This is because we were designed with an instinctual drive to know what is around the corner, what is hidden under the rock, and how the story ends. Of course, curiosity, if taken too far, can be dangerous. Yet, according to Scripture, the motivation to curiously pursue truth can be a commendable exercise. For example, Luke commends the Bereans' insatiable appetite for fact-checking the apostles (Acts 17:11); Proverbs 25:2–3 states that it is the glory of kings to search out the things hidden by God; and Paul himself takes advantage of the Athenians' curiosity by answering the long-standing question over the divine identity behind the statue to the "unknown god."

Curiosity, then, is a universally-experienced element within the human experience and could be leveraged for the sake of sharing the gospel with apatheists. Let us now consider possible strategies for each of the three apatheistic gods previously discussed: *Inratio, Incausam,* and *Involuntas.*

ENGAGING *INRATIO*

How can we leverage curiosity to engage spiritual apathy with those lacking the *reason* to care because of their confidence in the secular worldview? An obvious answer would be to poke and prod at the reasons they believe secularism is so incontestable in an effort to provoke curiosity of other worldviews. This provocation would entail walking the secularist propositions out to their logical conclusion to demonstrate flaws in a system that is considered flawless. Here is where apologetics plays an ancillary role to curiosity.

The moral argument, for example, shows that secularism has no basis for universal human morality. If God does not exist, what objective standard exists to define good and bad, right and wrong? It cannot be the individual since morality may vary from person to person (e.g., the legalization of marijuana). It cannot be culture since morality likewise varies from culture to culture (e.g., the promotion or rejection of segregation-era Jim Crow laws among the States). It cannot be societal law since, again, morality varies from society to society (e.g., the varying age of sexual consent among different countries ranging from fourteen in Germany to twenty-one in Bahrain). What, then, is the universal standard of morality, and from where does it find its origin and sustainment?

Secularism cannot answer this question, yet it presupposes that an answer exists. Thus, the apatheist may concede that another worldview might have the answer that secularism cannot offer.[6] Once the secular worldview is shown to be susceptible to

---

6. It must be said that this type of apologetic reasoning should not be seen as the end goal. Remember, apatheism is not an intellectual or

criticism, curiosity sets in. The apatheist may ask: "If secularism cannot account for certain things, what other worldviews can?" At this moment, the apatheist now has a reason to explore another worldview, to which a Christian can offer their faith as the solution. It is curiosity, not apologetics, that drives the apatheist to explore competing worldviews to secularism.

ENGAGING *INCAUSAM*

How can we leverage curiosity to engage spiritual apathy with those lacking the *motivation* to care? The problem for these apatheists is impatience, which lies in their unwillingness to sacrifice time to read Scripture and hold conversations about religion. If the Bible is presented in its metanarrative form, then perhaps the hearer may be more willing to sacrifice time to hear how the story unfolds. Again, as C. S. Lewis noted, narrative stokes human curiosity, which is especially true of millennials who grew up reading multi-volume sagas like *Harry Potter,* playing video games that placed them in the driver's seat of the story, and are currently fueling the wild success of a renewed comic book industry that commonly utilizes long, overarching narratives in its storytelling.[7]

Popular television series that have all struck a chord with this generation, like *Lost, Breaking Bad*, and *The Walking Dead,* have one thing in common—a long-range trajectory from beginning to end.

---

philosophical rejection of religion, but an emotional and psychological rejection of the same. Apologetics may blaze a trail towards curiosity, but it should not be the final destination. It is a useful tool to promote criticism that sparks curiosity.

7. For example, over 50 percent of movie-goers who viewed Marvel's The Avengers in theater were under 25. See Nikki Finke, "'Marvel's The Avengers': Records & Factoids" (May 6, 2012). Accessed March 15, 2016 at: http://deadline.com/2012/05/marvels-the-avengers-records-factoids-267389/. In Spring of 2016, DC Comics launched an ambitious project, DC: Rebirth, which has been extremely successful thus far as older millennials are returning to the comic book consumption they enjoyed in their youth.

Even popular sitcoms, once known as being a collection of one-off episodes, are most successful with long-lasting sub-stories woven into them, such as *The Office* or *Friends*. The millennial generation is one that appreciates good storytelling. Therefore, for many apatheists, evangelicals should present the Bible as it presents itself: a combined narrative with a single, long-ranging trajectory from Genesis to Revelation, from garden to eternal city, from the wedding of the First Adam and his bride to the wedding of the Last Adam and his bride, the church. In doing so, the same motivating curiosity that overcomes impatience and leads apatheists to sacrifice hours on end binge-watching a television series will likewise give them the motivation to hear the story of Scripture.

ENGAGING *INVOLUNTAS*

How can we leverage curiosity to engage spiritual apathy with those lacking the *will* to care? The problem is that the apatheist does not care to consider Christianity because they are fearful or undesirous to know its message. Unlike the rich young ruler who counted the cost of Christian discipleship and assessed it too costly for him (Matt 19:16–22; Mark 10:17–27; Luke 18:18–30), apatheists who lack the will do not even entertain the idea of counting the cost in the first place. In this instance, curiosity can be provoked in the form of challenging them to explore that which they fear, which is especially possible if the person has a reason and motivation to care, but remains apathetic because of fear. In the same way that curiosity drives the determination of explorers in the face of fear, it may likewise spur an apatheist with reason and motivation to overcome their fear and provide them the willingness to explore a worldview outside of secularism. They should be challenged with soul-piercing questions: "What are you afraid that you might find? Why do you allow this fear to arrest you? Should you not be more afraid of never even attempting to find what you are looking for?"

In conclusion, evangelical strategies for engaging secularism rightly include atheism and agnosticism but fall short when they exclude apatheism. Given the rise of Nones, especially in the millennial generation, apatheism cannot remain unaddressed. The local church should engage the new Western pantheon of apatheism at the local church level by leveraging human curiosity and presenting the gospel as it presents itself—as one grand narrative of redemption. This curiosity will offer an apatheist the reason, motivation, or will required to spark interest in spirituality, thus offering the Christian an opportunity to present the gospel. The Muslim missionary in Cambridge was correct in his assessment that apatheists "care nothing of God or spirituality." Our challenge, then, lies in offering apatheists a reason to care.

REFERENCES CITED

Bainbridge, William S. 2009. "Atheism." In *The Oxford Handbook of the Sociology of Religion*, edited by Peter B. Clarke. New York, NY: Oxford University Press.

Bengtson, Vern L., Susan Harris, Norella M. Putney. 2013. *Families and Faith: How Religion is Passed Down Across Generations*. New York, NY: Oxford University Press.

Bruce, F. F. 1977. *Paul: Apostle of the Heart Set Free*. Grand Rapids, MI: Eerdmans.

Buckley, Michael. 1987. *At the Origins of Modern Atheism*. New Haven, CT: Yale University Press.

Cabal, Ted, et. al. 2007. *The Apologetics Study Bible: Real Questions, Straight Answers, Stronger Faith*. Nashville, TN: Holman Bible Publishers.

Copan, Paul and Kenneth D. Litwak. 2014. *The Gospel in the Marketplace of Ideas: Paul's Mars Hill Experience for Our Pluralistic World*. Downers Grove, IL: IVP.

Finke, Nikki. 2012. "'Marvel's The Avengers': Records & Factoids." Deadline Hollywood. http://deadline.com/2012/05 /marvels-the-avengers-records-factoids-267389/.

Hedberg, Trevor. 2013. "Apatheism: Should we care whether God exists?" Nooga.com http://nooga.com/164154 /apatheism-should-we-care-whether-god-exists/.

Hedberg, Trevor and Jordan Huzarevich. 2016. "Appraising Objections to Practical Apatheism." *Philosophia*, 1–20. http://link.springer.com/article/10.1007/s11406 -016-9759-y.

Huxley, Thomas H. 1910. *Lectures and Essays*. London: Macmillan & Co.

Lewis, C. S. 1946. *George MacDonald: An Anthology*. New York, NY: The Macmillan Company.

Mavrodes, George I. 2005. "Atheism and Agnosticism." In *The Oxford Companion to Philosophy*. New Edition. Ed. Ted Honderich. New York, NY: Oxford University Press.

Oliphint, K. Scott. 2013. *Covenantal Apologetics: Principles and Practice in Defense of Our Faith*. Wheaton, IL: Crossway.

Pew Research Center. 2015. "America's Changing Religious Landscape." Pew Research Center. http://www .pewforum.org/2015/05/12/americas-changing -religious-landscape/.

Rauch, Jonathan. 2003. "Let It Be." In *The Atlantic Monthly*, May 34.

Strange, Daniel. 2014. *Their Rock is Not Like Our Rock: A Theology of Religions*. Grand Rapids, MI: Zondervan.

PRE-FIELD MISSIONARY ASSESSMENT IN THE CONTEXT OF THE LOCAL CHURCH

Nathan Garth

How could this happen? How could we have worked so hard, been so sure of our call and commitment to our people group, and now find ourselves broken and feeling alone back in the States? How could things go so wrong, so fast? These are the questions that run through the minds of Scott and Catherine Wright who left to serve as missionaries in Taiwan just eighteen months ago. They are gifted and competent people. They expressed a call to missions and were affirmed and sent by a respected missions agency. For the most part, they thoroughly enjoyed being on mission in their host city, but struggles came fast and overwhelmed them. They now find themselves back in the States, living and working in their hometown. They know that most people need to come off the field at some point, but this feels different.

The Wrights' story is an all-too-common story of missionary attrition—more than simply attrition, missionary failure. It sounds harsh to call the return of a missionary a failure, but there are times when people simply fail at the task they set out to accomplish. Businessmen fail at starting new businesses, church planters fail in starting churches, and missionaries fail at the task of taking the gospel across cultures. This is not a judgment of what defines success as a missionary but a simple observation that not all men and women are gifted or adequately prepared for the task of cross-cultural missions.

Missionary attrition can be defined as the premature return of a missionary from the field for any number of reasons. Some of the reasons for returning home are necessary, even appropriate, but not all reasons are equally valid. Not everyone who goes overseas as missionaries will remain there for a lifetime, but some causes of attrition can be avoided. Paul McKaughan calls this type of avoidable attrition, problem attrition. "Problem attrition occurs when missionaries, because of mismanagement, unreal expectations, systemic abuse, personal failure or other personal reasons, leave the field before the mission or church feels that they should" (McKaughan 1997, 18). Jere Phillips addresses this troubling idea of problem attrition when he writes, "Some missionaries leave the field because of stress but are reluctant to talk about it. Others who go home for a time overcome these difficulties and later return to their tasks. Another group transitions into other ministries. A few leave ministry completely" (Phillips 2013, 20).

Understanding the complexities and pain associated with missionary attrition is a difficult task. In fact, it is unlikely anyone can fully understand why missionaries leave the field and what leads to their early departure. One essential tool in seeing missionaries survive, even thrive, on the field is missionary assessment. Assessing missionary candidates before they leave for the field will not only lead to the decrease of early missionary departure, but also to the increased well-being of the candidate and the overall health of their ministry. By holistically assessing missionaries before they leave, churches give missionary candidates a deeper understanding of themselves. Churches can help missionary candidates identify both strengths and weaknesses as well as encourage them to grow in identifiable areas before being affirmed and sent overseas.

WHY LOCAL CHURCH ASSESSMENT?

The task of taking the gospel to the nations was given to the church and should flow out of local churches.[1] This is not a state-

---

1. This statement comes from the author's understanding of the five Great Commission passages: Matthew 28:18–20; Mark 16:15; Luke 24:47; John 20:21; Acts 1:8.

ment against agencies or parachurch organizations but instead a statement for local churches and their unique role in missions.

The outworking of mission, making God's glory known in all the earth, should not only happen across neighborhood streets but also across oceans and ethnic boundaries. Few in the evangelical world would disagree with this statement, but far too often the undertaking of missions has been led by mission agencies and societies. Though these parachurch organizations play a part, their role is to support and empower local churches to take the gospel to the ends of the earth. Thomas Hale stresses this idea when he says, "Yes, the Holy Spirit is the ultimate Sender but he sends us out as members of Christ's body, the church. The local church, as in the case of Paul and Barnabas, is the primary sender of missionaries" (Hale and Daniels 2012, 60).

George Peters emphasizes this same point. "The church and not the missionary sending agency, as such, is God's authority and creation for sending forth missionaries . . . The mission agency ought to be the church's provision, instrument, and arm to efficiently expedite her task. It can neither displace nor replace the church" (Peters 1984, 229). If indeed the local church is the one who sends out missionaries then the church should also take an active role in assessing gifts and readiness of those they send. The following are three additional reasons the local church should take the leading role in the assessment of missionaries.

To begin with, no organization or outside group knows the candidate as well as their local church. It is within the context of the local church, in the routine of daily life, that a person's true self is revealed. Through the ups and downs of ordinary life within the church, a person's character, gifts, and commitment to ministry will be discovered and cultivated. Indeed, the local church is the "ideal testing ground for potential missionaries" (Pirolo 2012, 56). Thomas Hale hits on this idea of life within the church when he says, "What do the people who know you best say about you? Because the single most important factor in predicting one's future missionary performance is one's past performance as a Christian" (Hale and Daniels 2012, 54). This seems like a simple idea. We can know how a person will behave and perform in future situations based on how they have behaved and performed in the past. However, this concept is troubling to many, especially those who have a romanticized view of missionary service. Often those with this view believe the myth that sharing their faith, discipling others, and life in general will become easier once they arrive on the field. Church-based assessment can debunk this myth by holding people accountable to a missional lifestyle here and now and by calling people to continual growth in their home context. The local church can and should use its intimate knowledge of missionary candidates to hold them to a high standard and speak into their lives, even when what needs to be said is difficult. Oftentimes, speaking hard truth to a potential missionary is the greatest gift a pastor or church leader can give.

A second reason churches need to take the leading role in missionary assessment is the fact that local churches are in the best place to help missionaries grow. The purpose of an assessment is not only to assess the readiness of candidates for service but to also encourage them toward growth in areas that have been identified as weaknesses. Church-based assessment should not be a simple pass or fail but a process of continual assessment and development toward maturity. The local church has the unique opportunity to help those within its congregation who desire to serve overseas because the missionary candidates live and worship with the church on a regular basis. Mission agency training, seminaries, and parachurch organizations are great tools to utilize in training people, but they can never replace the transformative work that the church, through the power of the Holy Spirit, can have in people's lives.

In Ephesians 4:11–16, we read Paul, writing to the church at Ephesus, urging them to use their gifts to build up one another toward maturity. He exhorts them "to equip the saints for the work of ministry, for building up the body of Christ, until we all attain to the unity of the faith and of the knowledge of the Son of God, to mature manhood, to the measure of the stature of the fullness of Christ" (Acts 4:12–13 ESV). It is within the context of the church that potential missionaries can continue their growth and development toward a healthy departure for life and ministry overseas.

Finally, assessment should take place in the local church because calling and affirmation come in community. In Acts 13:1–3, a group of elders from Antioch were fasting, praying, and worshiping the Lord together. While they were worshiping the Lord, the Holy Spirit spoke to them saying, "Set apart for me Barnabas and Saul for the work to which I have called them. Then after fasting and praying they laid their hands on them and sent them off" (Acts 13:2–3 ESV). In this passage, we see elders in the Church of Antioch hear from God, respond in obedience, and send out two of their own to be cross-cultural missionaries. It is important to notice that Paul and Barnabas's call came in community, the community of church leaders, to be specific. The church then affirmed, laid hands on them, and prayed over them. The model of calling and sending that the New Testament gives is one that happens within the community of faith, the local church. Churches must not assume that mission agencies will evaluate calling and capability. Local churches are the ones who know their people best and need to take a leading role in the evaluation of calling (Cook 1974, 267). Churches must also not depend solely on an individual's desire to be a missionary. A person's call and competency for the task must be more than a personal feeling. Michael Griffiths says, "The most an individual can do is express their willingness. Others must determine his worthiness. The individual may be free to go but only his church knows if he is really fitted to go" (1974, 15–16). Scott Moreau, in his book *Introducing World Missions* details this idea:

> Although the one who ultimately calls or sends is God, often in the immediate context it is a local body of believers who sense or confirm a call . . .

The body of Christ then has a significant role to play in the calling of people into ministry. As did the church at Antioch, they confirm and enact on behalf of God what the calling entails. The local body of believers, who usually best know the individual or team, should be able to affirm the call or leading and play a key role in helping the call to be fulfilled. (Moreau, et al. 2004, 170)

WHAT IS NEEDED IN MISSIONARY ASSESSMENT?

Once a church has understood its role in the process of assessing potential missionaries, the question must be asked, what is needed in a missionary assessment process? Four ideas are key when developing an assessment process.

First, as mentioned before, the process needs to be rooted in the local church. This is not to say that local churches should assess potential missionaries in isolation or apart from mission agencies or specialized assessment organizations. Many churches will find that partnering closely with organizations in the assessment process is the best model for them. The key is to take a leading role in the process. Do not simply outsource the process to others. Church leaders should ask questions of mission agency leaders, read books and articles on assessment, learn from other churches, and be intentional to create what fits their context. Above all, church leaders need to stay relationally involved in the lives of potential missionaries as they explore the process of being sent.

Secondly, assessment needs to be holistic. More than just looking at theology or activity, a church-based assessment process needs to look at people as a whole and evaluate them based on a deep understanding of who they are, how they function, what they know, what they believe, how they relate with others, and a spectrum of other areas. "It is more than what you know, what and where you have studied, and what skills you've developed.

Ministry flows out of being" (Hoke and Taylor 2009, 40). Because ministry involves the whole person, assessment must evaluate the whole person as well.

A third need in the missionary assessment process is to use the assessment as an opportunity to encourage ongoing growth and not pass final judgment. Very rarely should assessment be seen as a pass or fail test. Only in the most extreme cases should it be used this way.[2] Assessment is an opportunity for missionary candidates to examine themselves and to have others examine their call, character, and competency for ministry. The process should also provide a clear pathway toward continued growth. Assessment needs to be something people look forward to going through because they know it will point them to continued growth in their journey, not just in missions, but in life itself. Too often people think of assessment as a bouncer at an exclusive club. As they get closer to the front of the line they nervously wonder if they are good enough to make the cut. In reality, assessment should be more like an encouraging coach. Sure, he can keep you from getting in the game, but ultimately his desire is to teach and coach you in such a way that you play your best game. He is for you, not against you. Missionary assessment should be similar. As Zach Bradley says in his book on the sending church, "Robust assessment opens the door for great development" (2015, 75).

A final thought is needed when talking about developing an assessment process in a local church. Churches come in all shapes,

---

2. At Sojourn Community Church, we use the analogy of a traffic light when talking about assessment. A red light symbolizes a person we will not send. This rarely happens in the first assessment. This normally comes after time and many opportunities have been given to an individual. A yellow light is normal for an assessment. It means that a person can move forward with caution but has areas they need to work on before leaving for the field. A green light is used for a person who is good to go. This also rarely happens at the end of an initial assessment interview. A green light is normally given after growth in identifiable areas has taken place.

sizes, and personalities. Because of this, there is not a "one size fits all" assessment process for local churches. Churches should feel the freedom to assess according to their values, mission, vision, and commitment to the Word of God. What is needed then are flexible tools and processes that local churches can adapt according to their needs. As mentioned before, there are a plethora of great assessment tools that churches can customize and use as they see fit.

WHAT ARE THE IDEAL CHARACTERISTICS OF A MISSIONARY?

Along with assessment tools, local churches need to know what to look for as they assess their people for cross-cultural missions. What are the markers they evaluate people on? What traits and skills should church leaders look for in people they send out? What are the key qualities necessary for any missionary? The following are several different lists of key qualities a missionary should possess. These lists come from various sources, perspectives, and periods in history. What better place to start than with Scripture itself?

QUALIFICATIONS OF ELDERS AND DEACONS

Paul's writing in 1 Timothy 3 and Titus 1 provide a detailed list of the qualifications of an elder and deacon in a local church. Three lists of qualifications, two for elders and one for deacons, are provided in these two passages. While there is no biblical mandate that cross-cultural missionaries need to be elder or deacon qualified, it seems fitting to use these lists as ways to measure the lives of missionaries sent from churches. After all, the model we are given in Acts 13 is of a local church sending out two of their best leaders for missionary service.

In addition, Galatians 5:22–24 provides a list of the fruits of the Spirit, traits that are progressively true of those who follow Christ and are transformed by the work of the Holy Spirit. This list is helpful because it gives a picture into what the life of a growing believer should exhibit.

HUDSON TAYLOR

In his book, *A Biblical Theology of Missions*, George Peters offers a list from Hudson Taylor on what he believed were essential characteristics for any missionary.

Taylor's list includes: (1) A life yielded to God and controlled by the Spirit, (2) a restful trust in God for the supply of all needs, (3) a sympathetic spirit and a willingness to take a lowly place, (4) tact in dealing with people and adaptability toward circumstances, (5) zeal in service and steadfastness in discouragements, (6) love for communion with God and for the study of the Word, (7) some experience and blessing in the Lord's work at home, and (8) a healthy body and vigorous mind (Peters 1984, 229). What is most striking about Taylor's list is the life and ministry that came before it was written. Hudson Taylor created this list of expectations from a lifetime of his own missionary experience.

THOMAS HALE

Thomas Hale in his book, *On Being a Missionary*, provides a list of key qualities he believes mission agencies should look for in the missionary recruits they assess. This same list applies to local church assessment.

Hale's list includes: (1) insight, (2) adaptability, (3) perseverance, (4) a zeal for sharing the gospel, (5) ability to get along with others, (6) emotional stability, (7) humility, (8) spiritual maturity, and (9) a spirit-filled life (Hale and Daniels 2012, 47–54). Hale goes on to say the single greatest element of a missionary career is a Christ-like life, asking the question, "Do people see Jesus in this person?" (Hale and Daniels 2012, 54).

JOHN PIPER

In 1995, John Piper wrote an article entitled, "The Marks of a Spiritual Leader." In the article, he details the character and characteristics of spiritual leaders. Although his list is not specifically about the missionary context, his insights prove to be some of the most helpful in seeking to understand and assess the right people for missionary service. Piper defines spiritual leadership as "knowing where God wants people to be and taking the initiative to use God's methods to get them there in reliance on God's power. The answer to where God wants people to be is in a spiritual condition and lifestyle that display his glory and honor his name" (Piper 1995). This is the goal and aim of anyone seeking to be a cross-cultural missionary, that their life may "display his glory and honor his name." Piper breaks his "marks of a spiritual leader" down into two categories: the inner circle of spiritual leadership and the outer circle of spiritual leadership (Piper 1995).

The inner circle of spiritual leadership includes the following marks: (1) helps others experience the glory of God, (2) loves both friend and foe by trusting in God and hoping in his promises, (3) meditates on and prays over God's Word, and (4) acknowledges his helplessness and need for Christ (Piper 1995).

The outer circle of spiritual leadership includes being: (1) restless—a holy discontent with the status quo, (2) optimistic—confident based on the goodness of God, (3) intense—a zeal for life and what it holds, (4) self-controlled—someone who masters their drives through the power of the Spirit, (5) thick-skinned—able to handle criticism well, (6) energetic—one who has a work drive and is able to live under pressure, (7) hard thinker—thinks deeply and carefully about things, (8) articulate—can state their thoughts clearly and with force, (9) able to teach, (10) good judge of character—can detect the difference between those who have potential and those who are untrustworthy, (11) tactful—a quality of grace when interacting with people, (12) theologically oriented, (13) dreamer—has a vision of what the future could be,

(14) organized and efficient, (15) decisive—is willing to take risks rather than do nothing, (16) perseveres—commits to a task and finishes it even when it would be easier to quit, (17) a lover—loves their spouse deeply and sacrificially, and (18) restful—is able to put down work and rest (Piper 1995).

LARRY MCCRARY

Larry McCrary, executive director of the Upstream Collective, has created a list of key competencies from his years of experience as a North American church planter and missionary in the European context. McCrary bases his list of traits on the three overarching ideas of calling, character, and chemistry. McCrary prefaces this list by saying that all of these competencies should be observed and confirmed overtime in the context of the local church (McCrary 2011).

McCrary's list includes: (1) vision capacity—sees the future through the lens of faith and creates new things, (2) intrinsically motivated—demonstrates high motivation and passion for accomplishing God's will, (3) multiplies—creates ownership and reproduces leaders, (4) missional—has relationships with unbelievers and shares his faith, (5) discerns—has insight into people and circumstances, (6) teachable—learns from mistakes and adapts to change, (7) relates—has good interpersonal skills and shows genuine interest for others, (8) contextualizes—able to read and understand culture, (9) cultural adaptation—adapts well to other cultures, and (10) networking abilities—connects well with others for ministry purposes (McCrary 2011).

SOJOURN COMMUNITY CHURCH

The final list of missionary characteristics are ones I have created for our local church context at Sojourn Community Church in an effort to provide a grid for holistically assessing potential missionaries within the congregation (Garth 2015). Hopefully, this list can provide broad categories for other churches to evaluate the lives and ministries of those they hope to send overseas. From these broad categories, additional questions can be asked and areas of life examined.[3] This list is a gathering of ideas gleaned from various books, articles, like-minded churches, existing lists, and personal experiences as a missions pastor at Sojourn.[4] Staff and elders use these eleven attributes as a guide when they assess, develop, and send mid- and long-term missionaries.[5]

In addition to these attributes, Sojourn gives candidates, and others who are interested, a list of self-assessment questions.[6] These questions allow missionary candidates to examine themselves in three areas: knowledge, character, and skills.

A word of caution is needed here. The various lists of character traits mentioned above are not simply lists to check off in an assessment interview, i.e., if people meet these marks, they can go as missionaries; if not, they stay home. The intent of these assessment tools is far greater than a simple pass or fail test. Lists of competencies like these are intended to help churches, agencies, and those who are sent measure readiness for cross-cultural ministry. These same character traits can be used to create personalized development plans for individuals preparing to serve overseas.[7] In this way, these lists of ideal traits act as a jumping off point for further growth.

---

3. See Appendix 1 for a list of additional topics to explore with potential missionaries.

4. Many of the resources that influenced the writing of Sojourn's list of key character and behavioral traits are included in this paper.

5. See Appendix 1 for Sojourn's "Grid for Developing Healthy Missionaries."

6. See Appendix 2 for these self-assessment questions.

7. Personalized development plans can be used by churches to help missionary candidates grow in identifiable areas both during and after the assessment process. Often times, these plans list action steps to address weakness in candidate's lives. Areas may include marriage, counseling for past sin struggles, knowledge of the Bible, greater exposure to cross-cultural missions, and a variety of other things. Churches using personalized

It is helpful to remember that God often uses unlikely people to accomplish things that seem impossible. The Scriptures are full of unexceptional men and women who were used by God to accomplish exceptional things.[8] Modern day missions has also had a fair number of men and women who were not qualified to be missionaries yet were used by God to do great things. One such example was Gladys Aylward. At twenty-six years old, she applied to be a missionary with China Inland Mission and was rejected. One of the leaders at the time told her kindly, "You really don't have the capacity to learn a difficult language like Chinese and we prefer candidates who are younger and more able to adapt" (Voelkel 2007). In time, Aylward was able to get to China and was used of God to both bring the gospel to unreached areas as well as to help end foot binding and save the lives of many orphans. Stories like this are powerful but they are the exception and not the norm.

Too often we celebrate the lives of exceptional people like Gladys Aylward who were used of God but whose stories are almost too fantastic to believe. By doing this, we unintentionally set up the pioneering maverick personality as the missionary standard, men and women who overcome all the naysayers and win in the end. It is helpful to remember that for every Aylward who goes out and sees great things happen, there are a thousand others who get blindsided by their lack of preparedness, their own sin, or a host of other issues. They leave the field never to return again. As compelling as the exceptional stories are, the truth of community and godly counsel still hold true. "Where there is no counsel,

---

development plans include The Church at Brook Hills and Sojourn Community Church.

8. God often used men and women we would deem as unqualified to accomplish his purposes in the kingdom. For examples, see the stories of Moses in Exodus 3, Rahab in Joshua 2, David in 1 Samuel 16:1–13 and 17, Mary in Luke 1:26–2:7, and the calling of the Disciples in Luke 5:1–11.

the people fall; but in the multitude of counselors there is safety" (Prov 11:14 NKJV).

Church leaders need to be faithful to assess potential missionaries and be willing to say no to them if the situation demands it. However, assessments should also be flexible so that as the Spirit of God moves, church leaders are able to listen and respond, even if it means sending people who do not fit the ideal missionary profile.

SHOULD EVERY CHURCH DO ASSESSMENT?

One common question that is asked when churches start to think about assessment is the question of capability. Can small- to medium-sized churches that have little expertise in cross-cultural missions really do a faithful job in assessing missionaries? The answer is a qualified yes. Yes, any healthy church can play an active role in evaluating the readiness of its own people but not on their own or in isolation. Too often churches believe the lie that only churches with designated missions staff and large budgets are able to assess, develop, and send well. The truth is churches of all sizes have a vital role to play in sending their own people. Large churches may have more expertise and capacity, but what a small church lacks in one area, it may make up for in another. For example, a smaller church may not have a full-time missions pastor to assess and train missionaries, but what it does have is deep relationship with the missionary and more opportunity for one-on-one investment, something larger churches often lack the ability to do well. All churches are different, where one church excels another may struggle and vice-versa.

Churches, however, do not need to feel pressure to do everything well or everything themselves. A wise church is one who uses the resources and expertise available to them. One of the keys to being a great sending church is not totally recreating the wheel. Churches need to look to others, especially other churches, to gain insight, share in best practices, and find existing resources they can use to send well. Many churches are doing some sort of assessment of their own missionaries and have created tools they are willing to share with others.[9] Mission agencies are also great resources in these areas. They can come alongside the church and provide expertise in assessment and sending that churches will find invaluable. Many mission agencies have departments that are trained to help churches get more deeply involved in global missions and have the capability to assist in the assessment process.[10]

UNDERSTANDING THE ELEMENTS OF AN ASSESSMENT

Assessment is more than an interview. It is more than a simple evaluation of a person's character and competencies. If holistic assessment is the goal, which it should be, then the process of assessing missionaries needs to have some complexity to it—not complexity that creates confusion but complexity that involves multiple layers and angles of evaluation. Remember, there is no need to create the entire assessment from scratch. Churches can create or alter existing pieces according to their needs. Churches should do the parts of assessment they feel they are able to do. Either outsource the rest with caution or get coaching in weaker sending church elements.

When a local church begins developing an assessment process, they should strive to include some form of the following basic components: (1) evaluation of character and service, (2) fulfillment of requirements set by the church, (3) completing a formal process, and (4) assessing the candidate's ability to persevere.

---

9. Explore the resource page at the Upstream Collective for more assessment and sending church resources at http://www. theupstreamcollective.org/sendingchurchelements.

10. Asking mission agencies for their assessment tools can give churches deeper insight into what agencies are looking for in the missionaries they employ.

EVALUATION OF CHARACTER AND SERVICE

Before a church should think about any kind of formal assessment process, the first step should be an assessment of faithfulness to the ordinary. Are missionary candidates faithful members of the church? Do they serve on a regular basis? Do people in the church hold them in high esteem? Are they people who have proven character? Are they seen as leaders and people others can depend on? These and other questions provide an initial level of assessment that is vital to any assessment process. In fact, this may be the most important part of the process because how people have behaved in the past and present is a great indicator of how they will behave in the future.

One essential question to ask of potential missionaries is, do they regularly share their faith and disciple people? If the answer is no, then why would the church send them? Before people can live on mission in a cross-cultural context, they need to be on mission wherever they find themselves. Mission is less about geography and more about identity and obedience (Crider et al. 2013, 14).

Practically, this could include: expectation of church membership, faithful service in local church ministry over a period of time, faithfulness and fruit in evangelism and discipleship, and recommendations by members as well as church leaders.

FULFILLMENT OF CHURCH REQUIREMENTS

For any missionary working with a missions agency, certain requirements and expectations will need to be met before they are approved to go overseas. Everyone in missions knows and expects this, but what about the expectations of the local church? Too often the agency is the only one with an active voice in the area of setting expectations. This is not the agencies' fault. Local churches need to know what they expect and then make those expectations clear to their members. Providing a clear path to being sent is important for anyone who has a desire to go.

Practically, a local church's expectation for those they send could include: formal educational requirements, church-based training, a written application, a personality profile test,[11] marriage assessment, "tune up" counseling, and a host of other things the church deems appropriate. Be encouraged. Churches do not need to do this alone. There are many good books, agencies, and online resources available to assist in the process of creating an assessment process. [12]

FORMAL PROCESS

At some point in the process of assessing a potential missionary, there needs to be a formal assessment interview. This assessment interview can look many different ways but a face-to-face interview with clear expectations given to the candidate should take place. This interview can be based on a set of prearranged questions or based off a written assessment questionnaire they turn in before the interview. Consider providing a set of self-assessment questions to people considering missions so that they can begin to assess their readiness for missionary service long before the interview takes place. [13]

Make sure the assessment process is a place where hard questions are asked but encouragement is also given. A good assessment drills deep down into hard and painful areas. The deep things of the heart need to be revealed so that a plan for growth can be developed. The deep things of the heart will only

---

11. There are many types of personality profiles available today. These personality profiles are extremely helpful but should be used with caution. From my own experience in missions and missionary assessment, I would recommend the Enneagram, Myers-Briggs, and the D.I.S.C. assessments.

12. Churches should consider visiting an active sending church in their area to see firsthand what another church is doing. In addition, a great book to begin reading is David Horner's When Missions Shapes the Mission or Steven Beirn's Well Sent.

13. See Appendix 3 for Sojourn's "Self-Assessment Questions."

come out once the church has built trust through the assessment process and those leading the assessment are willing to ask the hard, poignant questions. For example, make sure to ask clear questions about pornography, masturbation, sexual abuse, hidden sins, health of the marriage, and other things that will strip away the false veneer we all present of ourselves. Candidates need to get raw about their sins, fears, and hidden expectations before an assessment team can take the proper steps of providing encouragement and a plan of growth. Given the potential intensity of these meetings, it would be wise to do these interviews in community with other leaders from the local church. Interviewing in community will allow for a variety of voices and perspectives on issues that arise.

The goal of an assessment interview is not to pass final judgment but to get a real picture of people's lives and character. An assessment interview is a tool to help people grow toward maturity—toward the place where they are healthy, maturing, and ready to leave for the field.

The result of an assessment process should be some sort of personalized development plan. This growth plan should act as a map for people, showing them where they currently are in the process and a clear path to get to a place where they are ready to leave for the field. Everyone has areas they need to grow in and thus everyone who goes through an assessment will have some sort of growth plan to work on. After the assessment, members of the assessment team should share ideas for personal growth and provide the potential missionary with a written development plan listing measurable action steps toward growth.

ASSESSING ABILITY TO PERSEVERE

The final stage of assessment is the perseverance it takes to actually get to the field. Roadblocks abound for those headed overseas. This can include significant spiritual warfare, delayed timelines, extended steps in the development process, support raising, and a host of other delays. The perseverance it takes to actually get to the field will act as a final assessment of the missionary candidate's commitment to their call and ability to follow through on hard things. Unfortunately, there are people who get caught in this part of the assessment process and never make it overseas. Make sure encouragement is a part of the process.

CONCLUSION

Assessment is essential in sending missionaries overseas. Too often we hear stories of attrition like Scott and Catherine Wright. This couple had the necessary formal training and theological education, were passionate about their call, were affirmed by an agency, but were only pseudo-connected to their home church. Scott and Catherine failed to draw near to their sending church and have them speak deeply into their lives. If their sending church had been more invested in their journey toward missions, maybe their story would have had a different ending.

When churches take an active role in assessing those they send out as international missionaries, they not only decrease the potential attrition of missionaries but they allow missionaries to go out healthier, better equipped, and with a greater opportunity to thrive in cross-cultural missions.

APPENDIX 1

GRID FOR DEVELOPING HEALTHY MISSIONARIES

Key Character and Behavioral Traits of an Effective Missionary
Developed at Sojourn Community Church, Louisville, KY

1. *Spiritual Vitality*
   Abides with Christ?
   Active devotional life?
   Commitment to the church and Christian community?
2. *Strong marriage and family*
3. *Theological foundation and clarity*
   Person of the Word and prayer?
   Ongoing theologian (always learning)?
4. *Missional Lifestyle*
   Shares faith regularly and disciples others?
5. *Emotional Health*
   Past sin issues/ baggage from life?
   Current sin struggles?
   Potential issues on the field?
6. *Leadership Ability*
   Self-starter?
   What have they created and maintained?
   Is anyone following them?
   Have they multiplied themselves/empowered others?
7. *Clarity and Strength of Call*
8. *Missiological Foundation and Clarity*
   Understanding of the world?
   Cross-cultural experience?
   Missiological knowledge (issues, history, best practices, etc.)?
9. *Intrapersonal Character Traits*
   Understanding of self?
   Understanding of suffering?

Deep dependence on God?

Abiding joy?

Track record of perseverance?

Interpersonal Character Traits

Flexibility and teachability?

Servant hearted?

Submissive to authority?

Team oriented?

Practical Skills

What assets and abilities do they bring to the field?

Do they possess the general life skills needed to thrive?

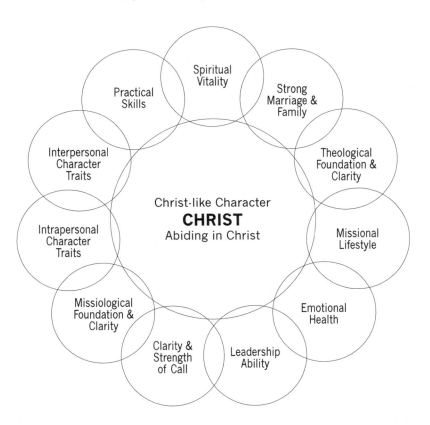

APPENDIX 2

SELF-ASSESSMENT QUESTIONS

The following are the three key areas for missionary preparedness. Take time to answer the following questions honestly and evaluate your own readiness for cross-cultural missions. *Developed at Sojourn Community Church, Louisville, KY*

KNOWING: KNOWING GOD, HIS WORD & HIS MISSION.

1. Do you have a deep understanding of the Bible— the unfolding of the redemptive story, general concepts, and major themes? Are you able to study the Bible for yourself and teach it to others?

2. Do you have a good understanding of theology? Are you able to articulate these truths and teach them to others?

3. Do you have a good understanding of global missions including biblical themes, history, best practices, current trends, practical issues, and definitions of major concepts?

4. Do you have a good understanding of the world outside of America, including world geography, different cultures, global trends, and the state of the global church?

BEING: BEING TRANSFORMED INTO THE IMAGE OF CHRIST

1. Are you practicing a planned and consistent devotional life personally and for your family? How can you grow in this area?

2. Are you being intentional to love and serve your wife/husband, children, and friends? Are you living in open and transparent community with other believers?

3. Do you consistently practice the disciplines of abiding in Christ, confession of sin, solitude, rest, self-denial, and humility?

4. Do you meet the qualifications laid out for elders and deacons in 1 Timothy 3:1–13 and Titus 1:5–16? Which of these do you need to grow in?

5. What emotional baggage do you still carry with you from your past? What are sin struggles you have dealt with in the past, and what are the sins you are currently struggling with?

6. What are character weaknesses that you see in your own life?

DOING: DOING THE WORK OF MINISTRY AND MULTIPLICATION

1. Have your skills, leadership, and calling been tested in the context of the local church? What has this looked like? How are you growing in these areas?

2. Are you living the life of a missionary here in your current context? Are you sharing the gospel with people on a regular basis? Are you discipling believers toward maturity?

3. Do you have significant experience in an international context? Have you spent time overseas (more than short-term trips)? Are you in relationships with internationals in your current context?

4. Outside of ministry skills: what experience, assets, and skills do you have to offer? This might include degrees, work history, hobbies, life experience, etc.

REFERENCES CITED

Bradley, Zach. 2015. *The Sending Church Defined*. Knoxville: The Upstream Collective.

Cook, Harold R. 1974. *An Introduction to Christian Missions*. Chicago, IL: Moody Press.

Crider, Caleb, Larry McCrary, Rodney Calfee, and Wade Stephens. 2013. *Tradecraft: For the Church On Mission*. Portland, OR: Urban Loft Publishers.

Garth, Nathan. 2015. "Grid for Developing Healthy Missionaries." SojournInternational. http://international.sojournchurch .com/wp-content/uploads/2015/07/Grid-for -Developing-Healthy-Missionaries.pdf (accessed July 18, 2015).

Griffiths, Michael. 1974. *Who Really Sends the Missionary?* Chicago, IL: Moody Press.

Hale, Thomas, and Gene Daniels. 2012. *On Being a Missionary*, rev. ed. Pasadena, CA: William Carey Library.

Hoke, Stephen, and William David Taylor. 2009. *Global Mission Handbook: A Guide for Crosscultural Service*. Downers Grove, IL: InterVarsity Press.

Judson, Edward. 1883. *Adoniram Judson, D.D. His Life and Labours*. London: Hodder & Stoughton, https://books.google .com/books/about/Adoniram_Judson_D_D.html?id= Wz4BAAAAQAAJ (accessed July 17, 2015).

McCrary, Larry. 2011. "The Sending Process." The Upstream Collective. https://www.theupstreamcollective .org/documents/missions-leader-assessment (accessed July 3, 2017).

McKaughan, Paul. 1997. "Missionary Attrition: Defining the Problem." In *Too Valuable to Lose: Exploring the Causes and Cures of Missionary Attrition*. Globalization of Mission Series, edited by William David Taylor, 15–24. Pasadena, CA: William Carey Library.

Moreau, A. Scott, Gary Corwin, and Gary B. McGee. 2004. *Introducing World Missions: A Biblical, Historical, and Practical Survey.* Encountering Mission. Grand Rapids, MI: Baker Academic.

Peters, George W. 1984. *A Biblical Theology of Missions.* Chicago, IL: Moody Press.

Phillips, Jere L. 2013. *The Missionary Family: Managing Stress Effectively.* Collierville, TN: Innovo Publishing.

Piper, John. 1995. "The Marks of a Spiritual Leader." Desiring God. http://www.desiringgod.org/articles/the-marks-of -a-spiritual-leader (accessed July 18, 2015).

Pirolo, Neal. 2012. *Serving as Senders Today: How to Care for Your Missionaries as They Prepare to Go, Are On the Field and Return Home.* San Diego, CA: Emmaus Road International.

Steffen, Tom A., and Lois McKinney Douglas. 2008. *Encountering Missionary Life and Work: Preparing for Intercultural Ministry.* Encountering Mission. Grand Rapids, MI: Baker Academic.

Voelkel, Jack. 2007. "Gladys Aylward: Small Woman, Big Heart, Great Faith." Urbana. https://urbana.org/blog/gladys -aylward (accessed July 18, 2015).

A MISSIONARY'S RELATIONSHIP TO SENDING CHURCHES

COMMUNAL AND EXCHANGE DIMENSIONS

David R. Dunaetz

When Joshua and Ashley were first appointed with their mission to a church planting ministry in Central Asia, they were thrilled and honored to be chosen to represent Christ in a country where the gospel had barely taken root. Their first responsibility was to raise financial and prayer support from friends and churches with whom they could share their vision. As millennials this was scary, but doable. Having been successful in everything they had always tried, they counted on God's grace for this undertaking. Sharing their vision and raising support from friends and other individuals with whom they could develop a relationship seemed fairly natural (after an initial period of hesitation). However, as they tried to develop relationships with local churches which had a history of supporting missionaries from their mission, they were not very sure of how to proceed. How bold should they be in asking for support? What did they have that they could offer churches? What did the churches expect of them?

When several churches began supporting them, the questions continued. Should they continue to develop the relationship with these churches or should they explore others? And once they arrived on the field, they still wondered about their relationships with the half dozen churches supporting them. What did the churches expect of them? How should they maintain the relationship? Should they let the churches know how difficult life was for them? Several years later, on their first "home assignment," Joshua and Ashley were still puzzled. How much time should they spend with their churches? How honest should they be about the difficulties they were experiencing on a notoriously discouraging field? Could they expect their churches to help more than they currently were?

To understand some of the issues that Joshua and Ashley need to deal with, as well as some of the concerns that members of Joshua and Ashley's supporting churches might have, we will examine several types of relationships that have been identified by social psychologists. These relationship types will provide a framework for understanding some of the important factors that missionaries should keep in mind in their relationships with their local churches. Missionaries, of course, live in a complex network of relationships that include relationships with various people in their home culture, other missionaries, and people in their host culture. This study is limited to describing one small fraction of these relationships: missionaries and people in their supporting churches.

It should be noted that the social sciences present many frameworks that can be used to understand mission-related phenomena. For example, social psychology, social identity theory (Hogg 2006; Dunaetz 2015), and organizational justice theory (Dunaetz 2010c, 197–221; Colquitt et al. 2001) have provided frameworks that has been applied to missiological topics. From the field of leadership, transformational leadership theory (Riggio et al. 2004) and leader-member exchange theory (Graen and Uhl-Bien 1995) are examples of theoretical frameworks that have many important missiological applications. None of these frameworks in themselves describe all mission-related behavior, and without integrating biblical revelation, they are not capable of giving a complete description of how humans ought to behave. In this study, social exchange theory (Cropanzano and Mitchell 2005) will be examined, specifically applied to relationships (Clark and Mills 2011, 232–50), in order to better understand how human nature plays out in missiological contexts.

COMMUNAL RELATIONSHIPS

A *communal relationship* is a relationship where at least one member responds to the other's needs non-contingently, that is, without condition (Clark and Mills 1979; Clark and Mills 2011, 232–50). A parent's relationship with a baby is a relationship that corresponds closely to the ideal of this model. Parents typically respond to a baby's needs without the requirement or expectation that the baby responds in kind or even thanks the parents for responding to his or her needs.   A young couple in love typically has a communal relationship as well. One partner does not keep track of the past responses of the other before meeting a perceived need. Each partner is intrinsically motivated to meet the other's needs out of love for one another.

Communal relationships are thus characterized by a concern for the other that is similar to the Christian concept of God's ἀγάπη love (John 3:16; Rom 5:8). Just as God loves humans unconditionally and sent his Son to respond to their need, a member of a communal relationship will respond to the other's needs unconditionally. Similarly, Christians are to respond to one another with unconditional love (Rom 13:8–10; 1 Cor 13:1–13).

This would seem to imply that Joshua and Ashley should seek to have a communal relationship with their sending churches. Shouldn't the sending churches respond unconditionally to the needs of the young missionaries, and shouldn't Joshua and Ashley also respond unconditionally to the needs of their supporting churches?

If Joshua and Ashley had a 100 percent communal relationship with their supporting churches, all the resources (including financial) that the churches possessed would be available for Ashley and Joshua and all of Joshua and Ashley's resources (including their physical presence) would be available for the churches. However, in most situations, this is not possible. Churches are constrained by their budgets and Joshua and Ashley will not be able to commute between their supporting churches and Central

Asia very often. The relationship between Joshua and Ashley and their supporting churches is different than a communal relationship between a parent and a child or between a husband and wife. It is, in fact, quite different. Neither Joshua and Ashley nor their churches can realistically expect the other to track and attempt to respond to all their needs. Although a communal relationship might be ideal, the limited resources of each party do not allow for this possibility.

It should be noted that these limitations in no way reduce the Christian responsibility to love God and other Christians with all the resources that one has. Whether one has one, five, or ten talents, the Christian is responsible for using them all for all God's service (Matt 25:14–30). Acknowledging one's limitations is simply a means of recognizing one's humble condition, a necessary condition for serving God (Rom 12:1–3).

EXCHANGE RELATIONSHIPS

In contrast to communal relationships, *exchange relationships* are characterized by an expectation that both parties will provide comparable benefits to each other (Clark and Mills 1979; Clark and Mills 2011, 232–50). Exchange relationships may be characterized by material exchange (e.g., hiring a plumber to unclog a drain), but most exchange relationships among people who know each other are better described by social exchange (Cropanzano and Mitchell 2005), an exchange of non-material benefits such as approval, trust, esteem, or support.

In the New Testament, various exchange relationships are assumed to play an important role in the life of believers. Employers must faithfully fulfill their commitments to their employees (James 5:1–6). Within the Christian community, Christians are expected to have mutually beneficial relationships, characterized by honoring one another (Rom 12:10), serving one another (Gal 5:13), and being kind and compassionate to one other (Eph 4:32).

Able people who do not contribute to their own needs are to be excluded from the benefits of being part of the Christian community (2 Thess 3:10–15). An especially important example of an exchange relationship is seen in Paul's appeal to Philemon to liberate his slave Onesimus, "If he has done anything wrong or owes you anything, charge it to me. . . . I will pay it back—not to mention that you owe me your very self. I do wish, brother, that I may have some benefit from you in the Lord" (Phlm 17–19 NIV).

Just as Paul and Philemon could expect, or just as a pastor and a church can expect a mutually beneficial exchange (e.g. salary and status for providing godly and biblical leadership to the church), Joshua and Ashley's churches might expect the young couple to faithfully proclaim the gospel and make disciples in an unevangelized area in exchange for their financial and prayer support. Similarly, Joshua and Ashley will carry out their ministry, report on the progress they make and the difficulties they encounter, and visit their supporting churches every few years in exchange for their continued support. If for some reason either Joshua and Ashley or one of their churches can no longer carry on this exchange, the other party will most likely graciously understand. The relationship will either end or, at least, become significantly different.

Although most likely neither party would want to sit down and define a contract or explicitly state that there are expectations that must be met for the relationship to continue,[1] understanding that Joshua and Ashley's relationship with their supporting churches has many characteristics of an exchange relationship can help them understand how they should interact with their supporting churches. It can also help their supporting churches better understand how to manage their limited resources to best respond to Joshua and Ashley's needs.

---

1. However, such contracts may exist. A biblical example is found in Acts 15 where the Council of Jerusalem requires gentile converts to abstain from certain behaviors (but not to be circumcised) in order for the relationship to continue in good standing.

BENEFITS MISSIONARIES AND CHURCHES PROVIDE TO EACH OTHER

Although an exhaustive list is not possible because of the unique situation and characteristics of both missionaries and churches, there are several layers of benefits that missionaries and churches provide to each other. There are both explicit and implicit reasons that missionaries and churches may enter into a relationship. None of these reasons would be true in every relationship between a missionary and a supporting church, but they may serve as examples illustrating the complex nature of these relationships.

The explicit reasons churches support missionaries include strategically spreading the gospel, making disciples among unevangelized people groups, and participation in relief and development ministries. However, there are other benefits that missionaries provide churches that are often not stated. Missionary families often serve as a model of a committed Christian family; in many churches, missionary families are the only families who are regularly invited on stage or who have their family portraits distributed via prayer cards and publicity materials. Missionaries also provide churches with ministry opportunities for short-term missions. Many youth groups seek to coordinate short-term travel and ministry opportunities with missionaries whom the church supports.

Missionaries also provide supporting churches encouragement and affirmation of the churches' values. Stories told by visiting missionaries serve as evidence of the gospel's universal relevance, affirming the foundational values of church members. Photos of missions work, especially relief work, provide motivating visuals for fundraising and offerings; it is easier for a church to collect an offering by mentioning relief work in a drought-stricken country than the salaries of the pastoral staff.

In special situations, missionaries may provide affirmation for doctrinal and theological distinctives of specific churches or denominations. A missionary church planter with a long history of success in evangelism and disciple-making was once told by a supporting church that funds would be cut unless he spent a certain number of hours per week reading and studying the Bible. This fit the missionary's theological framework, so he agreed to the commitment and the church responded by a very large increase in support. In another situation, a church went through a doctrinal shift and asked their missionaries to sign the new confession of faith which included a blanket condemnation of the present-day use of sign gifts, attributing their presence to Satan. Missionaries who refused to support the new confession of faith were cut from the budget.

The reasons that missionaries develop and maintain relationships with churches are typically stated less explicitly. It is generally accepted that within North American evangelical culture, apart from some specific denominations, missionaries must raise support from interested churches and individuals. The request for financial support is typically implicit when a missionary contacts a church. Nevertheless, it is acceptable, and even expected, for missionaries to specifically request prayer for their ministry. An explicit request for prayer support affirms both the missionary's and the church's belief in the omnipotence and benevolence of God. In contrast, explicit requests for financial support can make the missionary come across as self-centered or insensitive to the church's limited resources.

Emotional support is an important benefit that churches provide to missionaries. A church may send gifts or visitors to the missionaries while they are on the field, providing an opportunity to connect to their home culture and enjoy aspects of it that are not available in their host culture. Similarly, some churches may send short-term teams who may provide a useful service for the missionary. When the missionaries are on home assignment, the supporting churches may also provide affirmation through public presentations involving the missionaries. In general, the affirmation provided to the missionary is proportional to the status of audience (speaking to adults is more affirming than speaking to children), the size of the audience (Sunday morning worship service versus a home Bible study group), and the length of time allotted to the missionary's presentation.

UNDERSTANDING EXCHANGE RELATIONSHIPS

By understanding that their relationships with their supporting churches have many characteristics of exchange relationships, Joshua and Ashley can better understand how to maintain and develop these relationships. Several important phenomena which apply to exchange relationships have been empirically studied in social psychology such as cost-benefit analyses, power imbalances, relationship alternatives, and relationship investments (Kelley and Thibaut 1978; Emerson 2006; Cropanzano and Mitchell 2005). If Joshua and Ashley understand how these phenomena are likely to play out in their relationships with their supporting churches, they can better understand what they need to do to develop and maintain satisfying relationships with their churches, reducing (but not eliminating) the confusion and uncertainty that are associated with missionary-church relations.

COST-BENEFIT ANALYSES

Studies in social exchange theory (Kelley and Thibaut 1978; Kelley et al. 2003; Cropanzano and Mitchell 2005) have demonstrated that exchange relationships are maintained and developed when both parties view themselves as net beneficiaries in a cost-benefit analysis. A cost-benefit analysis is traditionally a tool used to determine if a business action should be undertaken or not. If the benefits are greater than the costs, then it will be a profitable enterprise. The costs and benefits associated with relationships range from the material to the emotional (Lawler 2001). The costs and benefits associated with entering into a relationship predict whether or not people will choose to enter into a relationship with each other. If the benefits of being supported by First Church are greater than the costs associated with the relationship, Joshua and Ashley will want to enter into a relationship with the church. Similarly, if the benefits to First Church outweigh the costs, First Church will want to enter into a relationship with Joshua and Ashley. Once they have entered into a relationship, the desire to maintain it will be greater if the cost-benefit analyses performed (typically subconsciously) by First Church and by Joshua and Ashley are both positive.

For Joshua and Ashley, this means that they need to demonstrate that they are worthy of support. They need to communicate a clear vision of what they believe God is calling and enabling them to do. Before they leave for Central Asia, they need to demonstrate through their vision and the ministry opportunities that they have in First Church that they will be worth more than the cost of money and prayer that First Church will provide them. Once they are supported, they need to clearly communicate what the benefits of their ministry are: what they see God doing, who is being changed by the gospel, how the gospel is taking root in their host culture. If the benefits for First Church outweigh the costs, the church will desire to continue the relationship.

Although cost-benefit analyses may seem cold and calculated when applied to relationships, the Bible provides several examples which assume that a social exchange analysis is rational and appropriate. Moses concluded that the costs and benefits of being identified with the people of God outweighed the costs and benefits of sin (Heb 11:25). Jesus told several parables illustrating the costs and benefits of the kingdom of God (the parable of the pearl of great price, Matt 13:45–46 and parable of the hidden treasure, Matt 13:44). He encouraged potential disciples to count the cost of following him (Luke 14:25–33). The costs of discipleship include forsaking family and wealth, but the benefits are a hundred times as valuable and include eternal life (Matt 19:16–30). Jesus's teaching that it is better to give than to receive (Acts 20:35) is an especially important illustration of social exchange: the social and psychological benefits of giving outweigh the material costs involved and are even greater than the receiver's benefits.

POWER IMBALANCES

In a typical relationship between a church and a missionary, the missionary needs the church more than the church needs the missionary. It is much easier for a church to find a missionary to support than for a missionary to find a supporting church. It may take several years for missionaries to build their support base before they can move overseas. However, churches may have several missionaries contact them each week seeking support. In the relational theory of power, the power that Person 1 has over Person 2 is defined as the degree to which Person 2 is dependent on Person 1 (Emerson 1962; Cook et al. 2006, 194–216; Wilmot and Hocker 2011, 115–117). Since Joshua and Ashley are more dependent on First Church than First Church is dependent on Joshua and Ashley, First Church has more power in the relationship. Joshua and Ashley will be more concerned about maintaining the missionary-church relationship than First Church will be.

Power imbalances have a number of important effects on the lower power member of the relationship (Keltner et al. 2003). First, people with low power in a relationship tend to experience more negative emotions than high power people. Second, they become very sensitive to threats from the other party in the relationship. In Joshua and Ashley's case, this means they are likely to be afraid if they sense anything negative happening in their relationship with their supporting churches. If someone from one of the churches is offended by something in a prayer letter or social media, or by something they say on home assignment, this will likely be a source of distress for them since it could potentially mean losing the church's support. Certainly, missionaries must always speak and act with integrity. But there is always a risk that whatever they say or do may be misinterpreted. However, "God has not given us a spirit of timidity, but of power and love and discipline" (2 Tim 1:7 NASB). Such a situation of weakness thus provides new opportunities to trust him.

A third consequence of low power is inhibited behavior (Keltner et al. 2003). Joshua and Ashley will want to continually make a good impression on their supporting churches and are likely not to share any information that would cast them or the effectiveness of their ministry in a negative light. They might be transparent about difficulties that they encounter (e.g., the difficulty of language learning or the people's resistance to the gospel), but they will not likely be transparent about their own weaknesses and mistakes (e.g., failing a language program or getting angry at a colleague). Such transparency could reduce their churches' perceptions of the benefits they are receiving from supporting Joshua and Ashley.

This means that Joshua and Ashley need to have close friends with whom they can share their struggles without the fear of rejection or damaging the relationship. This would most likely be a relationship with a peer on the field where there is no power imbalance (such as a fellow missionary or a national pastor). It could also be with an empowering supervisor if Joshua and Ashley could be sure that they would not suffer negative consequences for sharing bad news. However, if the supervisor cannot be trusted to respond in an encouraging way, the power differential is likely to prevent such communication.

COMPARISON LEVELS

Social exchange theory predicts that missionaries and churches are more likely to form and maintain relationships if the benefits for each party are greater than the costs. More precisely, the relationship will be satisfying if the benefits exceed the costs by a margin known as the *comparison level* (Thibaut and Kelley 1959, 21–24; Cropanzano and Mitchell 2005). This comparison level is the sum of all the expectations of what one party believes is the correct and appropriate net level of benefits that one should receive from the relationship. If the net benefits are less than the comparison level (less than expectations), the relationship will not be satisfying. For example, if a church expects Joshua and Ashley to regularly send encouraging prayer letters and to visit the church every few years, bringing their children to be seen on stage and to interact with others in Sunday school, Awana, and the foyer after the worship service, the church may not find the relationship very satisfying if Joshua and Ashley, in fact, leave their children with grandparents on most Sundays during home assignment.

The comparison level is thus the level of expectations that one party has for the other in order for the relationship to be satisfying, which increases the likelihood of it continuing. For missionaries, this means they need to learn each church's expectations and try to meet them. Each church may have different expectations and these expectations may change as pastoral staff and mission committees evolve. Joshua and Ashley thus need to get to know the expectations of each church that supports them. This may be difficult and time consuming, especially since the expectations change with time. In addition, once Joshua and Ashley begin to master their new Central Asian culture, understanding the expectations of their supporting churches may be even more difficult due to *cultural interference* (Mackey 2000, 26–54) in which knowledge gained from one culture interferes with being able to function in another in the most culturally appropriate way. Meeting with leaders from within their supporting churches, discussing expectations, and generally building up personal relationships are strategies that Joshua and Ashley can use to ensure that their relationships with these churches remain satisfying.

Social exchange theory also posits another comparison level, the *comparison level for alternatives* (Dunbar 2015; Thibaut and Kelley 1959, 21–24). This is the level of benefits that one could expect to have if one relationship is terminated in order to enter into another relationship. It is generally lower than the comparison level described above and sets the minimum level of satisfaction that one party must experience in order to maintain the relationship and not pursue another. For example, if First Church is disappointed in Joshua and Ashley's ministry, on-field communication, or home assignment presentations, they may consider supporting alternative missionaries instead. If there is a continual stream of attractive candidates who contact the church, the comparison level of alternatives may be relatively high. This means that not only should Joshua and Ashley try to meet the expectations of their supporting churches, but they should also try to provide benefits to these churches beyond what other missionaries seeking support can provide, especially if it is not possible to meet all of these churches' expectations. Although this may not be possible in every church, if Joshua and Ashley get to know the specific needs and expectations of their supporting churches and key leaders, they may be able to reach this goal with the churches that they know best.

INVESTMENTS

We can summarize social exchange theory up to this point with simple mathematical models. These models are not meant to describe precisely how these various factors relate to each other. Rather, they simply show which of the variables in question contribute to and which take away from the various outcomes. Many other variables influence these outcomes (ranging from personal differences in the people involved to divine intervention) which are not included in these models. In addition, we can only measure these variables roughly. God alone knows the true and ultimate value of all that we observe.

Our first model is an equation that gives a rough estimate of how satisfying a church-missionary relationship is:

$$\text{Satisfaction} = \text{Benefits} - \text{Costs} - \text{Expectations}$$

The church-relationship will be satisfying if the benefits received from the relationship outweigh the costs, and if this net difference is greater than the expectations for the relationship (used as the comparison level).

This satisfaction can be used to predict if the relationship will be maintained or abandoned, in light of the alternatives:

COMMITMENT = SATISFACTION – VALUE OF ALTERNATIVES

Each party will be committed to remaining in the relationship if the satisfaction obtained by a relationship (Equation 1) is greater than the value of the alternatives (the comparison level for alternatives). If First Church believes that their relationship with Joshua and Ashley is more satisfying than would be a new relationship with some missionaries who could replace them in the budget, it is likely that Joshua and Ashley will continue to receive support from First Church.

However, when actually measuring human behavior, Caryl Rusbult of the Free University of Amsterdam (Rusbult 1980; Rusbult and Farrell 1983; Rusbult et al. 2011, 218–231) found that adding a third term, *investment*, to Equation 2 produces a much more accurate model of human behavior over a wide range of contexts:

COMMITMENT = SATISFACTION + INVESTMENT – VALUE OF ALTERNATIVES

Investments refer to resources that are linked to the relationship and would be lost if the relationship would end (Rusbult et al. 1998). For a married couple, these investments might include happy memories, financial resources, possessions, common friends, respect in the community, and plans for the future. When the investment level is high, a couple is more likely to stay in a relationship. The same thing is true in other types of relationships, including missionary-church relationships. Investments might include memories and knowledge of each other, the church's financial investment in the missionaries, or visits made to the field by church members.

The range of investments can be quite broad, divided into two categories (Rusbult and Farrell 1983). *Intrinsic investments* are valuable resources that have been spent for the sake of the relationship. This might mean the time and effort that the missionaries have given to the church as well as the money that the church has provided to the missionary. On a personal level, the time and effort given by the individual members of the church and by the missionaries to develop individual relationships within the church may also be considered intrinsic investments. *Extrinsic investments* are valuable resources that have developed over time and have become linked to the relationship. This would include shared memories of past interactions, a sense of identity that has developed, and foreseen future benefits such as the fulfillment of the missionary's vision for ministry.

An important application of this model relates to how missionaries can maintain a relationship with churches even during the difficult times where the benefits provided by the missionary are low. Since the time of Paul, missionaries have passed through very trying experiences (2 Cor 4:8–9). This may be due to environmental and cultural stress (Dunaetz 2013), organizational dysfunction at the mission level (Dunaetz 2010c, 197–221), competition and conflict between organizations (Dunaetz 2010a), church dysfunction (Dunaetz 2008), missionary team dysfunction (Dunaetz 2010b), or many other problems that prevent missionaries from providing their supporters the hoped-for benefits of a fruitful ministry. If Joshua and Ashley experience trying times that prevent them from providing many benefits to their supporting churches, Equation 3 indicates that the church will remain committed to them, even if other promising missionaries are knocking on the door, if the churches and the missionaries have made sufficient investments in the missionary-church relationship.

If, in fact, sufficient investments have been made in the church-missionary relationship, the relationship begins to take on characteristics of a communal relationship, the type of relationship where all resources are shared regardless of the benefits that the church or the missionary receive from each other. Even if the cost-benefit analysis is negative, the relationship will remain intact because of the commitment to the relationship. As noted earlier, a communal relationship approaches the biblical concept of love and would be the ideal type of missionary-church relationship. The principle limitation mentioned earlier was that both the churches and missionaries have finite resources. However, when sufficient investments have been poured into a relationship, all the existing resources become available for meeting the needs that arise. Thus, it becomes clear for Joshua and Ashley, and for the sake of the mission to which God has called them, that they should do all they can to invest in the relationships with the churches who express an interest in supporting them.

APPLICATIONS

While the foundation of all missionary action needs to be based on a biblical theology, other tools such as history or the social sciences provide insight into how one can best serve Christ in one's specific cultural and historical context. In twenty-first century North America, social exchange theory is one such tool that can be used to describe relationships between missionaries and churches. Joshua and Ashley thus have several broad principles that they can use to help them decide how to best relate to the churches that support them. The first principle is that they should not assume that they have a communal relationship with their churches characterized by unconditional love and a complete sharing of resources. Rather, they should view their relationship as an exchange relationship, where both they and their churches have something that can benefit the other.

Their relationship will be at least minimally stable if they provide mutual benefits to one another.

A second principle is that Joshua and Ashley should provide as many benefits as possible to their supporting (and potentially supporting) churches to make the relationship more attractive. They will want to ensure that any subconscious cost-benefit analysis done by a church would indicate that the benefits that come from supporting them, both financially and with prayer, are greater than the costs involved. The benefits that they can provide the supporting church are numerous: the evangelization of an unreached people group, warm personal relationships with people in the church, a vision of how the gospel can transform a culture, interesting Sunday school lessons for both children and adults, and any other services that they can provide the church. Joshua and Ashley thus need to learn what aspects of their ministry are valued by each of their churches and clearly communicate to them how they are bringing about the desired outcomes in their host country as well as how they can provide desired services to the churches when they are serving in their home country.

It can be noted that these first two principles are also applicable to churches. Churches need to understand their missionaries' contexts well enough to know what their needs are. They should respond to as many of these needs as they can, not just to the financial ones. This will make the relationship stronger and provide a greater sense of partnership in fulfilling the Great Commission.

A third principle for Joshua and Ashley is that they should invest in their relationship with their supporting churches so that the relationship continues even when they pass through difficult periods of life and ministry. This means getting to know the decision-makers, gatekeepers, and key communicators in the church, building relationships with them, and continually sharing their vision with them. As the membership of the church evolves over the years, they need to continue to meet and develop relationships with each succeeding generation of church leadership, especially the lead pastor, the missions pastor, and mission committee members, depending on the structure of the church.

A final principle is that they need to trust the Lord, even in a position of weakness. Because they probably need financial and prayer support from the church more than a church needs an additional missionary family, Joshua and Ashley are in a position of weakness. Rather than fretting about their relationships with the churches, they should proclaim their vision with confidence in the Lord and work wholeheartedly toward achieving it, committing themselves completely to their ministry and to loving those who support them.

REFERENCES CITED

Clark, Margaret S. and Judson R Mills. 1979. "Interpersonal Attraction in Exchange and Communal Relationships." *Journal of Personality and Social Psychology* 37: 12–24.

———. 2011. "A Theory of Communal (and Exchange) Relationships." In *Handbook of Theories of Social Psychology*, edited by P. A. M. van Lange, A. W. Kruglanski, and E. T. Higgins. Los Angeles, CA: Sage.

Colquitt, Jason A., Donald E Conlon, Michael J. Wesson, Christopher Porter, and K. Yee Ng. 2001. "Justice at the Millennium: A Meta-Analytic Review of 25 Years of Organizational Justice Research." *Journal of Applied Psychology* 86: 425–445.

Cook, Karen S., Coye Cheshire, and Alexandra Gerbasi. 2006. "Power, Dependence, and Social Exchange." In *Contemporary Social Psychological Theories*, edited by P. J. Burke. Stanford, CA: Stanford Social Sciences.

Cropanzano, Russell and Marie S. Mitchell. 2005. "Social Exchange Theory: An Interdisciplinary Review." *Journal of Management* 31: 874–900.

Dunaetz, David R. 2008. "Transforming Chaos into Beauty: Intentionally Developing Unity in Church Plants." *Evangelical Missions Quarterly* 44: 358–365.

———. 2010a. "Christian Cooperation and Ministry Effectiveness: Insights and Applications from Empirical Research in Group Processes." *Dharma Deepika: A South Asian Journal of Missiological Research* 14: 17–26.

———. 2010b. "Good Teams, Bad Teams: Under What Conditions do Missionary Teams Function Effectively?" *Evangelical Missions Quarterly* 46: 442–449.

———. 2010c. "Organizational Justice: Perceptions of Being Treated Fairly." In *Serving Jesus with Integrity: Ethics and Accountability in Mission*, edited by D. Baker, and D. Hayward. Pasadena, CA: William Carey Library.

———. 2013. "Finding Still Waters and Green Pastures: Understanding and Reducing Stress in Urban Church Planting." *Great Commission Research Journal* 4: 235–50.

———. 2015. "Three Models of Acculturation: Applications for Developing a Church Planting Strategy Among Diaspora Populations." In *Diaspora Missiology*, edited by E. Wan and M. Pocock. Pasadena, CA: William Carey Library.

Dunbar, Norah E. 2015. "A Review of Theoretical Approaches to Interpersonal Power." *Review of Communication* 15: 1–18.

Emerson, Richard E. 1962. "Power-Dependence Relations." *American Sociological Review* 27 31–41.

Graen, George B. and Mary Uhl-Bien. 1995. "Relationship-Based Approach to Leadership: Development of Leader-Member Exchange (LMX) Theory of Leadership over 25 Years: Applying a Multi-Level Multi-Domain Perspective." *The Leadership Quarterly* 6: 219–47.

Hogg, Michael A. 2006. "Social Identity Theory." In *Contemporary Social Psychological Theories*, edited by P. J. Burke. Stanford, CA: Stanford University Press.

Kelley, Harold H., John G. Holmes, Norbert L. Kerr, Harry T. Reis, Caryl E. Rusbult, and Paul A. M. van Lange. 2003. *An Atlas of Interpersonal Situations.* Cambridge: Cambridge University Press.

Kelley, Harold H. and John W. Thibaut. 1978. *Interpersonal Relations: A Theory of Interdependence.* New York, NY: John Wiley and Sons.

Keltner, Dacher, Deborah H. Gruenfeld, and Cameron Anderson. 2003. "Power, Approach, and Inhibition." *Psychological Review* 110: 265–84.

Lawler, Edward J. 2001. "An Affect Theory of Social Exchange." *American Journal of Sociology* 107: 321–52.

Mackey, William F. 2000. "The Description of Bilingualism." In *The Bilingualism Reader,* edited by L. Wei. New York, NY: Routledge.

Riggio, Ronald E., Bernard M. Bass, and Sarah Smith Orr. 2004. "Transformational Leadership in Nonprofit Organizations." In *Improving Leadership in Nonprofit Organizations,* edited by R. E. Riggio, and S. Smith Orr. San Francisco, CA: Jossey-Bass.

Rusbult, Caryl E. 1980. "Commitment and Satisfaction in Romantic Associations: A Test of the Investment Model." *Journal of Experimental Social Psychology* 16: 172–86.

Rusbult, Caryl E., Christopher R. Agnew, and Ximena B. Arriaga, 2011. "The Investment Model of Commitment Processes." In *Handbook of Theories of Social* Psychology, edited by P. A. M. van Lange, A. W. Kruglanski, and E. T. Higgins. Thousand Oaks, CA: Sage.

Rusbult, Caryl E. and Dan Farrell. 1983. "A Longitudinal Test of the Investment Model: The Impact on Job Satisfaction, Job Commitment, and Turnover of Variations in Rewards, Costs, Alternatives, and Investments." *Journal of Applied Psychology* 68: 429–38.

Rusbult, Caryl E., John M. Martz, and Christopher R. Agnew. 1998. "The Investment Model Scale: Measuring Commitment Level, Satisfaction Level, Quality of Alternatives, and Investment Size." *Personal Relationships* 5: 357–87.

Thibaut, John W. and Harold H. Kelley. 1959. *The Social Psychology of Groups*. New York, NY: Wiley and Sons.

Wilmot, William W. and Joyce L. Hocker. 2011. *Interpersonal Conflict*. New York, NY: McGraw Hill.

15 EDUCATING TODAY'S PASTORS TOWARD AN APOSTOLIC IMAGINATION

J. D. Payne

The history of the seminary is closely connected to the training of pastors and missionaries to serve churches and advance the gospel. At a time when the discipline of missiology is going through changes, including a change in nomenclature (Newell 2015, 46ff), how can missiologists serving in academia better prepare pastors to lead churches in Great Commission endeavors? The purpose of this paper is to briefly address two challenges to this task and provide six guidelines to assist educators in the classroom.

Though the seminary trains students for a variety of Great Commission roles, this paper is written from the conviction that the pastor (i.e., lead pastor, senior pastor, primary pastor) is the most important individual when it comes to a local church understanding and engaging in the mission of God. John R. Mott stated it well in his 1904 publication, *The Pastor and Modern Missions: A Plea for Leadership in World Evangelization*:

> The secret of enabling the home Church to press her advantage in the non-Christian world is one of leadership. The people do not go beyond their leaders in knowledge and zeal, nor surpass them in consecration and sacrifice. The Christian pastor, minister, rector—whatever he may be denominated—holds the divinely appointed office for inspiring and guiding the thought and activities of the Church. By virtue of his position he can be a mighty force in the world's evangelization (1904, vii–viii).

Wherever you find a pastor with overflowing missionary zeal and knowledge, you will find an earnest missionary church (1904, 51).

The pastor's position gives him authority; his character and work give him vast influence. The pastor is the educator of the church. There is no other way to get the ear of the whole church save through him. It cannot be done through the women's missionary society, or the young people's society, or the Sunday-school. He has direct and influential access to all the members. Any idea which he persistently preaches and prays for in the pulpit will be gradually accepted as a rule of conduct by the people (1904, 51).

Apart from the pastor's direct leadership and regular attention to missions, a local church is unlikely to be involved in intentional, sacrificial, and perennial global disciple-making activities. The missiological education of today's pastor is critical to the Great Commission task.

METHODOLOGY

Much of my research methodology is based on anecdotal evidence gathered from conversations with other seminary-trained pastors and my ministerial experience. Regarding the former, I regularly find myself in conversations with pastors discussing matters related to equipping the saints for the work of the ministry (Eph 4:11–12). Such pastors are generally quick to share their thoughts on what is needed in the missiological education of pastors.

The second source of evidence comes from my personal experience over the past twenty-five years. Of course, evidence drawn from this source is biased and limited; nevertheless, there is much value in experience. As I enter into the latter half of my third decade of ministry, the Lord has graciously allowed me to serve in various capacities that have shaped my perspective on the topic of this paper.

Much of my journey has involved simultaneous ministry in the local church and the classroom. I served as a full-time missions professor for ten years at a seminary in the US. When part-time and adjunctive teaching are factored into my academic career, the duration of my teaching experience increases to eighteen years and counting. I also served nine years with a North American mission agency, with responsibilities involving recruiting, training, and networking church planters and pastors. In addition, over these twenty-five years, eighteen years have involved pastoral ministry with local churches. My present ministry as pastor of church multiplication includes the training of church members to be sent from our church to serve as church planters among unreached people groups and as pastors of established churches.

THE CHALLENGE OF DEFENDING THE DISCIPLINE

Missiologists face at least two challenges that work against the discipline of saturating the hearts and minds of a younger generation of pastoral leaders. The first challenge is the tension that often exists in academia between missiology and theology. Missiology has often been seen as a "Johnny-come-lately" by leaders in other theological disciplines. When it did arrive in the academy, according to Craig Van Gelder, the "focus was more on practices and pragmatics than on theology and theory" and it was seen as "a type of theological stepchild" (2014, 40). Van Gelder also noted that even today the discipline "still struggles to find its voice within the larger theological curriculum" (2014, 52). Sometimes missiology is understood as a sub-category of pastoral theology studies. Other times the discipline is allowed to have its own department, yet is looked upon with suspicion, considered non-theological, filled with pragmatists, and being primarily concerned with telling old missionary stories about jungles and eating bugs. This has often created an inferiority complex resulting in missiologists spending energies attempting to justify themselves and their teachings before their colleagues while simultaneously trying to teach students.

Related to this challenge is the desire to justify the discipline before a generation often disconnected from the discipline. If seminarians are only required to take one or two missiology courses (if any at all!), then the missiologist oftentimes finds him or herself spending class time giving an apologia for missiology in order to teach the content of the course. If missiology is not a value that permeates the academy, then in the mind of the student, those one to two courses are likely to be perceived as "hoops to jump through" on the way to receiving the coveted diploma.

THE CHALLENGE OF PASTORAL IMAGINATION

The second challenge is that a pastoral hegemony exists that allows little room for apostolic thought and the development of needed structures for mission.[1] Given the daily requirements of pastoral ministry, it is easy for the busy pastor to overlook the church's missionary activity or atomize missionary labors to an isolated department within the church's organization.

Yet, even the pastor with strong convictions regarding the evangelistic nature and practice of the church generally filters such convictions through a pastoral, rather than a missionary perspective. The result is the application of strategy and methods more conducive to local church growth and pastoral care. Rather than seeing the need to send teams of disciple-makers to plant churches from the harvest and raise up pastors from those new churches (e.g., Acts 13–14), missionary activity is more pastoral. This reality

---

1. At this point, it is worth reminding the reader that a pastor is writing this paper with high regard for the pastoral calling and ministry.

is seen in commonly asked questions. How do we find pastors to lead church planting efforts? Where will we find enough Christians to start a church? Do we have a praise team, children's leaders, and a bank account in the yet-to-be-planted church's name? The concern for global disciple-making begins with finding long-term kingdom citizens to self-identify as a church instead of reaching their community. Rather than beginning with a conviction of not building upon another person's foundation (Rom 15:20), the starting point is another person's foundation.

The heart of the shepherd should be set to care for the church of Christ (1 Pet 5:2–3). Numerous needs pull the pastor's attention in different directions. The challenge for missiologists is: *pastors need to be taught to think apostolically while remaining pastoral in their callings.* Pastors may pay attention if value can be shown in the discipline of missiology. And one of the many ways to show value is to teach them how to develop and use an apostolic imagination.

Part of the reason for the apostolic omission in the pastoral imagination is that the church in the United States defines ministry in pastoral concepts, methods, and strategies. Pastoral ministry is the default category, a matter that has been in place for centuries. Alan Hirsch and Tim Catchim commented, "the linguistic categories that an organization uses can shape how it conceives of core tasks" (2012, 12). What has been modeled before pastors is pastoral ministry. Therefore, even missionary activity, especially in the West, is now defined and organized in pastoral structures. When it comes to the missionary activity of the local church, pastors should be looking for and equipping apostolic-type individuals rather than the expected pastoral-type individuals. However, the present imagination only believes in the existence of the latter.[2]

---

2. An exception may be the openness to missionaries who are to serve "overseas." Of course, this exception raises the issue: if pastoral ministry is understood as "home" ministry, then what about the "missional" or "apostolic" at home?

If apostolic labors were not needed for global disciple-making, then the pastoral imagination would not pose a challenge. However, whenever pastors are expected to do missionary activities and missionaries are expected to function long-term as pastors, problems are likely to follow. There are differing gifts and functions in the body of Christ (Rom 12:4–6). Many pastors fail to recognize the apostolic nature and functions of the local church through her members. Practically, this means missiologists must teach pastors that missionary activity is here, there, and everywhere.

SIX GUIDELINES FOR EDUCATING PASTORS

In view of these challenges, what are some ways missiologists could serve the church (and academy) in the twenty-first century? What are some ways educators may provide both academic credibility and also pastoral value? The following are six guidelines to assist in educating pastors toward an apostolic imagination. While I am certain other important points should be added, this list serves as a starting point for missiologists to prepare for this Monday's lecture, next year's course, and the future of their department.

MAINTAIN HIGH ACADEMIC STANDARDS, BUT ANSWER THE "SO WHAT?"

As followers of Jesus, missiologists must be wise stewards with their scholastic abilities. Research must continue, but missiologists do not have the option of whether or not they will apply their missiology. Missiology that matters is missiology applied. However, those interested in the discipline seem to be divided into two camps with different concerns. In an article related to the future of missiology, Charles Fensham shared:

> Academics who are asking questions about teaching in the seminary and college appear concerned with graduate students in missiology and with further scholarship in the field.

> Practitioners and board/agency staff seem to be
> asking questions about pushing missiology out of
> the academy and more into the grassroots, where
> it can focus on the relationship between academy
> and church, and the definition of terms (2014, 86).

It is most unfortunate that this distinction is present. There should be no dichotomy between research and the application of such findings to the field.

While pragmatism is a philosophy that should be avoided by kingdom citizens, kingdom life is to be pragmatic. The church is called to make disciples (Matt 28:19) and bear fruit (John 15:5). In order for missiology to be relevant, it must move from the theoretical to the practical.

As a freshman in high school, I found myself frustrated, uninterested, and unengaged in algebra for one main reason: the teacher failed to show the class how the subject connected to life. On a few occasions, some brave student would ask, "But what does this have to do with life?" The answer was something to the effect, "It will prepare you for more advanced math courses." Missiologists seeking to develop an apostolic imagination in their students need a better answer than, "It is important to know this because you are likely to see it again on the final exam."

Pastors want to know what difference it makes to gospel proclamation and sanctification when they hear of theories of orality, honor and shame societies, or the methods of Cyril and Methodius. Multivariate statistics, regression analysis, and participant-observation are important and valuable to missiological research. But a failure to make the connection between the halls of the academia and the local church is another reason pastors will refuse to find value in the discipline.

If missiologists are not careful, the discipline will become more and more academic, eventually disconnecting from the local church. It was mentioned above that a present temptation exists for missiologists to defend the discipline in the theological academy. However, another related temptation is present before missiologists: the opportunity to become more scholastic so as to prove that they are equivalent to mainstream sociologists and anthropologists. Should missiologists draw from the best in the social sciences? Yes, but there should be no competition. If missiologists attempt to create a competition to prove that missiology, or intercultural studies, or whatever we are calling our discipline, is just as legitimate as something found in a secular academy, the church will lose every time. We should not feel inferior; the kingdom does not advance with the best offerings of Levi-Strauss, Durkheim, and Weber.

LISTEN TO THE CHURCHES, BUT LEAD TO AND THROUGH BLIND SPOTS

In an article on the application of theological studies to field practices, Arch Chee Keen Wong concluded that seminary faculty should spend more time listening to those in the field in order to have a healthy connection between the classroom and practice. He wrote: "Faculty must come to see that sustained interaction with both pastors and students must inform their teaching and scholarship if they expect their students to integrate formal learning and pastoral work" (2009, 251).

While a strong temptation exists to teach without understanding, the kingdom would be well served by missiologists who remain in close proximity with local churches. The writer of Proverbs noted: "A fool takes no pleasure in understanding, but only in expressing his opinion" (18:2 ESV). If the academy instructs missionaries to listen and learn so as to communicate clearly on the field, should not the academy apply such values to the classroom? Knowledge of present realities affecting local congregations is necessary for sustained influence from the missiological community. By listening with discernment, the missiologist is in a better position to assist pastors in developing an apostolic imagination.

Missiologists with an understanding of contemporary realities are likely to help pastors understand important matters affecting missionary activity. Missiologists must have the prophetic courage and humility to point churches to congregational realities in need of understanding and correction. Missiology has the potential to cause a cognitive dissonance among pastors while helping them think in terms of new paradigms and structures necessary for gospel advancement.

TEACH THEM HOW TO THINK ABOUT GLOBAL REALITIES

Much to my embarrassment, I was a professor before I understood the size and influence of the Majority World church. I was a professor before I understood the massive numbers of unreached people groups who have migrated from their countries of birth. I was a professor before I "discovered" that after India and China, the United States is home to the third largest number of unreached people groups in the world (Payne 2012, 63). If it took graduate and doctoral studies and research for a book to get an understanding of these realities, what might that reveal about the present state of pastoral understanding when it comes to global realities affecting the multiplication of disciples and churches? And what about church members' understanding of global needs?

While there are theological problems with the claim that "God Cannot Lead You on the Basis of Information that You Do Not Have," the reality is that God often uses the church's knowledge of reality to lead her to the peoples of the world (*Mission Frontiers*, 2008). Pastors need to understand that for two hundred years Protestant missionaries labored across the world and the Spirit did exactly as was promised. But not only do pastors need to know about the Majority World church, they also need to know of the 6,400 unreached peoples of the world (and the 570 who call the US and Canada home), including the three thousand unengaged-unreached groups (Payne 2013, 6).

Pastors need to know of the global forces shaping the face of the church and mission (cf. Payne 2013; Sills 2015; Johnstone 2011; Pocock, Van Rheenen, and McConnell 2005;

Guthrie 2000). They not only need to understand the grand issues of the day, but also how to maintain knowledge of contemporary issues. They need to be taught how to view such issues through a Great Commission lens and to develop a way of thinking that enables them to see the interconnectivity of global issues and their churches whether in rural Nebraska or downtown San Francisco.

HELP THEM THINK, BUT PROVIDE ANSWERS

Students need to be taught critical thinking skills. Wisdom and discernment are important components to life in the kingdom (Prov 1:7). However, missiologists absolutely must contend for the truths once delivered to the saints (Jude 3). While the Scriptures have not revealed the answers to all of life's questions, the Christian faith is built upon propositional truth claims. While claiming to know truths with certainty—especially those about theology—is often an affront to Western societies in general and definitely an assault on the general academy today, missiologists do not have the liberty to remain silent when God has spoken with clarity.

Evangelical pastors will fail to recognize the value of missiology if missiologists fail to speak with divine audacity about what God has already spoken. Yes, students should be led on a journey of discovery, and not of academic paternalism. But if Socratic pedagogy is always used in classrooms, books, reviews, and articles, then the busy pastor is likely to assume that missiology is irrelevant to the church and missiologists are people who always ask questions but never have answers. Busy pastors are not impressed when it takes twenty-two missiologists to answer the question: "Do Muslims and Christians Worship the Same God?"—a question many evangelical pastors would find irrelevant at face value. Those pastors, if they are willing to wade through thirty-two pages of material, might become frustrated at the missiological community whenever they discover that many of those writers did not answer the original question, but postulated other questions for consideration (Priest 2016, 1ff.).

TEACH THEM THAT THEOLOGY WAS BIRTHED FROM THE MISSION OF GOD

Missiologists must be experts in the field; this includes the realm of theology. David Kelsey wrote: "Theology is too important to leave to the systematic theologians, moral theologians, and historical theologians. Cultivation of the capacity to do theology is the task of the entire theological school" (1994, 134). If Kelsey is correct, how much more should the missiologist be intentionally involved in theological thought while attempting to equip others with an apostolic imagination?

Missiologists must lead others to the Scriptures as the source of the apostolic mindset. They must show pastors how all of Scripture was birthed from and relates to God's mission. In many cases, this will require an interpretative shift to a missional hermeneutic. Christopher J. H. Wright notes:

> For those who affirm some relationship (however articulated) between these texts and the self-revelation of our Creator God, the whole canon of Scripture is a missional phenomenon in the sense that it witnesses to the self-giving movement of this God toward his creation and us, human beings in God's own image, but wayward and wanton. The writings that now comprise our Bible are themselves the product of and witness to the ultimate mission of God (2006, 48).

This approach to understanding the Bible is likely to be a novel idea for some pastors. Two thousand years of history and well-developed pastoral ministry structures have contributed to an amnesia of the origins of the church, the Word of God, and theology.

Ironically, the theological academy (at times) fails to recognize the mission of God supporting and permeating the discipline of theology and the sending of the church. I remember hearing a reputable theologian preach a four-part sermon series on the church being "one, holy, catholic, and apostolic," with each expositional message addressing one of these four words. As a missions professor, I eagerly awaited the message on the "apostolic" nature of the church. Knowing this theologian did not have a reputation for emphasizing evangelism and missions, I hoped such a message would reveal a change in his theology and preaching. However, to my surprise, this brother managed to preach a message on the apostolic nature of the church by emphasizing the importance of the apostles' teaching while giving scant attention to the sent nature of the church.

If all of Scripture has been birthed from the outworking of God's redemptive and restorative plan, then it would seem that pastors should be able to understand this matter and allow these natural threads of the *missio Dei* to be revealed in their preaching. However, culture and tradition create strong forces that pose challenges to missiologists communicating a more excellent approach to understanding the Bible.

Mott was correct when he noted, "The pulpit treatment of missions should not be restricted to stated missionary sermons. The preacher must feel that missions is his domain, and not that he goes out of his way to preach on the subject" (1904, 69). If evangelicals fail to encourage a missional hermeneutic, then it should come as no surprise if missions is included in only a few sermons each year. A missional hermeneutic should not be an exceptional matter in the pulpit.

TEACH THEM TO STAND BETWEEN TWO WORLDS

The wise missiologist must understand that the call to be a pastor involves a call to stand between two worlds. The first world is that of the church; the second is that of the unreached peoples. Pastors with an apostolic imagination understand that apostolic workers are often members of their churches and need to be sent to the other world. They recognize that these members are to go with the gospel and simple disciple-making methods and church multiplication strategies. They are to be sent as ordinary believers, filled with the extraordinary Spirit. They are to be sent with their marketable skills and degrees so as to remain in their vocations while making disciples. Pastors with an apostolic imagination understand that church members are not sent to reproduce the complex ecclesiological structures modeled by their home churches. These laborers must keep their practices thoroughly biblical and highly reproducible among the unreached peoples.

Pastors with an apostolic imagination know that, for the most part, they are to remain between both worlds. This locus of ministry is a good thing. The church needs pastors; the unreached groups need missionaries. In general, pastors are not called to apostolic ministry. Pastors with an apostolic imagination recognize this reality and are comfortable with it. They know their role in the body of Christ and the role of the ones sent from their churches.

Missiologists must teach pastors that apostolic labors are not primarily defined by geographical boundaries. This other world may exist among an unreached people group across town or within another country. Teaching pastors to stand on the bridge with an apostolic imagination will require missiological thought that removes the dichotomy of North American and international missionary activities.

CONCLUSION

The education of today's pastors is one of the most important responsibilities of the missiologist. Few people have the influence to develop pastors with apostolic imagination. The missiologist faces significant challenges in this process. However, recognizing the need of the hour, understanding the challenges, and knowing a few guidelines is an excellent way to begin the transition to a new way of thought and action.

REFERENCES CITED

Fensham, Charles. 2014. "Group Discussion Conclusions on the Future of the Discipline of Missiology: Annual Meeting of the American Society of Missiology." *Missiology* 42(1):80–86.

Guthrie, Stan. 2000. *Missions in the Third Millennium: 21 Key Trends for the 21st Century*, revised and expanded. UK: Paternoster.

Hirsch, Alan and Tim Catchim. 2012. *The Permanent Revolution: Apostolic Imagination and Practice for the 21st Century Church*. San Francisco, CA: Jossey-Bass.

Johnstone, Patrick. 2011. *The Future of the Global Church: History, Trends, and Possibilities*. Colorado Springs, CO: Biblica.

Kelsey, David. 1994. Rethinking Theological Education. *American Theological Library Association Summary of Proceedings* 48:123–34.

Mission Frontiers. January-February 2008. http://www.missionfrontiers.org/issue/archive/god-cannot-lead-you-on-the-basis-of-information-that-you-do-not-have.

Mott, John R. 1904. *The Pastor and Modern Missions: A Plea for Leadership in World Evangelization*. New York, NY: Student Volunteer Movement for Foreign Missions.

Newell, Marvin J. 2015. "Symposium: The 'De-missionization' of Missions." *Evangelical Missions Quarterly* 51(1):46–51.

Payne, J. D. 2012. *Strangers Next Door: Immigration, Migration, and Mission*. Downers Grove, IL: IVP.

———. 2013. *Pressure Points: Twelve Global Issues Shaping the Face of the Church*. Nashville, TN: Thomas Nelson.

Pocock, Michael, Gailyn Van Rheenen, and Douglas McConnell. 2005. *The Changing Face of World Missions: Engaging Contemporary Issues and Trends*. Grand Rapids, MI: Baker.

Priest, Robert. 2016. "Wheaton and the Controversy Over Whether Muslims and Christians Worship the Same God." *Occasional Bulletin of the Evangelical Missiological Society*, Special Edition. https://www.emsweb.org/images/occasional-bulletin/special-editions/OB_SpecialEdition_2016.pdf.

Sills, M. David. 2015. *Changing World, Unchanging Mission: Responding to Global Challenges.* Downers Grove, IL: InterVarsity Press.

Van Gelder, Craig. 2014. "The Future of the Discipline of Missiology: Framing Current Realities and Future Possibilities." *Missiology* 42(1):39–56.

Wong, Arch Chee Keen. 2009. "How do Pastors Connect Their Academic Learning with Their Pastoral Practice? Negotiating the Tension between Theory and Practice." *Practical Theology* 2(2):241–52.

Wright, Christopher J. H. 2006. *The Mission of God: Unlocking the Bible's Grand Narrative.* Downers Grove, IL: IVP.